ADDITIONAL PRAISE FOR
THE WAR OF IDEAS AND WALID PHARES:

"Professor Walid Phares's *The War of Ideas* is a must read on the geopolitics of the war on terror. His book puts fifty years of Cold War and Jihadi offensives against democracies in an ultimate global perspective. This is a central resource for classrooms, newsrooms, and war rooms."

—Col. Kenneth Allard, USA (Ret.), former dean of the National War College, NBC Defense Analyst, and author of War Heads

"Dr. Phares understands like no one else the depth of Jihadi ideologies and how they have developed long-term strategies to counter and crumble free societies, both in the West and among young rising democracies in the Middle East."

—Richard W. Carlson, US Ambassador (ret.), former Director of Voice of America, former President and CEO of the Corporation for Public Broadcasting

"Walid Phares makes a compelling case for why winning the war of ideas is indispensable to winning the war on terrorism, and he points the way toward how to do so. It is a must read not only for policy makers and those who advise them, but for everyone with a stake in the fight of our generation."

—Clark Kent Ervin, former Inspector General of the Department of Homeland Security and author of Open Target: Where America Is Vulnerable to Attack

"If you want to understand the war of ideas being waged by Jihadists, Walid Phares is your man."

—U.S. Congresswoman Sue Myrick

"Walid Phares is both an incisive scholar and a skilled communicator. His insights into the psychologies and pathologies of the Middle East are unrivaled."

—Clifford D. May, President of the Foundation for the Defense of Democracies

"The Jihadists began their war of ideas against democracies decades ago. . . . a unique analysis of the roots and future of this terror campaign against the free world."

—Magdi Khalil, Egyptian journalist, Elaph.com

"I have followed and respected Dr. Walid Phares' academic work and reasoned commentary for years. He has a unique ability to articulate the central ideological conflict in the struggle against Jihadism. Dr. Phares consistently stands out as an invaluable resource and authentic voice in the global effort to understand exactly who the enemies of democracy are, what they believe, and how we can defeat them."

—Dr. Zuhdi Jasser, Chairman, American Islamic Forum for Democracy

"This book will change your way of seeing the war on terror. Professor Phares is the leading analyst of the war of ideas. His ability to see through the strategies and moves of the Jihadists in their quest to crumble democracies is unparalleled."

—Dr. Jacob Keryakes, NBC Senior Arabic Linguist

"Walid Phares is teaching the world about one of the greatest threats in history. Only a mind equally immersed in two civilizations and their ideologies can produce a book like *The War of Ideas*."

—Dr. Franck Salameh, Professor of Arab Culture, Boston College

"Walid Phares is the leading expert on the war of ideas between Jihadism and democracy."

—Alireza Jafarzadeh, Fox News analyst and author of The Iran Threat

THE WAR OF IDEAS

JIHAD AGAINST DEMOCRACY

WALID PHARES

palgrave
macmillan

WAR OF IDEAS

First published in 2007 by
PALGRAVE MACMILLAN™
175 Fifth Avenue, New York, N.Y. 10010 and
Houndmills, Basingstoke, Hampshire, England RG21 6XS.
Companies and representatives throughout the world.

PALGRAVE MACMILLAN is the global academic imprint of the
Palgrave Macmillan division of St. Martin's Press, LLC and of
Palgrave Macmillan Ltd. Macmillan® is a registered trademark in the
United States, United Kingdom and other countries. Palgrave is a
registered trademark in the European Union and other countries.

ISBN–13: 978–1–4039–7639–0
ISBN–10: 1–4039–7639–2

Library of Congress Cataloging-in-Publication Data is available from
the Library of Congress.

A catalogue record of the book is available from the British Library.

Design by Letra Libre

First edition: March 2006

10 9 8 7 6 5 4 3 2 1

Printed in the United States of America.

TABLE OF CONTENTS

DEDICATION

I DEDICATE THIS BOOK, THE *WAR OF IDEAS*, FIRST OF ALL TO ALL those dissidents in the Greater Middle East and in the Arab and Muslim world who have suffered and yet continue to strive for the liberation of their societies, and eventually for the rise of full democracy in their midst. I dedicate it to the women, youth, and minorities whose persecution needs to end and to the courageous people who stand by them; also to those intellectuals, authors, students, human rights activists, professors, journalists, singers, artists, and others who are the hope of the future.

I dedicate this book in memory of all those who have fallen as victims or have had to survive Terrorism, oppression, and intolerance ; also in memory of the soldiers from America and the free world who sacrificed themselves to free suppressed societies. And in support to those who have been suffering in jails and other detention centers across the land.

I also dedicate this book to those in the West and within Democratic societies who believe that the right for freedom is universal, and who stand for their principles: leaders, politicians, journalists, scholars, and citizens.

And finally, my highest dedication is in memory of my late father, Halim, who, as he shepherded me at home and stimulated my love of cultures and languages, taught me to serve the cause of justice and freedom by bringing education wherever I could.

Walid Phares
Washington DC, December 6, 2006

ACKNOWLEDGMENTS

MY FIRST ACKNOWLEDGMENT GOES TO MY LOVED ONES, THE FIRST ones to sacrifice for my reflections to become a book were those whose lives were directly affected by my hours and days spent in research, writing and editing instead of spending this precious time with them, enjoying what life provides you with a family and soul mates. In other words, I must thank my family and love ones first, for offering the best they have so that my readers can enjoy this book. I owe this sacrifice especially to the "Commander" and the "Scholar" for their understanding and patience; as well as to my beloved mother whose affection kept my hopes high and to my relentlessly supportive sister and her family.

My second acknowledgment goes to my professional house, the Foundation for the Defense of Democracies in Washington, which has been hosting me and providing me with an adequate intellectual environment since summer 2004. Since I was appointed a Senior Fellow at FDD by Cliff May I have had the opportunity to publish two books and dozens of articles and position papers. I also credit the European Foundation for Democracy for sponsoring my research in Europe. My thanks to Cliff, the leadership, the staff, and my colleagues at the Foundation, as well as its supporters, especially Mark Dubowitz; beyond hosting and supporting me, they have been at the heart of bringing awareness to the public regarding Terrorist threats and providing hope for Democracy to grow and rise. A thank you to my assistant, Adela, and my companions in the various NGOs, including Tom Harb and his colleagues, Behrooz Bahbudi and the Global Unity Partnership, as well as to the faithful managers of my web sites.

My third acknowledgment goes to my publisher, Airié Stuart, and my literary agent, Lynne Rabinoff, for their encouragement and permanent support as well as their insistence that I keep producing thoughts and sharing them with the readers. My thanks to the hard work of the editors of this book, as well as the art makers, who surely transformed it from a raw manuscript to a final product ready for the bookstore and library shelves; their notes, suggestions, and thorough editing helped significantly in the sculpting of the material into a final product—particularly Alan Bradshaw, Bruce Murphy, and Chris Chappell.

My fourth acknowledgment goes to my fellow travelers in this field of exchanging ideas and bringing awareness: Among them, especially, Andy Cochrane, the director of the Foundation on Counter Terrorism; William Smith, the publisher of the *World Defense Review*; Carol Taber, the publisher of *Family Security Matters*.

My fifth acknowledgment goes to the many journalists, anchors, show producers, and workers in the media who host, invite, and give me the opportunities to share my analysis and views in print, on TV, on radio, and online. This vast web of public mediators allows my ideas to be received and travel to where they may help shape a better debate on crucial issues—or eventually come back to me enriched and criqued. A special thank to the many readers, listeners and viewers who enjoy my comments, who have sent me emails and letters expressing their views, and who encouraged me to produce this book. This is to let them know that their messages, the simple ones and the heavy ones, have been a part of the making of the *War of Ideas*. For, ultimately, it is for the readers that I write, hoping that they will reward me with their appreciation. My thoughts go also to the many faculty and students I interact with on campuses around the country, especially those friends who have organized forums and lectures. These events have positively impacted my arguments and allowed me to discover the deeper thinking and concerns of current and future scholars.

My sixth acknowledgment goes to American government officials and legislators, representatives from the European Union and the Middle East, and diplomats at the United Nations and other international organizations who engage and value my research .

My seventh and last acknowledgment comes from remembering the actors from the earlier stages in my life. I wish to thank the publishers and the mentors who launched my first works, and before them the teachers and professors who educated me. And foremost among them, I owe the formation of my understanding of the world's politics and philosophies to my older brother Sami, my first teacher and a universal thinker.

INTRODUCTION

AT THE END OF THE TWENTIETH CENTURY AND THE BEGINNING of the twenty-first, we have witnessed a historic change in the approach to war and peace in international relations. In the wake of the Cold War, leaders and policy planners face new challenges. Efforts to persuade the public to support policies and ideologies have become an increasingly important activity of government in democracies, demanding ever greater resources, skill, and attention. Ideas now have to be presented, argued, and defended in public discourse. Although ideas have always been the engine of history, the audience for them has vastly increased with globalization and more widespread access to media (especially electronic media), and thus today a greater number of individuals influence whether a policy obtains support.

It is not only governments that have come to realize that there is now a global playing field in the struggle for control over which ideas are promoted. Militant organizations have reached the same conclusion: in times of war and peace alike, influencing the public by promoting ideas is a must. In democracies in general, this means debating and selecting from among many competing ideas. For radical groups, it means imposing one vision for the masses to follow. But regardless of party or group, in world politics, the promotion of ideas has become the prerequisite to action, including war.

In the last few years, especially after the September 11, 2001, attacks in America (and increasingly around the world as the so-called War on Terrorism spread to Afghanistan, Iraq, the greater Middle East, south Asia, Africa, Russia, and within the West), talk of a "War of Ideas" emerged in the media and to a lesser extent in academia. The first public statements about the concept were made by U.S. leaders such as President George Bush, Secretary of State Condoleezza Rice, and congressional figures from both parties. But other world leaders and politicians have also mentioned the roles of ideologies and doctrines in the context of counterterrorism efforts and confrontations with radical regimes and organizations. Among these leaders are British prime minister Tony Blair, French president Jacques Chirac, and Russian president Vladimir Putin. In the Muslim world, rulers such as Jordan's King Abdallah have also mentioned the clash of ideologies within Islam. But in the academic and intellectual communities in many democracies, the concept of a War of Ideas has been approached with suspicion and sometimes even disdain. Many of the gatekeepers of knowledge on campuses consider ideas to be their exclusive domain. They feel uncomfortable when nonprofessional thinkers, including statesmen and bureaucrats, meddle in academics. As a result, this major perspective—one that absolutely must be discussed and analyzed—has not thoroughly taken hold in the West, even though the War of Ideas has been mobilizing countries, regions, and armies across the globe in the first years of this millennium.

Particularly in the Arab Muslim nations, the War of Ideas is raging. It has inflamed millions of readers, viewers, and listeners, transforming large numbers of them into militants and demonstrators, some into suicide bombers, and many into voters. From websites to al Jazeera television, the flow and counter-flow of ideas are growing. In contrast to the people of the West, the Arab and Muslim masses are deeply engaged in the conflict of ideas, both old and new. Leaders in those regions, however, seem to espouse the same hesitant attitude as Western elites and merely attempt to maintain the status quo.

But regardless of who wishes for it, who is prosecuting it, and who prefers to think it isn't happening, the War of Ideas—call it a clash, conflict, dialogue, exchange, or search for alternatives—is occurring and will be for a long time. It has become the overarching framework of the twenty-first century.

In the early 1990s, I observed the post-Soviet intellectual debate, searching for new answers. Having lived in the Middle East throughout my youth and young adulthood, I saw firsthand the clash of ideologies, especially in the intellectual capital of the Arab world, Beirut. In 1990, the collapse of the Soviet Union ended not only the Cold War, but also the old East–West debates. With millions of Eastern Europeans demonstrating in the streets for democracy, one might have expected their counterparts across the Mediterranean to do the same. Unfortunately, they didn't. While the Iron Curtain collapsed across Europe, a fundamentalist curtain still surrounded the Middle East's civil societies. From Prague to Kiev, liberty was on the march, but from Beirut to Darfur, oppression remained widespread. As a result, most Iraqis, Syrians, Lebanese, Sudanese, Iranians, and others living under dictatorship, occupation, and radical ideologies felt hopeful at the sight of a wall falling in Berlin, the punishment of a tyrant in Romania, and the election of a Czech dissident as president. The end of the old bipolar paradigm of the Cold War may have brought freedom to the peoples of Eastern Europe, but not to those living in the Middle East.

I left the city of ideas overlooking the Mediterranean the year the world was changing, in 1990. But in the West, not all the changes I saw had been noticed yet. I was back on campus (in the United States after relocating in 1990), obtaining a Ph.D. in international relations and observing with great interest the evolution of political thinking in world affairs, from Europe to North America. At the time, the pressing debate was what a post-Soviet world would look like. To political scientists, it boiled down to this key question: Is there a global enemy anymore? To politicians dealing with the concerns of their public, the question was about mass security: Is there still a threat, somewhere in the world, that will shatter the daily lives of ordinary citizens? The answer of Western elites, both European and North American, was clear: world conflicts were over, security had been won, and there were now other issues to be addressed. It was at this time that Francis Fukuyama wrote his celebrated essay arguing that with the fall of the Soviet Union came the disappearance of global perils—the "end of History."

But a couple of years later, another leading thinker from the sole remaining superpower warned that the real threats were yet to be seen. To Samuel Huntington, the new world politics would be defined by what he called the "clash of civilizations." American and European academia split between two camps: those who dismissed this idea and those who agreed with it. I had another view: civilizations as identities never vanished, even during the Cold War. They were not referred to for decades, but deep down, they were the real tectonic plates of world politics. After the collapse of the Soviet Union, a new division emerged between those who wanted to reignite the clash, the jihadists, and those who didn't, democracies.[1]

The last decade of the twentieth century witnessed two parallel intellectual debates: one within the West, over which path to follow for the future, and another in the East, about which past to bring into the future—secular nationalism or Islamic fundamentalism. As classrooms and newsrooms in the democracies questioned whether a post-Soviet threat existed, in the east and south of the Mediterranean, the doctrine of Islamism was working its way deeper inside the social fabric. Confusion reigned in the industrialized powers, where ideas abounded but explanations were few. Why, for example, was the Arab-Israeli conflict not solved in the 1990s despite the internationally supported peace agreements of 1993? Who was sabotaging peace in the Middle East? Why was the Taliban able to brutalize women and minorities without being sanctioned by the international community? Why did the United States and Europe intervene twice to save peoples from ethnic cleansing and massacres in the Balkans but not to stop the genocide in the Sudan, which were taking place at the same time? Why are secular ideas valued over faith in the West but subordinated to religion in the Muslim world?

The West enjoyed the freedom to challenge ideas, but its public wasn't mobilized by these debates until September 11, 2001, when four planes flown by *"des fous d'Allah"*[2] massacred 3,000 people in 30 minutes in the most powerful nation on earth. From that morning on, the world changed dramatically, as did the meaning of ideas. Ordinary citizens started to wonder how all this could have happened so suddenly. In fact, it wasn't really sudden at all; rather, the debate over ideas hadn't reached the public, which hadn't been informed of the ideological conflicts raging worldwide. As I argued in my previous book, *Future Jihad*, the intellectual elites had failed their customers: for more than a decade, professors in the West had ignored the presence, growth, intentions, and misdeeds of those terrorists who went on to target the World Trade Center and the Pentagon, and later Madrid's trains and London's subways and buses.

The first question posed by Americans after the disaster of 9/11 was, Why do they hate us? Joe Public had no idea of the existence of an angry Mohammad Atta and a determined but patient Ziad Jarrah, both of them products of Jihadism. In fact, average citizens in the West, including the United States, knew nothing about Jihadism at all. Most of the 1,200 instructors of social science, Middle East studies professors, and "experts" on Islam from Oxford to Harvard had treated jihad as a benign spiritual tradition, like yoga.[3] It was the lack of an idea—or, more accurately, the insertion of a false idea (that Jihadism was a benign matter)—that made the public so unaware of the dangers we all faced. A missing political idea of that seriousness and gravity would allow the politics of war and peace to become very fragile.

It is not a secret that politics has long been a major reason behind war and peace among nations. It is also not a secret that economics has always been a major component of politics. Many civilizations have moved in different directions, both culturally and geographically, to satisfy their political economies: Assyrians, Persians, Romans, Chinese, Indians, Nubians, Aztecs, Europeans, and many others have followed their strategic interests in shaping their marches across the globe. Behind each historic speech and visionary plan have lain basic logistical needs: water, land, greenery, natural boundaries, room for expansion. To legitimize major decisions, strategies, conquests, sacrifices, and other collective human endeavors, ideas had to be structured, grounded in logic, accepted, and pursued. Rulers have used ideas to persuade, mobilize, and lead their followers. These visions have been the real engines of history.

IDEAS OF WAR AND PEACE

Ideas have been produced by philosophers, social visionaries, and politicians to guide people; however, religion has played the most powerful role in shaping the destinies of civilizations. Usually understood as a link between humans and the metaphysical realm, religions have been elevated to the highest levels of political inspiration: Moloch, Zeus, Baal, Zarathustra, Jupiter, Bophal, Buddha, Odin, El-lat, and other ancient deities were at the center of legislation, invasion, and exploration. Monotheist faiths such as Judaism, Christianity, Islam, and Bahaism were transported worldwide, changing humanity's policies and forming the basis of what would become international relations. Religions, beyond economics, produced the politics of war and peace. People of faith believe that all religious ideas come from the divine. In contrast, many social scientists believe that humans create religious ideas. Regardless, one fact remains unchallenged: ideas are at the center of religions; man-made or divinely inspired, they have moved people throughout history to change the world, their achievements seen by proponents as progress but by opponents as catastrophes.

In short, ideas are behind collective human behavior, whether political, economic, or religious. They describe the world and prescribe actions; they serve as fuel for war and as philosophies for peace. In the modern world, more than ever, ideas clash, and when nations and civilizations collide, they are prompted by competing ideas. The drama of human history is that men have acted and been violent under the auspices of ideas, often as a result of material needs. In these circumstances, ideas were "used" to legitimize physical goals. But the most dramatic developments in the history of ideas occur when communities actually act violently on the sole ground of differences in ideas, such as in theological wars, when, for example, adherents kill for the nature of Christ, for injunctions of the Qu'ran, or for doctrinal claims.

Such a dramatic conclusion leads us to ask why clashes of ideas become clashes of arms. Why cannot ideas clash with ideas and let human societies live in peace? These questions have confronted historians and philosophers for centuries with no real answers. They have become more difficult as massacres, genocide, and terrorism have come to define the twentieth and now the twenty-first century: Why would rulers, political leaders, militants, individuals, and terrorists kill, die, and destroy for mere ideas? Are these mental schemes, from divine or intellectual inspirations, connected endemically to human intentions? I believe that, while sociopolitical interests and religious beliefs have mobilized nations and civilizations to clash and strike back at each other, a more lethal form of modern commitment has led to the atrocities of recent history: ideology.

IDEOLOGY

Ideologies can be seen as the daughters of ideas—more complex, more determined, and by far more lethal. A history of ideology teaches us that modern conflicts, especially since the nineteenth century, are grounded in doctrinal roots. Nationalism is the earliest form of militant ideology in the contemporary West, followed by Marxism and fascism. In the Arab and Muslim world, religious fundamentalism took the lead in the nineteenth century, followed by extreme nationalism, which alternated with socialism and Islamism throughout the twentieth century. Similarly, East Asian and African cultures moved among nationalism, religious extremism, and Communism. In Latin America, the pendulum swung between left- and right-wing ideologies.

This is not to say that ideas have displaced practical or even cynical motives, such as expansionist designs, national rivalry, and sheer greed. In fact, ideologies legitimize and are produced by these designs. For example, in the early last century, nationalism and the balance of power combined to produce World War I. Bolshevism led to the massacre of millions in Russia, and in the

Spanish civil war, men and women killed and were killed for Marx and Lenin. During the 1930s, German Nazism and Italian and Japanese fascism decimated nations and ethnicities for "race, nation and purity."[4] Bloodshed resumed over Communism in the Soviet Union and China for another half century, with proxy conflicts in Asia, Africa, and the Americas all ideologically driven. The opponents of totalitarian ideologies, mostly liberal democracies, but sometimes nationalist movements too, faced off with the "isms" of Stalin, Hitler, Mussolini, and Yamato and continued to resist the Soviets of Khrushchev and Brezhnev throughout the Cold War. Between 1945 and the 1990s, many small regional conflicts flared up across the globe: Korea, the Arab-Israeli conflict, Vietnam, Cyprus, India-Pakistan, and so on. Civil and ethnic wars spread as well, in places such as Lebanon, Ireland, Sudan, the Philippines, and Nigeria. And insurrections and revolutions mushroomed in Cuba, Bolivia, Algeria, Hungary, Iran, and beyond. In all of these conflicts, and with leaders from Bismarck to Trotsky and from Hitler to Mao Zedong, ideologies were omnipresent: nationalist, socialist, communist, populist, anarchist, or ultrareligious, they all sought domination in the name of a higher calling, a divine, materialistic, philosophical, or historical ideal that claimed supremacy among human doctrines. Ironically, ideologies may start as an expression of age-old desires, such as lust for territory and domination, but as history evolves, they become self-fueled as a desire in itself, an autonomous wish to accomplish an idea regardless of its irrelevance.

THE HOUSES OF DEMOCRACY

All in all, the history of the twentieth century boiled down to a series of struggles between two major camps: the fortresses of authoritarianism and the houses of democracy. For example, the aging empires of Central Europe and the Ottoman Sultanate were pitted against the emerging democracies of Western Europe and North America. During World War II, the fascist powers of the Axis faced the mostly Western allies. During the Cold War, the authoritarian Soviet Bloc battled a mostly democratic NATO. And for decades, modern democracies opposed dictatorships, tyrannies, and authoritarian regimes.

Liberal governments weren't always on the side of liberty. Democracies possessed colonies and ruled other nations, notably in the past empires of Great Britain, France, Holland, Spain, Portugal, Germany, and even Japan. Later on, democratic powers and superpowers allowed their authoritarian allies to repress weaker nations: Indonesia and East Timor; Iraq and the Kurds; Syria and Lebanon; and South Africa are familiar examples. Democracies weren't and aren't perfect, but democracy was and remains the best form of government human societies have yet experienced. Democratic cultures ensure pluralism, open societies, rule of law, accountability, and eventually human rights and self-determination—all principles agreed on by the bulk of international society since the nineteenth century's series of democratic revolutions and the twentieth's rise of international law.

As we stated earlier, the engine of history in the modern era has been the spread of the ideas of democracy and freedom, successfully or unsuccessfully, intentionally or unintentionally, forcefully or peacefully, internally or externally; as a result of offensive or defensive wars, of civil conflicts or regime change, of one election or multiple elections; in one shot or gradually; as a result of an educational process or by elites, history has almost become the evolution of ideas and their results. All developments in world politics seem to indicate that the ideal governance is through the rule of the people and by the people. The growth of democracy has witnessed several setbacks since its inception and tragic ruptures with genocidal consequences in the twentieth century. Nevertheless, like a phoenix, it reemerges and takes off again. Russia knew multipartisanship for a few months in 1916–17 but was ruled by a one-party dictatorship for 73 years before reverting to a multiparty system in 1991. Modern Germany experienced a transfer from an empire in 1914 to the weak Republic of Weimar in 1920. The latter lasted 13 years, only to give way to the Third Reich, the most violent race-based regime in history. But half of Germany regained democracy in 1946, and the other half joined it in 1990. Egypt decolonized in the 1940s as a constitutional monarchy, lost its embryo of democracy under Nasser's dictatorship, and has been attempting to regain shreds of it since Sadat. Chile and Argentina experienced democratic elections before they were ruled by military dictatorships for decades, then returned to a free society. Other countries tasted some forms of democratic practice before internal wars devoured their liberties, for example Lebanon and Ivory Coast. Some countries split violently but preserved their democracies, such as Cyprus; others separated gently and maintained their open systems, such as Czechoslovakia.

Democratic forms of government evolved in different ways and under a variety of constitutions but converged toward similar principles: people elect their government and choose their laws. These basic principles, inherited from centuries of struggle and thousands of years of self-questioning, gained momentum decade after decade and one century after the other. Even dictatorships adjusted to the historical shift: most ideological and authoritarian regimes claimed to be serving a particular form of democracy or at least used the term in their names. The Soviet countries promoted a proletarian democracy; East Germany called itself the German Democratic Republic; Latin American populist governments cited democratic ideals as inspiration for their dominant party systems. Organizations seeking a one-party future state, such as the Democratic Front for the Liberation of Palestine, projected the same illusion. Furthermore, liberal elites attacked each other for not being democratic enough, as was the case between American and European establishments. Advocates of Third World ideologies criticized the "Western bourgeois" democracies of the North. The cacophony grew within world politics as it was debated whose democracy was better, fairer, and more suitable for just societies.

Democratization continued until a movement rose from the past to reject it altogether as an enemy of mankind, refusing the terms of debate and dragging a large segment of the international community back into a predemocratic era, or at least trying to do so. Some of the anti-democratic forces emerged from within Western civilization, such as fascism, Nazism, and Bolshevism. They struggled within their cultural zone over the control of countries and regions, but they were ultimately defeated. Still, other anti-democratic forces emerged from the Islamic sphere targeting power both within its own cultural zone and also beyond. These are the forces of jihad.

THE HOUSES OF JIHADISM

An old belief from centuries ago, jihad reemerged in world affairs slowly at first, beginning in the 1920s, growing steadily through the 1980s, and becoming more forceful starting in the early 1990s. While Communists and Fascists were battling capitalists, liberals, and nationalists for a half century, those who would label themselves as the jihadists of modern times waited for the right moment to unleash their War of Ideas. Self-described heirs of past powerful empires, the Islamic fundamentalists and their various precursors and derivatives are diverse and always changing, but they share one main goal: to bring down democracy.

Salafists, Wahabis, Takfiris, Tablighis, and other Sunni Islamists reject the concept of pluralism and radically oppose the rule of the people. Only Allah and his teachings, they postulate, are the basis for governance. The Shia-born Khumeinists condemn Western-style liberalism but co-opt concepts and words from international democratic institutions such as the idea of a republic. They installed an Islamic republic in Iran, but its mandate is believed to be divinely inspired and not subject to the approval of civil society. Islamists from all schools of thought, and violent jihadists in particular, have an ideology of their own, based on ideas diametrically opposed to classical liberal democracies. The jihadists aim at the re-creation of what they perceive as a caliphate, merging dozens of Muslim countries into one world power. They want to impose strict religious laws on the people of the caliphate and claim furthermore that this form of government is ordained by God. Hence they have no tolerance for man-made legislation, and politics is tightly scripted by the militant interpreters of faith. The followers of Jihadism, openly or discreetly, as well as those who share the Islamists' enemies, have moved worldwide to obstruct the rise of secular democracies, especially within the realm of the Muslim world. They plan to resume what they believe is a millennial project: world domination.

FORCES OF FUTURE AND PAST

Running against historical trends, the jihadists were bound to clash with democracies—all democracies—and are ultimately on a collision course with world civilization altogether, including with the allies they seek to enlist in their "holy" war. The rise of the contemporary jihadists has created a universal conflict between two camps: the forces accepting and promoting a future with multiple types of democracies, and those heading back toward the past, armed with extreme religious injunctions. Democracies are moving forward, though not without failures, while Jihadism is hurtling backward with occasional relative successes. The energies of the two outlooks have been unleashed against each other, willingly or unwillingly, culturally, politically, and increasingly militarily.

This monumental clash has been poorly explained to the public, especially in the West. Western elites have mostly failed to describe the conflict and, more particularly, refused to define the enemy of international relations in the post–Cold War era. In their own realm, the jihadists have subverted the understanding of the ultimate challenge. Although the clash of civilizations had subsided worldwide and was removed from Western agendas by the mid-twentieth century, the pioneers of the new caliphate and imamate argued otherwise to their masses. In an environment of forced backwardness and limited access to modern education, the societies of the greater Middle East and the wider Muslim world have been subject to the "explanations" of Islamists and other radicals. From China's borders to the Atlantic Ocean, masses are being taught to hate the other side of the world and blame it for all evil.

In between the two worlds, a marriage of convenience has developed between oil interests and ideology: the petro-jihadist connection. Spreading out in both directions, the hydra of the twentieth century's political economy aims at perpetuating the conflict into the twenty-first century. The jihadists have been waging a war of ideology against democracies, using the influence of their petro-economies, and democracies have fallen to a "global civil war" of ideas, politics, and interests.

A rising core in the United States, with support from growing political awareness in Europe, in the Arab-Muslim world, and in the international community, are facing off with a militant core within the Arab-Muslim sphere, in alliance with radical currents and sympathizers worldwide, including within the West. But while violent confrontations are located in Iraq, Afghanistan, Sudan, Lebanon, Chechnya, and many other sites of the War on Terror, the clash of ideas is universal, taking place at all levels and without interruption.

⋆⟫⟫ ⟪⟪⋆

On both sides, ideological fortresses and propaganda machines seek to blur the vision of the enemy and win the battle of legitimization in the eyes of potential supporters. For example, bin Laden, Ahmedinijad, Assad, and the plethora of militants under their umbrellas want the Western public to believe in the justness of al Qaeda, Iran's regime, and Syria's elite and punish the elected leaders of the West for their "aggression" toward the Arab Muslim world. On the other hand, policymakers in Washington, London, Paris, and many dissident pockets in the Third World hope the masses of Arabs and Muslims will embrace freedom and democracy and bring about the needed change.

Indeed, a War of Ideas is raging, relentlessly, behind the War on Terror. The outcome of the second is ineluctably conditioned by the consequences of the first. For the party that succeeds in convincing the largest numbers on the opposite side will eventually either stretch the war into the future or end it to its advantage. During the fall of 2001, Osama bin Laden said on al Jazeera that as long as he can reach the next generations of Muslims, he will be winning the war against his enemies. In fact, the central point in the entire war between Jihadism and democracy is this: All it takes for the jihadists to make progress is to continue to implant their ideology in the minds of the younger waves of followers. And all it takes for the supporters of the radicals within international society (and particularly inside Western democracies) is to prevent the public, especially youth, from understanding this equation.

In 27 years of observing, studying, and monitoring the conflict of ideas and the clash of ideologies, I have watched changing arguments used by the various parties. I have witnessed Western attitudes toward Islamic fundamentalism evolving from sympathy to concern, from a U.S. foreign policy that encouraged jihad in the Soviet-occupied Afghanistan of the 1980s to an American presidential speech blasting Islamist terrorism in 2005. And during that same period, I saw the Islamists changing their goals from a holy war against Communist atheism with the help of a "godly America" in the twentieth century to a jihad against the United States with the help of godless Marxists in the twenty-first century. Based on my years of following the evolution of the main players in world politics and closely analyzing the strategies of the two main camps in the current War on Terror, this book describes in detail the intellectual and other forces—the big picture—behind the ongoing world conflict. What are the aims of the jihadists and their allies, and how do they intend to reach them? How do they want their enemies to think, and are their strategies working? In fact, the ideological conflict and the War of Ideas overlap but do not coincide. Often, both democracies and jihadists moderate their idealism, make concessions on principles, depart from their ideals, and postpone their end games while finding rationales for these deflections. Ideologies are slower to change, but ideas that advocate them find ways to reshape strategies and tactics.

Observing the two sides is fascinating but troubling. By understanding the strategic intentions of the jihadists as of the early 1990s, you could see a 9/11 coming; by examining the level of consciousness of Western diplomacy, you could guess the upcoming failures. Al Qaeda's fatwas in 1996 and 1998, and the *New York Times* reporting of them during the same years, included a powerful message as to what was to come. Exploring Hezbollah's rationale for its October 1983 suicide attacks against the U.S. marines and French soldiers in Beirut and reviewing the media analysis of these events in Washington and Paris that same month presaged the future. And later on, even after 9/11, 3/11, and 7/7, the obvious goals of the terrorists, when put alongside the assessments of Western governments, create a deeply disturbing picture: even now, years after the jihadists made their ideology and intentions loud and clear, many in the West and in other democracies hesitate to accept a standing reality. From Berkeley to the Sorbonne, there is no war but imperialism; from the State Department to the Quai d'Orsay, the war exists, but it is on "terror." On al Jazeera, it is an "American War on Islam"; on Christian evangelical networks, it is "God sending Islam to punish the seculars." In Brussels, the European Commission's "experts" impose a deep silence about the doctrinal roots of Jihadism in order not to offend the "sensitivities of Muslims," as described by the jihadists. In Qatar, the World Union of Imams headed by Sheikh Yussef al Qardawi wants the United Nations to ban any criticism of Islam, religion and history. Across the Atlantic and Indian Oceans, an immense tower of Babel has been erected by the warriors of ideas: determined to win the final jihad against the infidels, the followers of Salafism, Wahabism, and Khumeinism indoctrinate their societies and attempt to mollify their opponents. As they proceed in their holy war of ideologies, they prosecute a very real War of Terror. The West and other democracies, on the other hand, respond with a War on Terrorism and sink their resources into Byzantine debates and intellectual dramas, and only in some instances display a will to reach out to the anti-jihadist Muslims.

Looking at both sides of this great chess game, I wanted to share my findings with readers across the globe. I wrote this book as a means to participate in the debate, but above all, to provide anyone, whether a beginner in international affairs or an academic expert, a glimpse of what the clash of minds looks like when the arguments are explored and compared.

In this book, my goal is limited to the warfare of minds. What do strategies aim at, what tactics and practices do they expect to see implemented, how do they read each other, how do they react and reshape their arguments? Ultimately I wish to show the ways that ideologies are constantly shifting, too slowly to detect easily but deeply influential over time. My objective is to open the eyes of the reader to the logic behind these ideas and their influence on the ongoing world conflict between Jihadism and democracy.

CHAPTER ONE

THE HISTORICAL DEBATES

THE IDEOLOGICAL CONFRONTATION BETWEEN JIHADISM AND democracy has spread into a vast array of areas, from international relations to legal interpretations and mass movements. In the 1990s, most of these debates were developing unilaterally. The Islamic fundamentalist intellectuals and their academic sympathizers in the West were "revealing" to the world their views on international politics, views they claimed had been suppressed by colonialism and imperialism for more than a century. Western intellectuals, in their overwhelming majority, made significant efforts to legitimize the arguments of their counterparts from the East, instead of debating them or at least investigating them.

In subsequent chapters, I'll expand on the key players in these historical debates on both sides of the Atlantic, the Mediterranean, and the Indian Ocean and will make the case that the dominant debate was not inclusive of all trends and ideas. In fact, the exchange of ideas on world politics wasn't taking place on merely a one-way street, but on a one-lane street: the public in the West was denied an alternative explanation of trends on the other side of the world, particularly after the collapse of the Soviet Union. The intellectual spokespersons of the Arab and Muslim world on both sides of the international divide developed a single dominant paradigm, ignoring opposing views. As I will show later, these elites claimed that the sole crisis in the Middle East was the Arab-Israeli conflict, and that all other problems were caused by it and would find their way to resolution only with the end of the Palestinian-Israeli quagmire. But had this unilateral debate been characteristic of the Eastern sphere only, Western pluralist culture could have helped generate a greater multiplicity of opinions among the Greater Middle Eastern elites toward international matters in general and political culture in particular. The drama after the Cold War was that Western elites largely reflected the views of their dominant counterparts across the water, and sometimes even the specific interests of regimes east and south of the Mediterranean.

The post-9/11 ideological debates and the War of Ideas between democracies and jihadists and their allies are not new. They are familiar in concept, substance, and subject. Most of the theses advanced by leaders, politicians, and opinion makers in the West are in fact either a reference to what their predecessors came up with, decades if not centuries ago, or fragments of previously marginalized concepts by various influential figures and authors. Indeed, the strategy of "spreading democracy" in countries still ruled by dictatorships and authoritarian regimes, advocated by the Bush administration and gradually considered by some of its allies, is a natural extension, although in radically different contexts, of the American and French Revolutions and of Western liberal doctrines toward Eastern Europe, Latin America, and even Africa. The novelty, perhaps, of Washington's grand strategy after the New York and Washington massacres of 2001 was to apply this old doctrine to countries in a cultural zone that had been forbidden from debating democracy by their own ruling elites and their allies within the West. The ideas of democracy, separation of powers, identity, equal opportunity, rule of law, secularism, and justice for all have traveled in time from Mesopotamia, Greece, Rome, and Enlightenment Europe to the League of Nations, the United Nations, and the Tribunal of the Hague. Other civilizations have reached democracy by their own different paths, via the same consensus of international principles: self-determination, liberty, and freedom for all humankind. These principles have been destined to be universal, not selective, even if historical circumstances impeded their implementation. The issue is one of essence, for the universality of these democratic principles is valid only if at every opportunity the international community works to expand them to reach more people.

Unfortunately, the story of the twentieth century was one of great exceptions—wars, genocides, and oppression. But fortunately, after every descent into cataclysmic bloodshed, such as World Wars I and II, the Soviet oppression, and the ethnic cleansings of the last quarter of the century, international principles still prevailed, recognizing the wounds of the victims, sometimes healing them but usually waiting for them to heal. Still, at least in the public declarations, foreign policies, and diplomatic announcements, democratic powers were unanimous that humans have rights inherent in their very nature. Whether these rights are respected or not, violated or protected, legislated or interpreted, at the end of the day, they are part of the constitution of the international society. The differences in putting them into practice come from how governments, organizations of states, political movements and parties, and economic interests perceive them and are willing to serve them. Contemporary world history has witnessed the recognition of these principles by stages and, despite raging conflicts, moved to shape them into documents. That is, until the jihadists began to wage war against democracies and against the ideas they had put forth for over two centuries.

To put it simply, the current War of Ideas is not introducing new ideologies and doctrines, but pitting against each other two forces with opposing world visions: democracies limping forward and jihadists rushing backward. The followers of fundamentalism, unlike their interlocutors across cultures, do not seek to integrate their views and values within the modern world; they reject the contemporary web of values and institutions. Instead, they propose, or in fact want to impose, a world of their own, wholly and holy, on the ashes of the current international society. Hence today's conflict of ideas is between the global consensus, reached by the international society, and the forces working to reverse or replace it. Between the mosaic of democracies and the panoply of Jihadism, the disagreement is philosophical, historical, and doctrinal: it is about how the world has functioned for centuries and how it should evolve. This debate bears on questions of war and peace, the clash or coexistence of civilizations, questions of nations and nationalism, and socioeconomics.

WAR AND PEACE

For all the progress that has been made in the modern world in diplomacy, signing treaties and making collective agreements on resolving conflicts, social scientists have largely agreed on the impossibility of eradicating wars and collective violence without a full satisfaction of human societies. Indeed, theologians discount the establishment of world peace short of divine intervention. Therefore, what modern international society has been able to achieve is a consensus on the principle that wars are the exception that should be limited, restrained, and, when necessary, bound to humane rules. In sum, peace should be the constant objective, and war the unavoidable evil to be contained.

In the current international legal system, which includes the UN Charter and the subsequent documents related to peaceful relations among nations and governments, legitimate reasons to go to war involve clear concepts such as defense of the national soil, rebellion against a foreign military occupation, or intervention to salvage a civilian population under threat of massacre. It took centuries to reach the present stage of consensus on war and peace—still imperfect, however. Without delving into the entire history of international relations, we can review the development of peace as a universal concept, efforts to challenge the legitimacy of all wars, and measures to protect the victims of conflicts including prisoners and civilians and to establish security systems to stop aggressors who breach the laws of war.

It was the Romans who introduced a now familiar nuanced justification of wars: the search for peace. From republic to empire, Rome developed two new components to the equation. One was to seek peace as a national policy, but only as a result of military might: *Si vis pacem para bellum* (If you want peace, prepare for war). An old precursor to the modern realism of the West, this rationale at least spoke of peace as a preferred state, though it legitimized power as the sole foundation for it. But this first component was coupled with another, showing the deeper sense of early realism: the Pax Romana (peace of the Romans). This was an attempt to provide a somewhat secular motive for conquests, other than divine sanction. It is in the interest of the conquered to be conquered, because of the "peace" that will be installed. The Romans, followed by most other empires, including Arabs, Europeans, and Asians, rationalized the conquests of other nations and territories by devising a doctrine of "in the name of future peace, we are now bringing war and invasion to you." The aim obviously was to legitimize conquest and ultimately colonialism, but the notion of "ultimate peace" signified that peoples were increasingly attracted to a "state of peace," even at a high price. In the path of the Romans and the Byzantines, for example, the Arab armies of the Rashidun caliphs and the following Umayyad and Abbassid dynasties claimed they were bringing salaam (peace) to the conquered peoples of the Middle East, such as the Arameans, Copts, Berbers, and Persians. In many accounts, Arab classical historians said the invading armies of the Fatah were actually "liberators" freeing the oppressed societies outside Arabia.[1] These armies kept "liberating" peoples, like the Romans had done before, until the "Arab Pax" reached the Pyrenees to the west and China to the east. Centuries later, Spanish conquistadors marched through the jungles and mountains of Central and South America, bringing "Iberian peace" to the Indians. So did the Anglo-Saxons and other Europeans in North America. The French added a new concept in the nineteenth century: *La mission civilatrice*, a special mission to "bring civilization" into North Africa. In other words, all these powers from antiquity to modern times invoked a state of peace that would be expanded in parallel with their colonial rule. And on top of sociopolitical values, religions often played a dominant role in justifying war and peace.

Before the main monotheist religions began to impact world history, almost all beliefs were used as incentives to territorial aggrandizement and overseas invasions. And even when polytheism receded in front of Judaism, Christianity, and Islam in Europe and parts of Africa and Asia, the "marching orders" of the monotheist religions continued to rely heavily on the divine. To ancient Hebrews, for example, the "marching order" was to head toward a specific land, Canaan, and seize it in the name of God. Christians received a wider marching order, to bring the "godly good news to all peoples." Islam went even further by following a more powerful marching order: to "bring all peoples under the word of Allah." Each one of these religious projects developed a different geopolitical history. An ancient Israel was established, with shrinking and expanding borders for centuries, with the Jewish religion as its soul, in war and peace. Christianity sought to separate the affairs of Caesar from those of God, rejecting violence among humans. Christian politics wasn't supposed to exist, let alone Christian wars. But Christian emperors and kings continued to clash as those before Jesus had. Islam expanded within Arabia and into the outside world as a result of major battles, with Fatah and jihad as the epicenter of the caliphates. In short, the divine remained involved in war and peace, regardless of how far and deep the theological, warlike orders from one religion against the other. Monotheist faiths and most other religions are part of the history of nations and civilizations, with their continuous conflicts. But with intellectual revolutions, enlightenment, political development, and reforms, a consensus emerged as the modern nation-state came into existence: more and more, political philosophies and cultures prescribed a more earthly source for the norms of conflicts, and the rationale for religious war slowly shrank. With the American and French Revolutions, British reforms, Italian-Vatican agreements, and the Russian Revolution, state and religion were separated, and theological regimes collapsed in the West. The last religious injunction for military action before the formation of the League of Nations was the Ottoman sultan's call for jihad against the Allies and in favor of the Central Powers during World War I. Indeed the call by the Ottoman sultan for state jihad in 1914 was the last before the fall of the sultanate in 1922.

But the disappearance of direct religious wars from world politics and of religious influence from the making of wars in the early twentieth century didn't stop nationalist and social ideologies from producing conflicts that were just as destructive, reaching higher levels of technological violence. In World War I, millions died for the sake of nationalism, but democracies emerged victorious. World War II witnessed Nazism and Fascism obliterating tens of millions of men and women before being defeated again by the forces of transatlantic democracies and their Soviet ally. A third global conflict resumed between Western democracies and the Communist bloc but did not end with a world war. The nuclear dilemma on both sides prevented mutually assured destruction. Although regional wars across the planet have taken place in subsequent decades, from the Middle East to South Asia, a belief in international peace has unified diplomatic claims on all continents, at least in theory. Since 1954, the United Nations—at least in principle—has elevated peace to a worldwide political philosophy. Under the United Nations, peace keeping and peace building received vast endorsement, albeit depending on state interest. But during the Cold War, the threat of destructive ideological wars persisted. Pro-Soviet forces and their allies often took to the battlefield to conduct wars against the "enemies" of the proletariat. From Vietnam, Cambodia, and the crushing of East Europe's popular uprisings to international Soviet-inspired terrorism, state Communism appeared to be the last threat to democracies. With the fall of the Berlin Wall in 1989 and the collapse of Moscow's Soviet establishment in 1991, world peace was supposed to have been reinforced. Without the nuclear duel between the United States and the USSR, the Cold War ended. On a planetary scale, it was thought that no global movement aimed seriously at world domination, or at least intended to reestablish a past empire. War obviously hadn't been eradicated, however, as nationalism, ethnic strife, and other tensions persisted across the continents. The two Yugoslav conflicts, the Rwandan genocide, Sudan's civil war, and a score of local violent conflicts proved that.

But democracies felt they had the upper hand in the 1990s and began to prepare for what they thought would be an advanced international peace process, with mechanisms and teeth. At the United Nations, the traditional Soviet veto was gone; Communist China didn't choose to replace the older Communist brother in world affairs but to secure its economic dominance first, learning from Moscow's mistakes. Multinational forces, mostly put together by an expanding NATO, seemed to be efficient in Bosnia and Kosovo. The Rwandan disaster, apparently, only encouraged the United Nations and Western powers to put more effort into preempting future catastrophes. And it appeared that the Arab-Israeli conflict could be contained by a Palestinian-Israeli peace process. Regional crises and local violence were thriving still, but the international community seemed able to close in on the renegades, though not without difficulties. South Africa was emancipated, Germany was reunified, East Timor was granted independence, and all former republics of the Soviet Union were recognized. In conclusion, the 1990s projected democracies as the long-term victors of a very bloody twentieth century.

This view of the world was enhanced by the fact that after the demise of the Soviet threat, there were no significant forces on the world stage challenging the very essence of international law or of the political philosophy hailed by Western democracies and their allies around the world. Even when governments, regimes, and organizations collided and fought against each other, they all referred to the same set of ideas and principles. Yugoslav president Slobodan Milosevic was tried in The Hague for "crimes against humanity," as were militia leaders from Africa. Israel and the Palestine Liberation Organization (PLO) disagreed on many items but referred to the same charter of the United Nations. Anti-Americans, antiglobalists, pro–free marketers, nationalists, secessionists, opposing political parties in Western democracies, transitional regimes in the former Soviet Union, Scandinavian social democracies, Japanese political parties, Arab and Third World dictatorships, regardless of the degree of democratization within one or the other system, referred to one higher set of ideals and overarching principles in international relations, of which they all claimed to be part. Liberal democracies such as Canada and New Zealand and oppressive regimes such as Zaire and Burma all knew the worldwide standards of respect for human rights, but applied them differently. In short, the international community seemed to have become a large basket of various governments and regimes, with a set of ideas about war and peace recognized in theory but practiced dramatically differently.

In this setting of the early 1990s, liberal democracies felt they were leaders in a unified vision of a world hoping for international peace, though there were obvious failures in reaching it. Unfortunately for these democracies, they were wrong in their assessment. For there were players on the world stage who not only disputed the leadership role of the advanced democracies in international relations, but also rejected the very system of values upon which modern society had based its advances. These were the jihadists.

Not unlike other ideological movements throughout modern history, the self-described jihadists of various doctrinal persuasions rejected the international system that had been reached by consensus, the political culture advocated by democracies, and the principles upon which human rights were declared to be universal and inalienable. After Nazism and Fascism claimed a racially and nationally based world order in contradiction with the League of Nations, and after Soviet Bolshevism rejected liberal freedoms, jihadi Salafism and Khumeinism announced to the world that they not only would reject the democratic basis of modern international relations for themselves, but also planned to impose their own totalitarian system upon all nations. This post-Soviet form of totalitarianism is something the world has had to face since the 1990s, at first in fits and starts, but then openly after 9/11, because it is at the roots of the War on Terrorism and more specifically Jihadism.

This new jihadist totalitarianism is a reality with dire consequences for the current equation of international relations and the search for peace—in the UN Charter, for example—for the simple reason that the ideology behind the new wars against the "infidels" does not see peace as most players in world politics do. To the followers of al Qaeda, Islamic jihad, Combat Salafism, Wahabism, and Hezbollah, to name the main players in the field, the concept of peace does not coincide with international standards, let alone democracies' expectations. Even Soviet Communists, who developed their own ideological notion of "final peace," nevertheless operated within diplomatic and legal debates under the same umbrella of ideas as others when negotiating peaceful resolutions to crises. Jihadists, in contrast, adopt principles radically opposed to those of all other players, liberals and Marxists alike.

The Islamists reject the transformations of international relations that have taken place over the centuries and have led to the new ideals of war and peace in the West. The body of intellectual achievements that have taken place in Europe, America, and the modernizing Muslim countries between the sixteenth and twentieth centuries are seen as null and void by jihadi ideologues. First of all, the separation of state and religion is not an acceptable concept to Islamists. This alone ensures that the universal results of the Western liberal revolutions, as well as of the Marxist attempts to create criteria for a modern society, and even the reforms embraced by modern Muslims, are all equally irrelevant: the jihadists of the twenty-first century consider themselves the direct successors of the Muslim dynasties of the Middle Ages. They believe they are actually the heirs of the previous caliphates and accept to a degree the formal legality of the Ottoman Sultanate. The world's democracies are coming to realize, not without pain, that the new enemies of international law have a vision of the future that is literally a restoration of the distant past. The notion of "peace" in jihadi thought is based on a millennial concept that, 13 centuries ago, was standing policy within the Islamic empire, in much the same way that "godly wars" were legitimate in biblical times and in the Christian medieval era. To democracies, and to some extent all members of the international community, world peace is the ultimate objective to reach and one of the highest values to spread. But to jihadists, "peace" is just a state of affairs between one war and another—or, to be more precise, an acceptable condition when it is part of the readjustment of the balance of power in favor of Islam or a path to the surrender of the infidel. For in the eyes of the *jihadiyyeen* (jihadists), history is nothing but a continuous "clash of civilizations," which can end only when the one they claim to represent finally triumphs over all others. Thus victory—theirs—is a prerequisite for lasting peace. It is not hard to see why, insofar as there is an "international community" based on democratic standards and the idea of universal human rights, the jihadists lie outside it. The "need" for a final victory by the jihadists is what makes the clash between civilizations in modern times one of their highest objectives.

THE CLASH OF CIVILIZATIONS

When Professor Samuel Huntington published his famous article in *Foreign Affairs* in 1993, "The Clash of Civilizations?,"[2] it triggered one of the 1990s' most intense debates. In America, and then around the world, the ideas advanced by Huntington created a wide divide between his supporters and the

dominant schools in international relations. A distinguished Harvard professor, Huntington argued that after the Cold War, large civilizations would
constitute the basis for interaction on the world stage. He identified the
major players in diplomacy, wars, and economics: the Western, Islamic,
Slavic-Orthodox, African, Latin American, Hindu, Sinic (Chinese), Buddhist, and so on. Huntington argued that countries would cluster politically
in "civilizations" instead of East-West or North-South groupings, and conflicts would arise among these large civilization-based alliances. In the following years, scores of American and European intellectuals, followed by
their counterparts in many other regions, criticized this as a "false and mis-
guiding" theory in international politics.[3] Earlier in the decade, Francis
Fukuyama had argued that the main global confrontations ended with the
collapse of the Soviet Union and that humanity is now seeking to solve problems other than those of identity and culture.[4] "The clash of civilizations
doesn't exist" was the response at every single meeting of the American Political Science Association (APSA) and other related social science forums after
the publication of Fukuyama's article in *Foreign Affairs* and the subsequent
book, which appeared in 1996.[5]

Western and international academic elites abhorred the Huntington vision, accusing it of "bringing the world centuries backwards."[6] In a nutshell,
the mainstream thinking argued that religious and cultural conflicts have existed for centuries, but "modern" clashes aren't about "civilizations" inasmuch
as they take place because of economic and national interests. In their response
to the theory, liberals and Marxists lined up behind a unified opposition to
Huntington's thesis. In the Arab and Muslim world, writers and commentators
joined the fray against the idea that Islamic civilization is fighting on several
fronts against "others." In his description of the conflicts, Huntington identified what he saw as the "bloody borders of the Islamic civilizations," with wars
in Chechnya, Sudan, Kashmir, the Philippines, and so on. Muslim intellectuals
blasted back by arguing that Muslim countries were under attack by the West,
not the other way around. Arab-American commentators such as Edward Said
accused the likes of Huntington, and before him Bernard Lewis, of legitimiz-
ing imperialism and neocolonialism. Thus, Western democracies' intellectual
establishment and its Muslim counterparts refused to admit that civilizations
were clashing—before 9/11.

The supporters of Huntington's theory formed a core group, which was
in the minority throughout the 1990s. The international intellectual consen-

sus ranged from far left to liberal. The Marxists claimed that "cultural civilizations do not exist; it is all about economic oppression."[7]

Liberals affirmed that "civilization is universal but parts of it are left behind by the more endowed parts, now in the West."[8]

But more scientific findings, identified as historicist-legalist, asserted that though indeed religious and geocultural civilizations had clashed for centuries from ancient times onward, enlightenment, industrial revolution, and democratization have actually shifted that clash and halted it. This theory accepted Huntington's assertion as valid, but only for previous centuries. Pre-9/11, democracies would at the most admit only that civilizations had clashed in the past, but held that they weren't anymore.[9]

With all modesty, I should mention that according to the Area Arab Studies of the Library of Congress, my own work on international relations of civilizations preceded Professor Huntington's by 14 years. In my book *al Taadudiya*,[10] I introduced the concept of a world divided into main civilizations, mostly religious, as a *summa divisio* (highest division) of nations and cultures. Titled "The Organization and Coexistence of Civilizations," a chapter describes the wider civilizational webs, linguistic subgroups, and national and ethnic entities. Despite the Cold War realities of the time, I argued that indeed civilizations exist not only culturally, but also politically, including via their votes at the United Nations. But I theorized that although civilizations have clashed throughout history, they can coexist like any other subgroups. They act like large and loose entities, often divided, but at some times united on global issues. Mainly, it is important to admit that civilizations do indeed exist as world realities; that they do have historical differences, but that evolution in international relations and law has been able to reduce and in many cases reverse these tensions. According to Professor Huntington's theory, however, the clash is unstoppable.

Strangely, unexpected endorsers of the theory of civilizations have been the jihadists. Since the launching of their movements in the twentieth century, both Salafists and Khumeinists asserted strongly that their struggle is about the *umma* (umma in Arabic language means literally "nation" but could also mean "universal community"), which in their view *is* the global Islamic civilization. Contemporary jihadist ideologues, such as Abdel Wahab (nineteenth century), Hassan al Banna, Sayyid Qutb, and Imam Khumeini (twentieth century), based their doctrines on the fundamental belief that a *Hadara Islamiya* (Islamic civilization) continues to exist, despite the collapse of the caliphate in the 1920s, and is under attack by the forces of *kufr* (infidelism) worldwide. These militant currents, self-identified as *Islamiyun* (Islamists), borrowed the previous self-identification of the highest religious and political authority in the Muslim world, known as the sultanate under the Ottomans and the caliphate under the Arab dynasties. Before the collapse of the Turkish Empire in 1924 at the hands of secular general Mustafa Kemal, the Muslim world was ruled (at least nominally) by a supreme authority, the caliph.[11] Since the seventh century, with no significant interruptions, Muslim dynasties have ruled vast parts of Asia, Africa, and Europe, assigning regions and countries to *walis* (governors). The Muslim empires, as in other areas of the world, have led their subjects in wars and political crises. For centuries they clashed with other empires, including Christian, Hindu, and African. The caliphate represented Muslim civilization in the same way as the Papacy and the Byzantine Crown represented Christian civilization at some stage of history. Muslim geopolitics were influenced by Islamic theology a great deal, as were Hebrew geopolitics in biblical times and the actions of Christian empires during the Middle Ages.

But while ancient Israel came to an abrupt end in 70 AD/CE, the Hindu religious kingdoms under the Moguls in the fifteenth century, and the various Christian empires (as well as the papal states) by the end of the nineteenth, the last Muslim empire ended only in the early 1920s. Historically, by the beginning of the twentieth century, international society had withdrawn its recognition of universal religious empires and instead viewed nations and states as sole representatives of peoples. The League of Nations, followed by the United Nations, didn't include a concept of civilizations, but only nation-states. The idea of civilizations remained a vague cultural reference in academic, literary, and popular circles. However, nationalist ideologies would often exacerbate the "civilizational" affiliation of their nationality. Found mostly on the right, as in the case of extreme British, French, German, Russian, and Hindu nationalisms, these attitudes were also predominant among Arab nationalists, from both right and left wings.[12]

In the mainstream Arab Muslim intelligentsia, the wider *Hadaara* (civilization) became a center of pride and a serious component of public policy. A sense of belonging to a Muslim civilization became part of almost all political ideologies, from Nasserism to Baathism, even though secular. However, it was the Islamists who took the concept of global Islamic civilization literally; the Islamists in general and the jihadists in particular, since the 1920s, were bent on reconstructing the caliphate as a hub for the *umma*, the wider house of the "civilization of Islam." In practical terms, this means that the jihadists not only believe in the continuous existence of a civilization as a real political entity, but also are committed to removing any obstruction to its revival, including 21 Arab governments and more than 50 Muslim states—all of which are to be subsumed under the caliphate. And beyond the rebuilding of the caliphate, the Islamo-jihadists are committed to pursuing past conquests into infidel lands, "at the discretion of Allah and the orders of a reinstated Caliph."[13] In sum, not only do jihadists believe in the clash of civilizations, but they are consciously practicing it. It is not merely a passive clash of divergent civilizations, but an active war. In fact, while mainstream Muslim governments have integrated international law and global institutions, the Salafist and Khumeinist long-term objective is to dismantle international relations as we know them and reinstate *dar el Islam* (house of Islam).[14]

More pertinent for the War on Terrorism and its overarching War of Ideas is the fact that the jihadists are ready to kill and die for the *idea* of an *umma* civilization. And that fact was mostly missed by Western democracies until very recently. Instead, intellectual leaders in the international community, both liberals and Marxists, attempted to address the economic root causes of terror and violent crisis but again failed to understand the Islamist paradigm.[15]

THE ECONOMY DEBATE

Centuries before the Marxists reduced all social movements to the economy of social classes, thinkers, politicians, and diplomats from all cultures used water, agriculture, booty, lands, gold, silver, technologies, and goods as "material" roots for war and conquest. Put in simple terms, all wars and conflicts, even the most religious and theological, had economic goals at their center. A debate rages and probably will continue to rage between believers and atheists, as well as among people of divergent beliefs, as to whether, and how, a deity intervenes in or directs human history. Existential reflection on human origins and the human condition will always swing radically between the "scientific idea" that humans are material beings who rose to consciousness, and the "spiritual idea" that all existence, including human, is of divine origin. But underlying the philosophical and theological debate about human destiny, geopolitics attempts to explain social actions regardless of the unsolved mysteries of the universe. And here debate rages as well, among those who see the history of religion as strictly an economic one, those who see it as a spiritual one, and those who see it as a combination of both.

To take one example, the Bible reports that God ordered the Hebrews to move toward the land of Canaan. But a socioeconomic interpretation of these events links them to the migration of ancient Semitic tribes to lands with water within the Fertile Crescent. In Christian theology, God sent his Son Jesus to save humanity from sin. Historians, on the other hand, speak of the maturing of the Greco-Roman civilization toward monotheism. In Islam, Allah ordered Mohammed to reveal a new religion and spread it to all peoples. A sociological analysis shows that extreme, harsh conditions inside the Arabian Peninsula pushed the nomadic tribes to conquer the northern and more arable lands of Syria, Mesopotamia, and beyond.

Theological and sociological interpretations of world events intertwine and mingle; but after centuries of evolution, the international community of modern times has come to see in economics a human need in itself, to be addressed as such, regardless of religious imperatives. With the Enlightenment, Industrial Revolution, liberalism, and the rise of behavioral and other social sciences, a consensus grew within the international academic elite on the centrality of economics in historical movements. Although the debate about the explanation of these economics, their cultural impact, and their future evolution has remained lively, a consensus in political thought has emerged: economics can affect, and indeed radically change, the thinking, policies, and strategies of ideological movements, particularly those inspired by theologies.

In Marxist thinking, economics constitutes the entirety of what ideological movements are about. Hence, changing the economics of social classes would transform movements, including religiously motivated ones, into mostly social energies. In liberal thinking, economics is the "dominant part" of ideological currents, but other ingredients, such as cultural, historical, and political forces, have to be factored in as well. To conservatives, economics is only one component of the political thinking process (including ideological movements).

Political systems find their places along this continuum as well. Unlike dictatorships and autocracies, democracies include and tolerate all types of economic thinking, as an expression of pluralism. But by the end of the twentieth century, and as political violence grew exponentially across continents, the most common international attitude toward terrorism has been an agreement on the so-called root causes. The common thread has been to consider that the most important reason behind the rise of terror—including fundamentalist terrorism, and especially jihadi terrorism—is the so-called inequalities, the postcolonial and socially frustrated segments of the economically disfavored and underdeveloped areas in the Muslim world. A consensus among world elites that crosses political divides has developed based upon this view of jihadi terrorism.

"Why do they hate us?" asked America in the wake of 9/11. "Because of their economic conditions," answered the overwhelming majority of social scientists, both Marxist and liberal, and more intensely the Middle East Studies elite in the West. Falling into a familiar trap, the leading thinkers of democracies confused the Third World as a whole with Islamic fundamentalists, and Muslim societies with jihadists. For even if economics can be used to explain most historical events and analyze ideologies, a global explanation of any social phenomenon, such as terrorism, and Jihadism in particular, has to factor in other psychological, political, and historical ingredients. Democracies looked at Jihadism as one of the religiously inspired ideologies that can relate to the universal socioeconomic order, over which right- and left-wing ideologies struggle. And here was the analytical mistake of international elites, from the extreme left to the extreme right: Jihadism is not *another* ideology competing for the existing world order, with its economic, social, and financial incentives. Rather, it is an ideology trying to destroy the current order and replace it with another world order altogether. Philosophical nuances can make great differences in real politics, as with the different economic visions of capitalists, Communists, Fascists, and even conservative and religious movements. Democracies believe they can accommodate all economic views and ideological visions—as long as the overarching objective is the "democratic state," where all can coexist. But liberal democracies, and with them entire societies, have paid dearly for this conceptual mistake, as when Western democracies trusted Nazi and Fascist regimes, and when the Free World abandoned Europe and Central Asia to a Soviet occupation that some argued was building a "just society." It is happening again when Western elites affirm that jihadist groups and Islamist regimes are nothing but an expression of transitional economies and social frustration.

As I will note later, the jihadist ideology is not economically inspired, even though its elites profit from its political success—for example, the Taliban, the Sudanese regime, and Iran's ruling establishment. The leaders of the Islamist movements, from Abdel Wahab of Arabia, to Hassan al Banna and Sayyid Qutb of Egypt, to Salafi clerics such as Ibn al Uthaymeen and al Albani in the Saudi Kingdom, and many others around the globe, have been very clear in their writings and speeches: it is not about economics, nor about enhancing the socioeconomic conditions of Muslims; the *Aqida al Islamiya* (Islamist doctrine) is about the "will of Allah." It is about the spread of an ideology, mainly through jihad, first within the Muslim world and then beyond. Once the caliphate is reestablished, then "justice," including social and economic justice, will prevail. It is supremely ironic that though many intellectuals in the West attribute the claims and actions of the Islamists and jihadists to "dire socioeconomic conditions," the Islamists themselves declare just the opposite! Osama bin Laden, the Saudi multimillionaire, has no economic agenda for the *umma*. When he speaks of its resources as being plundered by the "Crusaders and the Jews," he intends to regain it so as to reinstate a caliphate as rich as the lost sultanate. Ayman Zawahiri, al Qaeda's number two, was a medical doctor in Egypt, not a proletarian. On al Jazeera TV (generously funded by Qatar's oil industry), the prominent cleric Sheikh Yussef al Qardawi tells his audience, "Your jihad is wealth in itself. You're not here on this Earth to reach material equality or financial prominence; you're here to spread the *deen* (religion) of Allah."[16] Indeed, Jihadism has recruited rich and poor, bourgeois and workers, immigrants and natives alike. Its outreach is vertical across classes and horizontal across nations. Democracies have missed this enormous "detail" just as much as they have confused nationalism and fundamentalism.

THE NATIONALISM DEBATE

The most debated phenomenon over the past two centuries in the industrialized world and many colonial regions has been nationalism. The idea of a nation is old but has witnessed a constant evolution. Linguistically, it has meant many things to many cultures and peoples. Attempts to define the concept of "nation" have been continuous and varied from school to school in social science. The classical German school, known as "objective," claimed that a nation is defined by history, language, geography, and sometimes race. In contrast, the French school, using the "subjective" concept, argued that a nation is determined by the will of its members to live together as a nation. Jean Jacques Rousseau and others sympathized with the right of self-determination. More modern approaches, using an American perspective, have viewed the legitimacy of a nation through its functionality: if it functions like a nation and looks like one, then it is one. More hybrid approaches have attempted to include all of the above parameters; that debate is still open, particularly with the emergence of the ethnic factor. But whatever the definition of a "nation," it is its derivative that has caused trouble in all stages of world history and particularly the modern era: nationalism.

Defining the collective identity of a nation is one thing. Struggling or even making war on behalf of this identity, under the ideology of nationalism, is something else. Nationalism has served positive purposes but has also caused human devastation. Nationalists have helped determine the identity of peoples, draw borders, liberate countries from foreign occupation, and protect cultural identity. They have played a significant role in bringing tyrannies down, ending absolutism, and opening the path to modernity. But extreme nationalist movements have also caused civil wars, occupations of other countries, colonialism, isolationism, and even global wars. The exaggeration of German, French, Italian, Spanish, English, Turkish, Arab, Russian, Japanese, Chinese, and many other nationalisms in the modern era has led to the Holocaust, genocides, massacres, and oppression. German Nazism and Italian Fascism are only among the worst examples. Russian extreme nationalism, even under a Marxist regime, was responsible for the suppression of non-Russian nationalities. Arab nationalism has oppressed numerous minorities in the Middle East. In the current state of international relations, democracies recognize nationalism as a legitimate movement when it expresses the will of a national resistance against occupation, such as during World War II, and when the nationalist "resistance" is a form of decolonization. But democracies have come to realize the excessive role of nationalism in such cases as the ethnic cleansing in Yugoslavia or the nuclear arms race between India and Pakistan. However, Western democracies have not consistently exposed such nationalist "excesses" in the twentieth century. For example, the United States and Europe rushed to condemn Yugoslav ethnic cleansing, and rightly so—but not Sudan's similar drama. They spent energy to solve Cyprus's crisis in 1974, but very little to help Nigeria in its civil war in the 1960s.

Despite these inconsistencies, democracies have at least been attempting to better understand "national-ethnic" crises around the world, as in Darfur, Iraq, East Timor, and other comparable cases. What Western democracies have failed to see clearly is the relationship between nationalism and Jihadism, especially in the context of the War on Terror. As mentioned above, many in the West confused the jihadi movement and its overarching Islamist current with a reaction on behalf of "underdogs"—victims of colonialism, neocolonialism, and underdevelopment. The same misguided application to jihadis of the rationale of economic factors was also committed with regard to national identities. A main argument floating among elite thinkers and commentators in the United States and Europe has been—and remains—that the jihadists in different geographical locations are the expression of the "national frustration" of the populations they represent. Hence, during the 1990s, the Wahabis of Chechnya were presented on both sides of the Atlantic as a "nationalist resistance, who happen to be Islamists."[17] Similar interpretations were applied to Jaish e Taiba and Jaish Mohammad in Kashmir, Abu Sayyaf in the southern Philippines, and to a certain extent Hezbollah in Lebanon.

The analytical mistake made in the West after the Cold War was to not understand the very nature of the jihadi ideology: it is a pan-nationalist, cross-national, and theologically inspired doctrine. The Salafi vision of the international struggle opposes what they perceive as *dar el Islam*, the abode of Islam worldwide, with the rest of the world, which they dub *dar el harb* (the war zone). The Islamists may well operate in the midst of a specific nationality (Arab, Turkish, Asian) and in the context of a particular country (Egypt, Saudi Arabia, Indonesia), but their aim is for the whole *umma*, which theoretically would include all 52 Muslim states. The jihadists are ideological internationalists by definition. Mohammed Atta, an Egyptian, and Ziad Jarrah, a Lebanese, along with 15 Saudi citizens perpetrated the attacks of September 11, 2001, against a country designated as an enemy of "all Muslims" by al Qaeda. Abdallah Azzam, a Palestinian, was fighting the Soviet Russians in Afghanistan instead of the Israelis at home. More recently, American citizens, supporters of al Qaeda, have conducted warfare in central Asia, thousands of miles away from their homes.

Western intellectuals, in the main, have reacted too fast to the attacks of 9/11 by imputing them to a so-called global frustration by Arabs and Muslims over the problem of Palestine. By doing so, they have confused international jihadists and Palestinian nationalists. In the jihadi view, expressed by bin Laden, Zawahiri, and many radical clerics such as al Qardawi, Palestine is one issue among many in the greater confrontation with the *kuffar* (infidels). It may be the main issue, especially to Palestinian Islamists, but not the single jihadi issue worldwide. For whereas the PLO's first objective is to establish a Palestinian state on as much land as possible, al Qaeda's agenda in Palestine is to dismantle Israel, then merge the "province" of Palestine into the greater caliphate. In short, the jihadis are not nationalists, but internationalist Islamists. Such nuances are crucial in the War of Ideas.

Policy planners commit tremendous mistakes if they confuse a nationalist claim with a jihadi one. The two may overlap in political propaganda and on the battlefield, but they are distinct spheres with opposed agendas. Jihadism, in its various robes—Salafism, Wahabism, Deobandism, Khumeinism—can easily use nationalist causes, take over these causes, and fuel ethnic strife. But at the end of the day, nationalism has its own logic and Jihadism another, and democracies must understand the differences if the War of Ideas with the terrorists is to be won with the support of nationalities and not against their will.

CHAPTER TWO

THE ANTIDEMOCRACY AXIS

IN THE GLOBAL CONFRONTATION BETWEEN DEMOCRACIES AND Jihadism, international observers have noted an odd convergence between diverse Islamist movements on the one hand and a world array of totalitarian ideologies on the other. Adding to this strangeness, Jihadism, Communism, Fascism, extreme nationalism, Nazism, and other radical, totalitarian isms, which clashed against each other with raw violence throughout the twentieth century, have now come together to face off with their ultimate common enemy: democracy.

The collaboration of the antidemocratic isms is one of the most fascinating phenomena in modern international relations. For example, Arab nationalists, such as the Baathists and followers of Egyptian leader Gamal Abdel Nasser, engaged in brutal oppression of the Muslim Brotherhoods for decades. But Syria's Hafez Assad, while a devout secular Baathist and socialist (as he pretended to be during the Cold War), struck up a strategic alliance with Iran's Khumeinist—and very Islamist—regime. This alliance produced a more politically incorrect (from the socialist angle) cooperation with ultra-Islamist Hezbollah in Lebanon.

Other convergences of interest between jihadists and their archenemies, the Communists, are the growing cooperation between the Islamists and the Venezuelan populist regime of President Hugo Chavez and the international collaboration with twenty-first-century Trotskyists of the so-called Anti-War Movement. The jihadists—as Mujahideen first—fought the Soviets desperately in Afghanistan but did not hesitate to form an axis with the Latin American friends of the former Soviet Union, such as Castro and Chavez. Perhaps most shocking to the Western reader is the behavior of the Islamists in the 1930s and 1940s, peaking with World War II. Muslim Brotherhoods, as well as Arab nationalists, allied themselves with Hitler and Mussolini, hoping to defeat the British and French. And more recently, while the debate was raging about Iraq, all indications were that Baathist Saddam Hussein had a convergence of interests with the anti-American jihadists in the region. In every single case, the purpose was to come together with archenemies to oppose the surge of freedom and democracy.

It's important to note, though, that Western governments have also allied themselves with one or more of these antidemocratic isms. But in most cases, it was to serve an overarching necessity of defending a democracy at risk or because of a global conflict with greater dangers to humanity. Examples can be easily cited: during World War II, Western democracies allied themselves with the Soviet Union, which was ideologically opposed to the essence of liberal democracy. But the rationale was simply to defeat a greater Fascist threat. During the Cold War, the Western democracies, particularly the United States, had to back up the Islamic fundamentalists in Afghanistan and other parts of the Middle East, but in the logic of the time, this was to contain and weaken the greater danger of Soviet Communism. Without doubt, democracies, and especially their foreign policy establishments, have and will commit serious and sometimes dramatic mistakes in these unnatural alliances with totalitarian isms. But in sum, democracies seek to further freedom, liberty, and the survival of modern achievements, notwithstanding the great damages they inflict on their own values as they strike illogical alliances. On the other hand, Jihadism, sometimes with its interim allies, seeks the reversal of modernity and the defeat of secular democracy and universal human rights: two different and contradictory world agendas. As we will come back later to examine how democracies and the jihadists apply their agendas to international relations, let's compare the agendas of some totalitarian ideologies with those of the jihadists.

ANTIDEMOCRACY IDEOLOGIES

The most basic tenets of democratic movements and governments are freedoms of thought, expression, political action, and the formation of political parties—in essence, pluralism and the *droit à la différence* (right to difference). Antidemocratic ideologies do not grant the common citizen the right to differ, oppose, or organize outside the realm of the dominant doctrine. A common trait of all antidemocratic movements is the claim of "higher inspiration" and therefore legitimacy. In the center of totalitarianism, a source of power and truth overrides all other considerations, from popular will to intellectual difference. By contrast, the basic unit in democracies is the will of an individual human being, as it finds its expression in groups, from a political party to an ethnic nationality all the way up to the largest social entities.

Today's political scientists note that democratic culture and processes are only a small part of a universal human history that has been mostly authoritarian. That is to say, most of the recorded history of nations is obviously one of obscurantism and oppression, of boundless conquests and genocide. From monarchic city-states, such as Greece and ancient Rome (even if sometimes called republics), to the greater colonial empires of Byzantium, the Sassanids, the Umayyad, Carolingians, Abbasids, Habsburgs, Mameluks, Tsars, Huns, and Ottomans, it has taken the whole history of empires and nation-states to firm up and finalize the principles of democracy and its derivatives. From bloody revolutions, such as the American and French, to slower constitutional reform, as in Great Britain, a long trail of struggles has produced international norms and modern freedoms. Though democracy was principally practiced in the West and by similar entities overseas, democratic principles challenged centuries of raw realism, both domestically and internationally. Inside nation-states, the principles of freedoms and human rights had to be imposed through waves of revolts and debates. Between nation-states, the ideas of self-determination, independence, and sovereignty had to be slowly introduced and negotiated, not without major ruptures of global security. Ironically, endless wars have planted the seeds of most if not all of the democratic principles entrenched today in charters, declarations, and constitutions.

With the end of World War I—the war that was supposed to end all wars—Woodrow Wilson declared his points, and some imagined that peace and democracy had finally brought about the "end of History." The Paris Peace Conference of 1919 and the emergence of the League of Nations in the 1920s were heralded as the end of oppression and repression. In fact, the *principles* of peace and freedom were being consolidated but were to be violated tragically throughout the whole twentieth century. The explosion of antidemocratic ideologies was not confined to a particular region or culture; they emerged from all continents, most nations, and in different shapes and forms. From primitive extreme nationalism turned fascist to socioeconomic doctrines turned imperialist to militaristic turned populist, many currents sank the twentieth century into continuous havoc and bloodshed. But ironically, the principles of democracy continued to make progress. Western democracies, particularly in Europe, spent many decades sloughing off the weight of their former colonial empires, not without dramatic mistakes and delays. But at every Western pull-out, democracy made progress. And Japan, following World War II and the loss of all its territorial possessions, became an Asian democracy. So on the one hand, all democracies evolved into more experienced ones, with internal and external transformations and laws emancipating greater sectors of their own populations, including women and minorities. But on the other hand, antidemocratic ideologies continued their relentless attempts to reverse the historical process of democratic modernity.[1]

Latin America

In Latin America, officer juntas and family dictatorships dominated many countries, while populist leaders such as Juan Peron and parties such as the Institutional Revolutionary Party (PRI) in Mexico also instituted authoritarian rule. The right wing used such concepts as *personalismo, continuismo,* and *machismo* (individual leadership, continuity of rule, and manly personality) to affirm their legitimacy. The left wing was the alter ego of this phenomenon. In Cuba, Fidel Castro's regime modeled itself on Stalinism. In Nicaragua, the Sandinistas borrowed from Vietnam's regime. Across the region, radical groups emulated Trotskyism and Maoism. Until the collapse of the Soviet Union, antidemocracy forces in Latin America prevailed.

But by the end of the century, authoritarians had retreated and democracies moved forward: Chile, Argentina, Uruguay, Brazil, Nicaragua, Mexico, El Salvador, Haiti, and others developed multiparty systems. Cuba's monoparty regime alone withstood the trend toward freedom, awaiting better times and future partners in the hemisphere, such as Venezuela's populist president Hugo Chavez and Bolivian president Evo Morales of the early twenty-first century. And in more recent years, Middle Eastern radical regimes and organizations have introduced another antidemocratic ideology to the region, aiming at converging with the local radicals.

Africa

Africa has witnessed an evolution some describe as too abrupt, from tribal societies into independent states, after decades of Western colonialism. At the end of the nineteenth century, the entire continent—with the exception of Ethiopia—was under colonial rule. For the previous three centuries, the north of Africa was under the Ottoman Sultanate; and since the seventh century, all lands between the Sinai and the Atlas Mountains were submitted to Umayyad or Abbasid caliphates. Freedom came back to Africa gradually with European decolonization in the second part of the twentieth century, but most of its countries were dominated by ruthless elites: military juntas, dictatorships, and dominant elites ruled the continent from South Africa to Egypt almost without exception.

After the departure of the Europeans, Arabs and blacks were ruled by their own kind, but these regimes mutated into an internal colonialism, often more oppressive than that of Western democracies' governors. Egypt got its Nasser, Zaire its Seku Toure; Libya got its Ghaddafi, and Uganda its Idi Amin. Claiming a Marxist agenda but ruling as absolute monarchs, Africa's leaders were the continent's worst threats to liberty for decades. Yet the most deprived continent of all has moved forward in the past 20 years. South Africa reversed apartheid and elected black presidents without ethnic cleansing of white Africans. Although facing crisis after crisis, multiparty and multiethnic elections have been taking place against all odds and despite the dissatisfaction of many forces on both sides of the former racial divide. All colonial powers have ceased on the mainland. Civil wars have erupted in Sierra Leone and Liberia to the west; tribal genocide in Rwanda and Burundi in the center; Eritrea seceded from Addis Ababa, and the power of the military is still omnipresent elsewhere, but elections are taking place in most countries. In sum, postcolonial Africa is attempting to cross the dangerous path from Third World drama to transitional democracy. But with the War on Terror looming from all directions, the continent has to face the wrath of a new antidemocratic ideology, which could destroy the small achievements it has made since decolonization. Jihadism could thus plunge Africa back into the authoritarian past.

Asia

Asia didn't escape the rise of dangerous antidemocratic regimes and ideologies. The most eminent mid-twentieth-century phenomenon was undoubtedly Japan's militaristic imperialism. But dictatorships and authoritarian regimes abounded elsewhere: Burma, Indonesia, and Pakistan are just a few examples. Asia's first giant, China, fell to Communism in 1949 and has remained under this form of government to this day, the most populated non-democratic country in the world. North Korea under the Kim Jong regime is perhaps the most repressive worldwide since Stalin. Indochina too fell to Marxism-Leninism and its one-party repressive system. Because of the Asian Communist bloc, liberties on the continent have been curtailed for decades.

But even as Communist Asia has survived the fall of the Soviet Union, democracies have advanced, both horizontally and vertically, over the past few decades. Japan moved from Fascist empire to multiparty democracy. The Philippines followed, and South Korea, Taiwan, Singapore, and Thailand have enhanced their free societies. India has consolidated its position as the single largest democracy in the world. Even the Communist countries, with the one exception of North Korea, have made internal changes toward openness, mostly economic, but with slight political loosening. Twenty-first-century China and even more so Vietnam are modernizing at a rapid pace, not without concessions to their populations—though liberties are far from meeting the minimal requirements to be considered democracies. In the Muslim part of Asia, trends have been different. Although multiparty elections have been the rule in most Muslim countries since decolonization, as in Pakistan, Bangladesh, Indonesia, and Malaysia, serious challenges have begun to impede the advance of the democratic cultures of these countries. Authoritarianism plagued some and militarism others, but across the board, a radical Islamist ideology has forced leaders to slow the democratization process and in some cases reverse it significantly.

The West

It goes without saying that democracy has been thriving in the West, in an international space that transcends geographical, political, and religious divisions. Since the Peace of Westphalia in the seventeenth century, the march toward reform, reformation, industrial revolution, and enlightenment has produced a political development leading to what we know as modernity. Democracy as a concept may well have been forged through the ages in various cultures, but in modern times it has taken roots among societies on both sides of the Atlantic and in the overseas communities that subscribe to its principles. The American and French Revolutions, the British constitutional reforms, and other European democratic achievements form the basis of international law and human rights. However, the West has not been consistently democratic. Indeed, European societies haven't been ruled systematically and equally by liberal governments, even though European democracy as a whole was leaping ahead of other cultures. Authoritarian regimes such as those in Portugal, Spain, and Greece coexisted with the most advanced democracies of Sweden, Holland, and Belgium. But by the 1970s, the anomalies within Western Europe were gone: all members have become equally democratic. And during the same decades, most European colonies were surrendered to their indigenous populations. In reality, the most antidemocratic threats Europe has experienced were home-grown ideologies that caused tremendous destruction, the death of millions, and an immense loss of freedoms: Fascism and Bolshevism.

For decades, the dire ideological enemies of democracies emerged from their own birthplace. Nazism and Soviet Communism obliterated entire societies that were naturally evolving toward liberalism. Destroying authoritarian tsarist Russia in 1917, Bolshevism preempted the country's social-democratic revolution, throwing Russians and other neighboring peoples under the yoke of Stalinism and "Sovietism" for decades; millions of citizens perished. German Nazism and Italian Fascism crumbled their own weak democracies, leading the continent and the world to global war and genocide; many more millions were massacred. Fortunately for the peoples of the continent, Hitler and Mussolini were defeated with the help of the United States in 1945, and later the Soviet Union defeated itself, again under America's pressure.

Europe's democracies since the early 1990s have been pushing eastward, slowly but surely. However, the danger of totalitarian isms has not vanished. With 9/11 in New York, 3/11 in Madrid, and 7/7 in London, the West has witnessed the rise of another deadly ideology, reemerging out of the past and promising perhaps the longest war of all against democracy. This ideology is Jihadism.

The Greater Middle East

Europe's paradox is not unique; that of the Greater Middle East is comparable even if dissimilar. Europe practiced democratic values but witnessed major totalitarian exceptions in the twentieth century. In contrast, the Arab and Muslim Middle East were and continue to be ruled by dictatorships but are witnessing the beginning of democratic exceptions in the early twenty-first century. As in other regions, the area stretching from Morocco to China and covering North Africa, the Levant, the Sinai Peninsula, and the high plateau of Asia Minor and Iran had to deal with its own isms, as repressive and lethal as the authoritarian regimes and ideologies of other continents. And like its neighbors across the Mediterranean and the Indian Ocean, the Middle East has been ruled by empires and dynasties thirsty for warfare and conquests: Abbassids, Mameluks, Seleucids, and Ottomans were striking examples. The Muslim sultanate finally fell to European mandates and secular Turks in the 1920s. And as soon as British and French colonial powers withdrew from the region, in stages, the weak elites installed by the Europeans—mostly inclined toward liberal evolution—collapsed dramatically under the pounding by authoritarians, whether absolute monarchies or Pan-Arabist socialists. Egypt got Gamal Abdel Nasser; Iraq, Saddam Hussein; Syria, Hafez Assad; Libya, Muammar Qadhafi; Sudan, Omar Bashir; and Algeria, Boumediene. Other Arab countries fell under dynasties, and Iran was ruled by the shah.

As in other continents and cultures, the region's antidemocratic ideologies have had a devastating effect on people's freedoms and security. More importantly, they have survived the decades of political change that impacted other nations around the world. Virulent nationalism to the extreme of ethno-imperialism has characterized most nationalities in the Greater Middle East: Pan-Arabism, Pan-Turkism, Persian nationalism, and even smaller ethnic groups have been adamant about rejecting the idea that other "identities" would be allowed within their national boundaries. Minorities have paid a dear price for these irredentist attitudes: Kurds in Iraq, Armenians in Turkey, Berbers in Algeria, Africans in Sudan, Arabs in Iran, Copts in Egypt. Extreme nationalism has been another brand of antidemocracy, especially when coupled with militaristic regimes as in Baathist Iraq and Syria, populism like Nasser's, or religious fundamentalism as with the Khumeinist regime in Iran.

But even in the Middle East—the last space where antidemocracy thrives and threatens freedoms greatly—the challenge to oppression is also manifest. Liberal democrats, in the Middle Eastern sense, are very active; minorities haven't let their struggle lapse, and they rise up at every occasion. Women's movements are alive despite great oppression, and youth and intellectuals are more determined than ever. Democratic forces are struggling against extreme nationalism and ethnic racism from Sudan to Iran, and the regional forces of social change are determined to crumble authoritarianism, local fascism, and militarism as well. But as witnessed in the last few years, the most lethal force at work in the region—the enemy of all democracies—is without doubt Jihadism, omnipresent from the Atlantic shores of the Arab world to the Indian shores of the Muslim world. The oldest of all isms in ideological terms, it has assembled resources including oil dividends, fundamentalist religious zeal, oppressive regimes, sophisticated elites, propaganda machines, efficient organizations, global lobbies, and the inhuman power of terrorism unbound by any principles—all in order to deliver war against the struggling and unaccomplished democracies. One can see that the central battlefield between the forces of Jihadism and the weak but equally determined pockets of democracy is the Middle East itself. Over the past few decades, socialist Baathism and Islamist Jihadism have become like enemy brothers—they used to try to slaughter each other, but they have now come together in a global effort to stop democracy.[2]

BAATHISM

Originally influenced by European classical nationalisms of the nineteenth century, the early intellectuals who claimed Arab nationalism were not all, nor necessarily, totalitarians. Many among the founders were poets and writers. The first wave of manuscripts left to readers in the early twentieth century was mainly focused on bringing down the Ottoman occupation of the Arab Middle East and chanted freedom and liberty in a manner mirroring Rousseau and Garibaldi. According to a number of modern students of the phenomenon, in its initial stage, Arab nationalism (*al Qawmiya al Arabiya*), wasn't even a mass movement among Muslims. In fact, Arab-speaking Christians living under the sultanate, themselves members of religious and ethnic minorities, were the ones to launch the idea that a "secular" national identity grouping Muslims and Christians would defeat the idea of an absolute Islamic caliphate. Hence, according to this historical explanation, non-Arab and non-Muslim minorities "constructed" an imaginary community of Arabs but removed the connection to religion. In reality, these intellectuals were attempting to seduce the Arab Muslim majority into separating from the wider "Ottoman identity," which retained the Islamic legitimacy of the caliphate. In short, they set the Arabs against the Turks and tried to enlist the former into choosing a secular instead of religious identity, so that the Christian minorities of the Arab world would find a political space among a new Pan-Arab identity not restricted to Muslims.

This early attempt to "manufacture" a national identity for all Arabs outside the Islamic reference failed. As of the beginning of the twentieth century, and increasingly after the collapse of the Istanbul sultanate, ironically at the hands of a new secular Turkish nationalism spearheaded by Mustafa Kemal "Ataturk" in 1923, Arab nationalism was taken back by Islamic feelings and aspirations. Muslim intellectuals, politicians, and cadres saw a historic link between the *Urubah* (Arabness) and the Islamic identity. This marriage between the two ideas produced an interesting hybrid. Officially, Arab nationalism was presented as somewhat secular, in the sense that it would encompass Muslims and non-Muslims alike, but it was connected organically to historical Islam. Michel Aflaq, the founding father of the Baathist ideology—a Christian Orthodox from Syria—said in this regard, "Islam is to Arabism what bones are to flesh."

But by the 1930s, Pan-Arabism stood for more radical goals:

1. The first tenet of Pan-Arab nationalism was removing all non-Arab presence from all "Arab lands." This raised at least two questions. First, what is an "Arab land"? Is it defined by language, ethnicity, self-determination? Arab nationalists, distancing themselves from the pro-self-determination French school of nationalism, rejected any debate or even democratic consultation on Arab identity. There was no discussion of it, only an acceptance by its subjects. The only objective component of this nationalist identity that was ultimately retained was language: you speak it, therefore you're an Arab. But many non-Arab ethnics spoke the language in the region, including Kurds, Assyrians, African Sudanese, Berbers, Aramaics, Hebrews, and others. With the exception of the Jews, all these pre-Arab indigenous ethnicities were "forced" into "Arabism." In a show of early anti-Semitism, Jews were excluded from being considered as cultural Arabs. Hence Arab nationalists argued that first Europeans had to leave the greater Middle East, including the French civilian population of Algeria, then the Jews of Israel—those who had immigrated from overseas. Finally, all other minorities were to declare their allegiance to "Arab nationalism, or else."[3] In other words, a preemptive strike by Pan-Arabists aimed at

cleansing all non-Arab identities from Morocco to Iran. The move was later labeled as Arabization *(Taareeb)*.

2. The second tenet was to unify all these "Arab lands" by all means, including by force if needed. The influence of European nineteenth-century national unification was a factor: Bismarck in Germany and the Pan-Italian nationalists provided a precedent. But the *Qawmeyeen Arab* (Arab nationalists) made the unification an overarching objective of their takeover of governments in the region. Nasser built his career on the necessity of unification with other brotherly Arab entities, called *Qutr* (a segment or piece of a larger entity). He forged one with Syria, imposed another on Yemen, and attempted a third with Libya. All Arab nationalists—those in power and those who were in the opposition—looked at the independent sovereign countries in the Arab world as just *Aqtar* (plural of *Qutr*), whose destiny was to melt into the wider Arab nation, or *al umma al Arabiya*. Pan-Arabist intellectuals, many of whom, ironically, graduated from the American University of Beirut and various colleges in Cairo, Damascus, and Baghdad, were mostly urban people with petite bourgeoisie tendencies, tilting toward left-wing doctrine but practicing right-wing policies. Comparatively, the Arab nationalists were swinging between Hitler's social-nationalism and Stalin's Marxist-Leninism. The few liberals among them weren't successful in gaining ground by the 1950s. The radical nationalists were the ones to launch the mass movements and in some cases take over regimes.

3. The third tenet was to transform the *umma Arabiya* into a modern superpower. Ideologues who have promoted this idea argue that "once upon a time, the Arabs formed a formidable empire, stretching from Spain to China and they defeated other great empires on two continents" (Asia and Africa). Today, they continue, "Arabs have oil, large lands, and strategic locations (the Suez Canal, access to the straights of Gibraltar, Hermuz, and the Bab el Mandeb); this should enable the Arab nation to build all that world powers have, including nuclear weapons, a seat on the Security Council, and the ability to defeat their enemies swiftly."[4] This third concept, very popular in the 1970s and 1980s, flirted with the notion of an Arab imperialism that would bring back "past glory" and project a future of expansion.

In a global comparison, the evolution of Pan-Arabism (Baathism being one of its emanations) has resembled German national socialism and Italian Fascism more than French, British, and Italian liberal nationalisms. For Arab nationalism, like the movements led by Hitler and Mussolini, based itself on cleansing its national territory of ethnic minorities and did not recognize any other nationality within its imaginary Lebensraum. In many cases where Arab nationalists took over power in one *Qutr* or Arab country, the triangular fascist equation was repeated: *umma waaheda, shaab wahed*, and *qaid awhad*: "One Reich, one people, and one Führer."[5]

The ideology of Pan-Arabism rapidly became expansionist, fascist, and populist. Many manifestations within the Arab world produced a variety of parties, movements, leaders, and regimes: from Nasser to Arafat, from Assad to Saddam, they developed identical core values and cultivated extreme cults of personalities. One of these ideologies was the Baath Party's.

Founded by two Syrian intellectuals in the 1950s, Michel Aflaq and Salah Bitar, the Arab Baath Socialist Party was the most advanced among all similar movements. In fact, the only real competing Pan-Arabists were Egypt's charismatic Gamal Abdel Nasser and the Baath parties of Syria and Iraq. The latter started as a seriously socialist and secular party but was extremely chauvinistic. Interestingly, the Baath ideology disagreed with Islamist doctrines and in fact clashed with them, but it waged war against the same enemies, wanted the same Arab territories, and told the same tales of past Arab glories. The Baath, in other words, wanted to be more politically correct in the second part of the twentieth century, when religion was not well regarded by progressives around the world and certainly wouldn't have attracted the support of the Soviet Union. *Baath* means "renaissance," to indicate the rebirth of Arab identity. The Baathists took power in Syria first via a series of coups d'etat in the early 1960s. Years later, they grabbed power in Iraq. In 1970, Hafez Assad seized power in Damascus, and by the end of the decade, Saddam Hussein was installed in Baghdad.

Other than the genocide perpetrated in Sudan by the Islamists, the two Baathist regimes combined to produce the highest volume of oppression and violence in the modern history of the Middle East. Baathism, next to Jihadism, has been one of the worst bullies in the region. With an ideology that gives no space for pluralism, differences, and liberties, the Assad and Saddam regimes practiced almost all types of human rights abuses—collective, ethnic, cultural, political, and humanitarian. In Syria, the Baathists suppressed the opposition for decades, massacred more than 20,000 victims in the uprisings of 1982 in Hama, tortured prisoners, and occupied Lebanon and assassinated its leaders. In Iraq, their counterparts gassed and murdered tens of thousands of Kurds in the 1980s, massacred at least 300,000 Shiites in the 1990s, tortured Sunni opponents, and suppressed Christians and other minorities. Furthermore, Baathism systematically obstructed an Arab-Jewish reconciliation and all attempts at a peace process between Palestinians and Israelis. Thus Baathism, as the most powerful expression of Arab national-ism, has played a central role in denying Arabs and minorities in the region historical opportunities to let their reforms develop naturally and join the in-ternational political culture of democracy. But this doesn't mean that a new Arab nationalism can't reform and democratize. What it does mean is that it will take historic efforts by new generations of Arabs to reverse the colonial-ist trends of twentieth-century Pan-Arabism and achieve a new liberal and pluralistic sense of identity, with either progressive or conservative color-ing—but in either case, with democratic inspiration. This is the challenge of the first decades of the twenty-first century. It will be a difficult path, in view of the rising and widening growth of Jihadism.[6]

JIHADISM

As I defined it in my previous book, *Future Jihad*,[7] the world jihadist move-ment emanates from well-defined ideologies, with adapted strategies and a wide variety of tactics, dictated by political realities. As discussed earlier, con-trary to assertions by many intellectuals in the West and the many anti-West-ern propagandists worldwide, Jihadism is not a mere reaction to the foreign policies of industrialized powers, nor is it a collective response by a frustrated Muslim world to American, European, and allied "aggression." These classic stereotypes, often depicted in Western classrooms, read in the mainstream press, or heard on al Jazeera and other Islamist media, are the result of a global War of Ideas waged by the defenders of the strategic interests of regimes and organizations that are challenged by the rise of new democracies in their midst. The camouflaging of what Jihadism is or isn't is in fact a main component of this War of Ideas. For as I will explain later, the current battle of arguments on the world stage is about defining the concept of jihad, Ji-hadism, and jihadists. Depending on which definition is held by Western democracies and their allies, the War of Ideas could be won by the jihadists and their allies, and the War on Terror might be prolonged for an additional number of decades. This is why it is important, in this book and in future research, that the doctrines upon which Jihadism and Islamism are based are clarified to the reader, so that the public is able to better understand the players and their plans. Elsewhere I have offered a comprehensive analysis of Jihadism, as a concept and as an ideology, and attempted to project its trajectory into the future. In this book, I will try to show by way of comparison how Jihadism as a movement is in a state of complete conflict with democracy, not only in terms of principles, but also in the realm of geopolitics and power politics.

Defining Jihad

Jihad as a concept was developed in the early seventh century by the founders of the Islamic state in the Arabian Peninsula. The state concept of jihad was certainly inspired by the citations of *al-Jihad* in Islamic holy scriptures, including the Qu'ran (the revealed word of Allah to Mohammed) and the *Hadith* (the Prophet's sayings and acts). So one root of jihad is theological. It is summarized as "constant effort on behalf of Allah" *(al-Jihad fi sabeel Allah)*.[8] From this perspective, it has a divine cause.

Some commentators in modern times, both Muslims and non-Muslims, have argued that there are two jihads, the military one and the spiritual one. In fact, in its inception, it was one jihad with multiple faces or dimensions. What is overarching in *al-Jihad* is not just the effort, but the objective of it, which is to propagate the *rissala* (mission). For there is no jihad outside its essence, and that is the *rissala*. The question has been to determine the needs for this "mission" and the legitimate "authority" that can lead it. And to complicate the matter, Muslim theologians are in disagreement on the place of jihad in the basic tenets of religion. The more moderate argue that jihad is the sixth unofficial pillar of Islam next to *Shahada* (witness), *Zakat* (alms), *Hajj* (pilgrimage), *Salaat* (prayer), and *Sawm* (fasting). But more zealous clerics affirm that *Jihad* is a central tenet. "It is a duty, which has been neglected too long," declared Ibn Taymiya in the Middle Ages.[9] However, without dodging the research question of jihad's place in religion, I postulate that it is a theological issue and should be addressed by theologians and legislators in the context of religious and historical studies, interfaith activities, or when legislation is debated regarding the coexistence of Sharia laws (Islamic laws) within secular contexts. I'll come back to this question later in the book.

The relevant question is about jihad's historical and later ideological meanings, notwithstanding the outcome of the theological debate (though admitting that the latter can influence future political actions). In short, what was the reality of jihad as a concept through centuries of practice, and what does the specific ideology of Jihadism claim? In my previous book, and in many similar works, it is clear that historically, jihad was a state tool for war mobilization under Arab and Ottoman caliphates and various Muslim dynasties, such as the Umayyads, Abbasids, Seleucids, Moguls, Mameluks, and many others. The official references to jihad and the number of fatwas (religious edicts) authorizing it are too voluminous to ignore. Throughout the centuries of early Islamic Fatah (conquest) of Syria, Iraq, North Africa, Persia, and all the way to Spain, thousands of jihad speeches and declarations legitimized state expansion into these vast lands outside Arabia.[10]

The jihad policy was not an individual choice during the first centuries of the Islamic empire. It was decided by caliphs, legitimized by imams, and archived by the bureaucracy. The supreme commander of the believers, known as *Ameer al mu'mineen*, issued jihadic edicts as declarations of war and for mass mobilization. Nowadays, Islamist intellectuals and Western academics insist on a jihad with a spiritual dimension. Although this is theoretically and philosophically possible, jihad throughout history was a state public policy on war and peace, and it was sanctioned by religious edicts. The Ottomans, taking over the caliphate from the Arabs in the sixteenth century, resumed their own jihad throughout Europe, with as many conquests, wars, and peace treaties as their predecessors of the seventh century. To the east, the Mogul Muslim dynasty conquered territory as far as India and China, also with the legal help of holy war declarations. Below the level of caliph and sultan, local emirs and *walis* (governors) also used jihad fatwas against the infidels and even against each other.

Historically, the state form of jihad lasted about 13 centuries on three continents: Asia, Africa, and Europe. The very last caliph-sanctioned jihad was during World War I by the Ottoman Sultanate against the Allies, just before the Turkish imperial armies collapsed. By 1924, Islamic state jihad, or global war by Muslim powers based on the caliph's decision, was over. In comparison, "Christian wars" have also been halted by religious developments, as a result of the Reformation, the Vatican agreements, and the rise of the secular state in the West. "Jewish Wars" ended physically in 70 AD/CE with the fall of Jerusalem. But from the rubbles of the sultanate, jihad has been seized upon by a movement that has constructed an appropriate ideology and put it into practice as the twentieth century unfolded.

In the 1920s, two movements surfaced in Arabia and Egypt calling for the resumption of the caliphate and claiming they had the right to resume jihad as a way to "return to the path of the predecessors,"[11] known in Arabic as the *Salaf*. The Salafists defined themselves as the truest of all Muslims and promoted Jihadism. (Other similar schools of thinking emerged in south Asia, such as that of the Tablighis. Many militants, influenced by the thinking of the doctrinaire Sayyid Abul al Maududi, expanded an Indian version of Islamism. In Arabia, the dominant confederations of tribes from Najd adopted Wahabism as a doctrine, in reference to Mohammed Abdel Wahab, an ideologue who influenced the Saudi tribes in the nineteenth century.) Inspired by the radical interpretations of Islamist Sayyid Qutb in Egypt, a doctrine of *Takfir* (rendering opponents infidels) spread among the Salafists. The whole movement was initially impacted by ideas promoted in the Middle Ages by a doctrinaire who opposed reform, interpretation, and moderation in the Islamic empire: Ibn Taymiya. His followers, over the course of a thousand years, became the Islamists. In modern times, and after the caliphate fell at the hands of the first Muslim secular power in history, Turkey, the Islamists saw themselves as the sole jihadists. It was upon them, they were indoctrinated to believe, that the resumption and succession of the *rissala* (mission) rested. And from then on, the global jihadi ideology with its various schools and doctrines defined its mission: reeducate the Muslims, rebuild the Islamic states, repel the infidels and the apostates, reestablish the caliphate, and ultimately resume the Fatah to expand all of the above. In sum, it is a universal, comprehensive, relentless, unstoppable, nonnegotiable program of world domination.[12]

Jihadists, like all other totalitarians, such as Bolsheviks, Nazis, Fascists, and extreme nationalists, believe ideologically but proceed rationally. They analyzed international relations, studied the balance of power, decided on timing, devised strategies, and chose appropriate tactics. In the 1920s and 1930s, they launched their platforms; in the 1940s, they hoped for an Axis victory over the Allies so that they could recapture the Muslim colonies and turn them back into a caliphate. During the first part of the Cold War, from the 1950s to the 1970s, they spread within the Arab and Muslim world; during its final stage, in the 1980s, they moved forward to establish the legitimacy of jihad against infidels, including atheist Soviets in Afghanistan, apostate Muslim regimes such as Anwar Sadat's, and Zionist Israel. In that decade, other jihadists joined the fray: the Khumeinists. Emerging among Persian Shiia, the Islamists of Iran opted for their own doctrine of *Vilayet e faqih* (announcing the future return of the lost Imam and postulating that an Islamic republic was the best institution for resuming jihad against the *Isti'laa'*, the contemporary power of the infidels).[13] While Salafi Jihadism focused on the main Soviet enemy in the 1980s, Khumeini Jihadism engaged the American enemy during the same decade. But both were committed to the destruction of Israel, the "reassembled and arrogant *Kafir* state of the Jews."[14] And both ideologies demonized moderate Arab and Muslim governments as well as liberal elites.

In the 1990s, Jihadism leaped forward to meet the challenge of the fall of the Soviet Union. Both Salafists and Khumeinists saw the opportunity and the challenge. Who would replace Soviet dominance and Communist influence in the Muslim world? The Islamists felt they were the best placed to fill the gap. That was the opportunity; but the challenge was omnipresent too. Thinking steps ahead of the West, Wahabis, Muslim Brotherhoods, Iranian Islamists, and others watched with consternation the power of the people bringing down the Wall in Berlin, dismantling dictatorships, and installing democracies. The jihadists quickly realized that if they didn't move quickly to establish Islamist states in the region, democratic movements would beat them to the punch.[15]

The West did not understand during the 1990s that a race was taking place between democracies and Jihadism in the Greater Middle East and throughout the Muslim world. The Islamists had watched the Allies and the Soviets defeat Nazism and Fascism, and then the West face off against the Soviet empire. Democracy, followed by pluralism, was installing itself in many regions around the globe and in areas too close to the "Muslim borders," as they considered them. Historically, the jihadist ideology had to engage the enemy before the latter's ideas reached and possibly infected the heart of the caliphate-to-be. In short, Jihadism had to spread itself at home to deter the outside enemy, and destroy the enemy at home as much as possible so as to control as much land as possible for the *umma*'s territories.

Thus, since its inception, Jihadism was doomed to collide with democracies and their values. The trajectory of the jihadists crossed decades and battlefields before they came face-to-face with their ideological foes. Inter-estingly—and as in classical international relations—Jihadism and the other totalitarian isms confronted each other when they chose but united against democracies when they needed.

CHAPTER THREE

IRRECONCILABLE VIEWS

IN THE GLOBAL WAR OF IDEAS BETWEEN DEMOCRACIES AND JI-hadism, the two "foes" have divergent views on very fundamental issues affecting international relations, from the most philosophical questions to the most practical answers. Based on diametrically opposed perceptions of world affairs, the international community of nations and the transnational webs of Salafism and Khumeinism are in conflict over the issues that matter most: life and death, civilization, the status of women, sexual freedom, the role and place of religion, self-determination, sovereignty, international law, the United Nations, genocide, art, and the concepts of war and peace, among others.

LIFE AND DEATH

The sanctity of life is perhaps the highest point of consensus in international relations and the political philosophies that lie behind the values shared by the international community. It took centuries of conflicts, violence, authoritarianism, revolutions, religious wars, reforms, and all sorts of human drama for the world community to agree that, above all, human life should be protected. The first line was drawn in the sand when a distinction was made between allowing lives to be taken at the discretion of leaders, religions, and ideologies and sacrificing lives during conflicts that aimed to save multiple lives. In the history of war and peace, the Enlightenment, reforms, and the rise of democracy slowly drew a thick line between the ability of rulers to take the lives of their citizens at will, bringing them under the rule of law, and the ability of religious or ideological leaders to condone the taking of lives at their discretion. Philosophically, the international consensus of ideas forbade diminishing the value of life, either as property (slavery) or through disposition or sacrifice (such as at the discretion of the divine). The secular revolution and the political development of most societies rejected the ownership of human lives by anyone other than the individuals themselves. Only by law may an individual's life be taken in times of war.

History is always steps behind the evolution of human thinking, and the various declarations of principles regarding the sanctity of life continued to be violated in practice. The horrors of World War II, inflicted both by the Nazis and by others (the Holocaust and other genocides in particular), showed the dangers that still hampered the progress of democracy and humanity. The UN Charter of 1945 and the Universal Declaration of Human Rights in 1948 were abused many times during the second half of the twentieth century: Soviet oppression of its peoples, and massacres in Nigeria, Sudan, Chile, Argentina, Cuba, North Korea, Lebanon, Syria, Rwanda, and elsewhere. For decades, the humanitarian debate worldwide centered on the principle of defending lives, even at the height of wars and bloodshed. Even when nations and alliances fought fiercely, the rest of the international community, especially democracies, looked at ways and means to limit the killings, to separate non-combatants from fighters, to try the abusers, and to further consolidate the principle of the value of human life. The major difference between totalitarian ideologies, such as Nazism, Fascism, extreme nationalism, and Soviet Communism, and racist ideologies lies in the absolute sanctity of individual lives and the legal and political protection and autonomy granted to them. But that is not the view of Jihadism.

In one of his most important speeches, delivered via audiotape and aired by al Jazeera during the fall of 2001, al Qaeda leader Osama bin Laden said solemnly, "We [the Jihadists] love death in as much as you in America [West and infidels] love life."[1] This slogan has since become a central theme for recruitment and mobilization among Salafi, Wahabi, Deobandi, and all jihadi Sunni movements. On the Shiia side, Khumeinist leaders, such as revolutionary leader Ayatollah Khamenei and the current president Ahmedinijad in Iran and Hezbollah secretary general Hassan Nasrallah, also promoted death in jihad *(al maout fi sabeel al Jihad)* as an ultimate value. Both trees of Jihadism, Salafism and Khumeinism, praise death as a weapon to bring about victory, but they also worship the concept of killing for the sake of ideology. *"Naashaq'ul maout kama taashaqun al hayat"* ("We are in love with death")[2] proclaim the imams of radicalism when they harangue their potential suicide bombers and assassins.

The doctrinal rationale of the jihadists is said to be drawn from religion: they argue that Allah ordered them to take into their own hands the decision of life and death, as long as they are on a mission for the sake of the *deen* (religion). And taking such control—in the minds of radical Islamists—is complete, unbound, and sanctioned by the divine through religious scholars. Moderates (such as Sufis) and realists (such as secularists) reject the jihadi argument. But it is this doctrine that motivates the counter-democracy movement worldwide, not the reformists and the liberals.

⇀⇒⊙ ⊙⇐⇀

The *ushq al mout* (love of death) is the backbone of suicide bombing and gives terrorism its most frightening firepower. Indeed, once the fear of death is subtracted from political planning and public concern, there are no limits to the power of Jihadism. Hence arose the concept of *Istishaad*, translated hastily as "martyrdom" in Western languages. But the concept is different from what martyrdom means or has meant historically. In Christian religious history, a "martyr" was a person who sacrificed himself or herself to give witness to their beliefs. Linguistically, the word comes from *muerte, mort,* or "dying for." *Istishaad* includes dying for one's belief, but it also includes taking other people's lives. Dying for religion is martyrdom; killing as well as being killed for religion is the jihadi concept. The philosophical difference is enormous. In history, both Muslims and Christians at times have twisted the theological understanding of sacrificing one's life. Caliphs and emperors, imams and bishops used martyrdom and *Istishaad* at will, depending on the geopolitical situation. Other religions struggled with similar challenges. Dying for one's nation, mission, ethnicity, or ideology was dominant in war rhetoric for centuries. But with the modern era, the international community has settled on a vast consensus, regardless of religion and interpretation; they have agreed on the separation of theology from international law. Religious debates on these matters should remain in the religious realm only. Life and death, in the sense of war and peace, are matters to be decided by national governments and global society. In short, in the present international context, individuals and political movements may not legislate or license killing, suicide, or massacres based on divine, theological, or ideological grounds. In this respect, democracies and Jihadism are irreversibly opposed.

Bin Laden, Ahmedinijad, Nasrallah, and Sheikh al Qardawi cannot legitimize killing by Allah's orders, because human life is not their theological property—that's what moderate Muslim clerics have theorized, though they still promote this view only shyly. It is also what democratic societies have committed to. Critics of the distinction will argue that at the end of the day, there is no practical difference between democracies taking lives on the battlefield, authoritarians carrying out mass killings, and jihadists practicing *Istishaad*. I argue otherwise. When democracies make war, these are exceptions that allow the risk of being killed but not the certainty of sacrificing lives on ideological grounds. When oppressive regimes use lethal force, they are knowingly breaking international law. When jihadists claim they have a divine right to kill and be killed, notwithstanding international principles on the sanctity of life, not only are they breaking international law, but they are rejecting that law completely and thereby removing themselves from the world consensus and creating a new category of persons opposed even to our most basic ideas of humanity. The Salafist-Khumeinist vision of life is embodied in their outlaw doctrine of death. It cannot coexist with the internationally agreed-upon principles of civil society, enshrined in the many declarations on human rights and self-determination. The jihadists have awarded themselves full discretion over the life and death of every person on Earth. It allows them to recruit militants ready to offer their lives at any time, under any circumstances, and against any man-made laws. It allows them to cross any legal, ethical, and moral boundaries. Al Qaeda and Hezbollah's real strength isn't their terrorist capacity, but the ability of their ideologues to incite and take control of the minds of their adherents to the highest level of threat—against the very idea of life.

This jihadist ideological path transgresses the most fundamental shared principles of the international community, of ameliorating life on earth. While Communists, Fascists, and extreme nationalists adhere to the idea of self-sacrifice for the empowerment of a social class or the grandeur of the nation, and democracies honor those fallen for a cause greater than themselves, jihadists perceive individuals as either followers of the divine sanctioned path, which is jihad, or enemies of that path. Those in the first category have the duty (*Wajib*) to die for religion (*deen*); the latter are doomed to be killed or surrender.

All monotheistic religions, including Islam, Christianity, and Judaism, believe that what you do in this life will have consequences in the eternal one after. Historically, this was an incentive for people to do good. But the jihadi creed has transformed the afterlife from an incentive to act humanely into a reward for fighting at the service of a particular political project on earth. The young soldiers of jihad will offer their lives so that the rulers who send them to death can reestablish the caliphate and enjoy its very earthly power. The *Istishaadeyeen* (would-be martyrs) have an ironclad vision, offering rewards in this life and the next. Those who choose to fight for the caliphate will have it both ways: If they win the battle and survive it, they will have pleased Allah and hence deserve privileges within the *umma* (nation) and later on will enjoy heavenly pleasures. If they die while they are performing their duty, they will be instantly transported to the afterlife, where they will be rewarded immediately. However, the most fortunate are those who choose to pass the frontiers of life willingly in the cause: the suicide-jihadists, the suicide bombers. These *Istishaadeyeen* are the most advanced product of Jihadism of all time. Regular soldiers in holy wars offer to sacrifice their lives but leave that decision to the discretion of God; modern jihadists force the hand of Allah. Their clerics, particularly contemporary Sunni Salafists and Shiia Khumeinists, have gone to incredible lengths. Khumeini, Sayyid Qutb, and Yussef al Qardawi, considering themselves guardians of the true path, have established the parameters of "jihad suicide." Twisting verses in the Qur'an (although a debate is still ongoing on this matter between theologians and historians), the neo-Islamists have brought about a code of suicide. "If you please Allah, and we will tell you how, you would be gratified by His endless bounties."[3] The rewards are described graphically: women, honey, milk, peace, and all that may have attracted a seventh-century desert Bedouin. The secular norms of the international community, on the other hand, aren't governed by rewards, but by principles and laws. Jihadism intertwines politics and theology and makes each one organically linked to the other, with an irreversible impact on individual lives and humanity.

Hoping that the divine will sanction a sacrifice done within the internationally accepted context is legitimate. If one or more individuals believe that by dying on the battlefield they will defend their society or please God, that is their belief. But if these individuals or groups decide on their own to respond to a divine call, wage a war based on this call, kill and be killed, they transgress all norms of war and peace as agreed on by modern society. When a suicide bomber takes lives because he believes he will be meeting 72 virgins, he is disqualified from the status of a legitimate resistance, liberation movement, or self-defense of a country. For one cannot be a soldier operating under the legal norms of wars and at the same time perform violence to obtain the benefits of afterlife. It is either about the society—Gaza, southern Lebanon, Iraq, Chechnya, Kashmir—or about honey and milk. It is either about economic and social miseries or about sexual gratification in heaven. It cannot be both, logically at least. A mujahid throws himself into a bus or flies a plane into a building because he is convinced (or more exactly, someone has convinced him) that Allah wants him to do so and that he will be rewarded instantly after death. If that suicide bomber or jihadi isn't convinced that Allah has ordered him or that he will be gratified as described, that person has no reason to kill, let alone kill himself. All rests on the teachings that convince the militant that life *(al hayat)* and his life are not worth living if Allah is not pleased. The jihadi teaching determines the mindset of potential jihadis, and that teaching has removed the belief in the inherent sanctity of individual lives and replaced it with the collective identity of the projected *umma*. And that "community," in the mind of the ideologues, has a mission that is inescapable, unavoidable, and relentless: moving forward until humanity submits.

DAR EL HARB AND THE INEVITABLE CLASH

The second systematic conflict between democracies and Jihadism stems from the latter's vision of an inevitable clash of civilizations. The international community, after centuries of bloody wars and revolutions, has reached the global consensus that countries, civilizations, and cultures should not have aims of world dominance. Even if they have a particular ideology of primacy or claim affiliation with a religion, nation-states, or any other actors in international relations, should not conquer and subdue at will. After Hitler, Mussolini, Japan's imperialism, and Soviet Communism, open declarations of missions to subdue, occupy, or obliterate neighbors or other nations are not accepted. But all jihadists subscribe to the overarching doctrine of *dar el harb*, linguistically translated as the "house of war," but ideologically meaning the "zones of the enemies," which are the target areas of Jihadism, so to speak. In other words, contemporary radical Islamists believe not only that world politics are animated by an ongoing and uninterrupted clash of civilizations, but that their principal mission is actually to win that conflict and defeat all other civilizations.[4]

The idea of the clash of civilizations was presented in the first chapter. Historically, most civil societies in the world have undergone a clash of civilizations in one form or another. European Christians, Muslim Arabs, Turks and Moguls, Chinese Confucians, and others have been involved in wars against different cultural-religious coalitions—civilizational conflicts. The most notorious in medieval history were the initial Arab Islamic Fatah invasions of the seventh to ninth centuries, followed by the Christian Crusades of the eleventh to thirteenth centuries, and later the Ottoman Islamic Fatah of the fifteenth to seventeenth centuries. Historians have also interpreted several regional movements in history as civilizational conflicts, pitting dynasties representative of one universal religion against those of another. Examples are the Mogul Muslim conquests of India and the tsars' orthodox domination of Muslim central Asia. But the era of religiously based civilizational wars, as noted earlier, ended with the fall of religious empires on both sides of the Mediterranean: Christian kingdoms have fallen to republics, and in some cases replaced by constitutional—mostly folkloric—monarchies. And the Islamic caliphate was brought down by Muslims who chose the secular mode of government.

Yet certain ideologies around the world have maintained their attachment to the old form of universalistic struggle based on religious missions. Among Jews, for example, many ultrareligious regarded the "return" to Palestine as a strictly religious duty, in contrast to the Jewish Zionist majority, which perceived it as a national-secular objective. Many Christian religious movements still regard world politics as directly tied to God's will. Conservative Catholics of Opus Deus wish to see governments under Church influence. And more important, the U.S.-based and influential evangelical charismatic community sees direct links between the formation of the state of Israel and divine prophecies, with real world consequences. In the Muslim world, the question of the religious and the secular is still at the center of crucial debates. Yes, the universal Islamic state (Ottoman Sultanate) has fallen at the hands of secular Muslims (Turks), but the religious power bases across the Muslim world didn't bless that revolution. Indeed, while Muslim governments have subscribed to international law and integrated with the United Nations, clerical hierarchies haven't clearly cut the cord with the caliphate of the past. In other words, whereas the Vatican, for example, rendered religious wars illegal and rejected the return to a Christian empire, the sheikh of al Azhar[5] has not yet forbidden jihad as a concept or practice, nor expressly stated that the caliphate is over. Between the silence of the moderates on the question and the disparate use of the concepts of jihad and caliphate by various regimes, organizations, and intellectuals, the jihadists fell through the cracks. In other words, because the official Muslim institutions and intellectual establishment have been wavering, selective, or silent on the matter of global concepts of Islamism, the more radical groups—Salafists and Khumeinists—got hold of the past legacy and transformed it into a contemporary, ongoing duty, in full contradiction with the modern world. By doing so, the radicals have cornered the Muslim world with a tough challenge.

Since the 1990s, the jihadists have moved to resume an old struggle that was controlled by the caliphate, an institution that has disappeared. Modern Muslim nation-states such as Egypt, Indonesia, Iran (before the revolution), Morocco, Nigeria, and others have subscribed to the body of international law that forbids religious wars and policies. But the Islamists operating within the Muslim countries, and sometimes in control of regimes (in Afghanistan, Sudan, Iran, and to some extent Saudi Arabia), haven't subscribed to modern international laws and principles, even though they tolerate its diplomatic and technical appearances. Hence an ideological sector within the Muslim world is in conflict with the consensus reached by international society. Moreover, these Islamists have profited from the fact that their ideology wasn't officially banned by international and most national Muslim institutions, which has given them a free hand in starting, waging, and managing wars outside all international norms. Logically, Muslim countries should have banned the Muslim Brotherhoods, Salafi movements, al Qaeda, Hezbollah, and other jihadi groups not only because they were a threat to their own governments, but also because they endangered world peace by attempting to incite entire religions against others or against the rest of the world. The Taliban, and Sudan and Iran's Islamist regimes, should have been isolated and refused recognition by the rest of the Muslim world before they began to sponsor terror, precisely on the grounds of their adoption of jihadi ideology.

And yet, the international public wasn't apprised of the global objectives of the jihadists. As described in *Future Jihad* and many of my other books, articles, and lectures, contemporary jihadists aren't some radicals who want to reform or change the system or are frustrated with injustices within global society, as was the prevalent academic analysis before 9/11. The jihadists are outside the world system and aim at destroying it altogether and replacing it with their own ideological system. Their view of humanity is simplified: it is *dar el Islam* and *dar el harb*. The first one is the world as they see it perfected, under the rule of a caliphate and with the strict implementation of the Sharia laws (Islamic laws). *Dar el Islam* is not simply the "Muslim world" where Muslims live; it is where the Islamic state rules or where the jihadists are struggling for it. Obviously, the entire Muslim world is potentially *dar el Islam;* the struggle there is to bring down the apostate regimes and replace them with the true Islamist governments of the Sharia. Examples are Egypt, Algeria, Jordan, Oman, Morocco, and Turkey. *Dar el harb*, which many translate as "war zone," is not just that; it is the rest of the world outside *dar el Islam*. In radical ideologies, war and jihad are permissible in these areas with a particular logic, endorsed by the righteous Ulemas who subscribe to Jihadism. The managers of Jihadism are the ones who decide which country, government, or group to target first. During the Cold War, the Soviet Union and Communists were targeted, even though Israel was rejected as a Jewish entity and the West was described as "infidel." After the collapse of the Soviet Union, multiple jihadi battlefields were opened, including Russia, India, Northern and sub-Saharan Africa, and Israel—and the campaign against America began as well. After 9/11, Afghanistan became the center from which to launch violence, followed by Iraq. The logic of Jihadism is global and sophisticated. Ireland and New Zealand are infidels but not part of the "war effort" yet—not because they aren't engaged in the confrontations, but because their turn hasn't come. Denmark crossed the line with Jihadism with the cartoon affair: it has since become a prime foe.

The *dar el harb* doctrine is the proof that the jihadists are not only aiming at, but already performing a war of civilizations. All other civilizations, including the moderate part of the Muslim civilization, are their enemies. In fact, Jihadism might be depicted as a radical piece of one civilization attempting to create a collision course between it and all others, breaking all norms of coexistence and transforming current frontiers into fault lines, old feuds into new ones.

THE UNITED NATIONS

Along with international law, jihadists oppose the United Nations and all international institutions. To the stupefaction of the public, but not to those who have been attentive to bin Laden's speeches since 2001, al Qaeda treats the United Nations as an enemy, "at the service of Crusaders, Kuffars and Jews."[6] In more than one speech, Osama bin Laden equated the organization with *kufr* (infidels), and he once called UN Secretary General Kofi Annan a "criminal." The smaller tree of Jihadism also despises the United Nations. Tehran's regime since the coming of Khumeini, and clearly in the statements of Mahmoud Ahmedinijad, describes the United Nations as a tool of the *Istikbar* (world infidel powers, in Khumeinist rhetoric). Many observers of the debate on the United Nations, and most academics in international relations, confused the jihadi criticism of the organization with the mainstream critique of its policies and actions. There are very few governments and nongovernmental organizations (NGOs) that haven't criticized the world body since its inception; the attitudes toward the UN are obviously reflective of world politics. The Soviet Union saw "capitalist control" in it. The majorities at the General Assembly criticize the veto power in the Security Council. The United States is uncomfortable with the ideological trends in the General Assembly; many large or economically powerful countries (such as Brazil, Japan, Germany, India, Nigeria) are frustrated at not being represented on the Security Council; and many Muslim countries are advocating the creation of a permanent seat representing an Islamic bloc. Lately, criticism has mounted against the mismanagement of UN funds and the inefficiency of the body in the War on Terrorism.

Yet all these types of criticism are aimed at ameliorating the defects of the organization, pushing opposing agendas in its debates, or shifting the center of gravity inside the organization. Indeed, the United Nations has tilted to situate itself at equal distance between the Islamists and the rest of the world, as it was about to do with the Communist-controlled Third World Movement in the 1970s and 1980s. Democracies are in dispute over the efficiency of the organization, its fairness, and the timeliness of its interventions in resolving conflicts, but democracies in general believe in the United Nations and the reasons behind it and tend to make sure it is able to survive as the keeper of global peace. The UN Security Council is still the highest level of reference when a crisis explodes, and UN relief agencies remain among the most accepted internationally.

But here again, the jihadist attitude is radically different: it rejects the legitimacy of the organization as such and wishes to do away with it. Why? The answer is also ideological. The United Nations, in the eyes of Salafists and Khumeinists, is *kuffar*-made. "The infidels created it, and shaped it so that it would constitute their best tool in the War against Islam," said al Qaeda's number two, Ayman Zawahiri,[7] repeating what many radical scholars have stated before him. Thus because the organization is a construction by non-Islamist governments, it can't represent the *dar el Islam*. Moreover, as bin Laden lamented, "The UN was unfair against Muslims and has been used to subdue them."[8] He considered the UN protection of East Timor as an aggression against a "Muslim" country. The basis of the complaint is the identity of the parties, not the relationships. The jihadists blast the United Nations for monitoring Iraq's weapons under Saddam, asking Syria to withdraw from Lebanon, and intervening in Darfur, on the very simple ground that one of the parties is Muslim or Islamist. In other conflicts, where the United Nations was waging a war against governments at war with Muslims, such as in Yugoslavia's Bosnian and Kosovo conflicts, the perception by Islamists didn't fair better. "They [the United Nations] came late to save the Muslims. They did it on purpose to see Bosnia and Kosovo defeated."[9] In international crises, the jihadists describe the organization as anti-Muslim. Ahmedinijad blasted the UN Atomic Agency, as it requested inspections, and accused it of being anti-Islamist, even though its director is Muslim.

On many occasions, from official speeches to chat rooms, jihadists have rejected the principle of the United Nations not just on the grounds of perceived unfairness, but also on a theoretical level. To Salafists, there shouldn't be an institution that Muslims should respond to that's higher than the caliphate. "Muslim states shouldn't accept resolutions produced or coproduced by non-Muslim states and particularly by foes of Islam."[10] To the jihadists, the United Nations doesn't fit with the vision of the world divided into *dar el harb* and *dar el Islam*. It doesn't represent the Islamic *umma*, nor does it allow Jihadism to fulfill its mission. Therefore, and despite the membership of dozens of Muslim countries within the United Nations, the Salafists paint a dark tableau of the Manhattan-based institution. The jihadists deem it responsible for the failure of many Islamist projects, such as the following:

- The UN partition plan of Palestine, November 29, 1947, seen as anti-Muslim because it gave half of Arab Muslim Palestine to the Jews and allowed the creation of the "illegitimate" state of Israel.

- The UN nonrecognition of the "Muslim" Turkish state of Northern Cyprus in 1974.
- The UN nonsupport of the separation of the "Muslim" southern Philippines since the 1970s and its support for the establishment of a non-Muslim state in East Timor, detaching it from a Muslim country, Indonesia, in 1999.
- The UN Security Council Resolution 1559 of 2004, forcing a Muslim state, Syria, to pull its troops out of Lebanon, under the pressures of mainly Christian Lebanese lobbies overseas for the restoration of a multireligious state in Lebanon.
- The UN's listing of al Qaeda as a "terrorist" organization.
- The UN nonrecognition of the Islamist jihadi claim for the establishment of a caliphate.

With this comprehensive rejection of international law and the United Nations, the jihadists find themselves in full confrontation with almost the whole international community, including not only all democracies, but also many Muslim states. The moderate countries that identify themselves as Muslim are fully engaged with the international community on legal and organizational levels. They assume their roles as nation-states within the United Nations, as all other countries do, thus rejecting the call of the more radical Islamists for the withdrawal of Muslim governments from the international organization and the formation of one of their own. Some Islamists have suggested forming an "Organization of Muslim States," which would become a world entity parallel to, and not at a level under, the United Nations.

TWO WORLD ORGANIZATIONS

As viewed by the ideology of Islamism, world affairs should be resolved by two organizations: a world Islamic organization and the United Nations. The first would include all Muslim states under its wings and represent them in war and peace, and the second would represent the rest of the world. Such a situation would, in radical Islamist thinking, bring international relations as close as possible to the image of an "apple divided in two." The United Nations would represent the "infidels," while a resurrected caliphate would manage the affairs of Muslims everywhere. This would reflect, according to Islamic fundamentalism, the historic realities that have been twisted by secular, modernist, or realist Muslim leaders worldwide. Clearly, such a jihadi division of the world into two rigid and confrontational blocs would undermine the authority and sovereignty of all Muslim member-states of the United Nations. The idea that an Islamic world bloc would supersede the powers of Muslim presidents, prime ministers, and monarchs would lead to the other, more challenging idea of an international authority that would become transnational and impose war and peace at the discretion of a single Muslim world leader—in essence, a caliph.

Such a new order, sought for by the jihadists and their ideologues, would challenge modern Muslim states to their core. Can 50 Muslim countries concede their sovereignty to a new emerging caliph or a world organization with similar powers? Would Morocco be ruled from Damascus or Baghdad? Besides sovereignty, Muslim societies—in order to accommodate a new international status—would have to abandon their democratic achievements and revert to the strict application of the Sharia laws as prescribed by Salafists or Khumeinists. This would compel Muslim countries that have moved toward democratic institutions and multiparty systems to revert to absolute rulers in the name of holy scripture. The world's democracies would certainly oppose this challenge, in the same way they have opposed illiberal regimes and authoritarian governments in the past. At the same time, Muslims who have chosen democratic principles, methods, and customs since the 1920s would find themselves faced with a gigantic choice: following the renewed caliphate or rejecting it. As recent history has shown—in the Algerian civil war, the deep cultural divide in Turkey, the reformist spasms in Iran, and elsewhere throughout the Arab and Muslim world—millions of Muslims have reached a stage in their history beyond the return to the Salafi Caliphate. Therefore, if the Islamists attempt to split the planet in two, many Muslims would be forced to confront the jihadists and extremists, and long before the democracies would; this would be the only chance for moderate Muslims to salvage a modern way of life that provides them with pluralism, freedom, and relationships with other nations in the world that accept the global consensus on international law and peace.

CHAPTER FOUR

THE JIHADI WAR ON
INTERNATIONAL PRINCIPLES

IN THE WAR OF IDEAS BETWEEN DEMOCRACIES AND JIHADISM, THE center of the battlefield is political culture. Twentieth-century international relations, emerging from the rubble of two world wars and the Cold War's many low-intensity conflicts, had moved away from the past centuries of bloody identity confrontations—or so the world thought after the collapse of the Soviet Union and the start of a Middle Eastern peace process in the 1990s. Wars to impose religious, cultural, and ethnonational affiliations were believed to have become a thing of the past. Accordingly, this post-Soviet understanding pushed the West to intervene twice, and decisively, in the Yugoslav ethnic conflict and to extend diplomatic backing to the Palestinian-Israeli peace process, despite multiple setbacks even after the 1993 peace agreement was signed. After World War II and the Cold War, Western elites and their secular counterparts worldwide planned for a brave new world, free from apocalyptic conflicts and visions. Hope for peace had dwindled while the Soviet threat loomed over the Free World; it took four more decades of perseverance against the Red Menace in both Europe and the Third World before the Gdansk workers, Russian reformists, and German youth completed the destruction of the Berlin Wall. As the Scorpions sang the day that wall was about to fall, "the winds of change" were blowing full force.

In a few months, democratic culture swept through Central and Eastern Europe all the way to Vladivostok, leaving the end of totalitarian Communism to be decided at some point in the future by the Chinese, Indochinese, and North Koreans. But as of 1991, democracies had advanced not only in geopolitics, but also, above all, in the War of Ideas. In Latin America, military dictatorships on the right and left had been dislodged with the help of Western pressure. Elections replaced juntas in Chile, Argentina, Brazil, and Uruguay and Marxist dictatorships, as in Nicaragua. When needed, direct action by democracies was used to dislodge military elites, as in Haiti. Some totalitarian regimes in the hemisphere, like Cuba's, remained exceptions. Democratic culture was also moving forward on other continents, even though not yet up to the level of liberal democracies in the West. In South Africa, the apartheid regime collapsed—also under international pressure, mainly from democracies. The world community began to monitor other African transitions from tribal affiliation to post-colonial modernity, with all the pitfalls and drama that accompany this evolution: Ethiopia, Nigeria, Kenya, Mozambique, Angola, and others. In Asia, existing democracies further reinforced their free societies and principles, as in Japan, the Philippines, South Korea, and India.

Thus a global assessment of the post-Soviet era showed that the democratic political culture—the one mainly advanced by the West—was establishing itself as the international norm for national and international practices in human rights and free societies. After centuries of wars for religious identities, democracies seemed to be offering an alternative ground for world politics. Secularism was supposed to have granted religions the space they needed and shielded societies from the wrath of religious wars. Religion was thought to have been contained within its theological dimension on the one hand and its sociological impact on the other. But democracies overlooked the unabated character of the jihadi ideologies; the collision between democracy and Jihadism on the level of political culture suddenly became the most dramatic theme of the twenty-first century. Past and present explosively collided, leaving the future of the international community open to uncertainties.

THE WARS FOR RELIGIOUS IDENTITIES

For centuries, kingdoms and states claimed they defended the same culture but insisted they practiced it better, or believed they were warring for their culture against those who intended its destruction. Christian monarchs in Europe waged endless and sometimes senseless bloody wars against each other, "for the righteous faith" to which all claimed affiliation. French and

English, both Christians, battled each other in the Hundred Years' War while fighting for the same values. The conflict, rather than being about spiritual or philosophical values, was really about land and elite powers. In the Muslim caliphate, *walis* (governors of provinces) and other sultans devastated each other's countries, though battling under the same banner of Islam. Umeyads, Abbassids, Fatimids, and Mameluks plunged the empire into internal wars, each of them claiming to represent the "true" religion. History tells us that these were power struggles over the control of the state and the spoils of war. History has also witnessed many conflicts between different religious cultures and the political powers that represented them. First there were the Arab dynasties spreading Islam into the greater Middle East during the Fatah era, clashing with the Byzantines, "beholders of Eastern Christianity,"[1] and conquering the region. They continued the Fatah into Christian Spain and Europe; later, European crusaders unleashed military campaigns against Muslim dynasties and provinces in the Eastern Mediterranean to recapture the Holy Land for Christendom. The Ottomans conquered Christian Constantinople and Eastern Europe to further spread Islam, and the Moguls conquered most of Hindu India to bring it under Islam.

For centuries, religious conquests and imperialism overlapped with each other. The Arab Bedouin of the seventh century, leaving his native desert of Arabia, thought he was on a mission from Allah to defeat the *kuffar*. Thousands of them marched and fought through alien lands, all the way to France, in defense of Islam. What was established as a result of these colonial wars was a caliphate and governorates dominated by rich elites vying for power and more wealth—just as the European peasant would later leave the green pastures of France and England on a "mission from God" to retaliate against the *infidèles* who had conquered the Holy Land. In crusader Palestine, barons and princes reproduced the pattern of Europe's dynasties and mirrored their endless internecine feudal conflicts. Ironically, the Islamic conquests starting in the seventh century and the Christian Crusades of the Middle Ages resembled each other: constant warfare to advance what each believed was a fight for the divine against the "other."

It should be noted that many commentators and social scientists today focus on one particular phase of these conflicts and wrongly draw contemporary conclusions. For example, many Western academics call the Crusades the beginning of Western religious wars on Islam but neglect to place them in their historical context, namely, as a response to the Fatah invasions that had started some three centuries earlier and had brought the armies of jihad to the gates of Paris.

Similarly, other (mostly Western) historians treat the Spanish *Reconquista* as a unilateral advance by Christian European armies into Muslim Andalusia, omitting the fact that seven centuries earlier, Abbasid Muslim armies had conquered the Iberian Peninsula and its Christian native cultures. What modern liberal academics have failed to understand or teach is the classical dimension of these cross-Mediterranean wars. Both Islamic conquests and Christian counterconquests from the seventh to the nineteenth century were at the heart of the times' international relations. Jihad and *Guerra Santa* (Sacred War) were equivalent to preventive and defensive wars conducted by contemporary powers. Not to legitimize these conflicts, but to put them in context, one has to read their events with the mindset of their era. From when Khalid Ibn al Walid invaded Syria in 634 AD/CE until Saint Louis landed in Egypt in the twelfth century, and from when Suleiman's armies pounded the walls of Vienna in the sixteenth century until Napoleon crushed the Mameluks on the Nile Delta two centuries later, this back and forth between Christian Europe and the mostly Muslim Middle East was a standard feature of the religious and colonial culture of the times.

Hence the link some Western academics establish between today's U.S. and European policies and the crusader era is unhistorical. For the democratic revolutions in the West ruptured the chain of events; in today's political culture and under international law, a crusade is considered illegal and unacceptable by the mainstream in civil societies. Democracies do not send troops to fight for a faith or to resume past religious wars; the U.S. Congress and the European Parliament do not declare wars in retaliation for the Islamic conquests of centuries ago or to resume the failed Crusades. For the West—and the international community that accepts modern international law—that era is over, and even though historical resentments may persist despite the passage of time, academics cannot deconstruct the policies of today based on the behavior and feelings of armies and peoples a thousand years ago, let alone launch "apologies" movements for the Crusades or the Fatah conquests. If such apologies are to be made, they would be on the grounds of mutuality and commitment to the culture of democracy and human rights. The descendants of all conquerors, if they wish, can symbolically testify to the wrongs of the past as stages that have ended. But for contemporary Westerners to build policies based on their perception of past centuries would twist history and be a disservice to future generations.

Another mistake made by Western elites has been to consider Arab Muslim societies incapable of bypassing religious political culture, hence condemning them to remain theologically driven forever. Here again, many intellectuals living in democratic societies are blind to the causal relations that keep religiously grounded cultures under the influence of ideologically based political cultures. If some Muslim societies are still influenced by past historical eras and relive them in modern times, it is because of the ideological movements that are in control of the political culture of these societies. It wasn't so long ago by historical standards that Europeans were operating under (perceived) Christian politics. Today European MPs and U.S. lawmakers do not refer to the battle of Poitiers (or Tours) of the eighth century (won by the Christian Franks) when they endorse antiterrorism policies. Russian politicians aren't mobilizing for revenge for the battle of Yarmuk of the seventh century (lost by the Orthodox Byzantines) when they devise strategies to combat Wahabi terrorism in Chechnya. But jihadists do refer to historical events involving Islamic warfare centuries ago in justifying their actions today. Bin Laden often cites military confrontations that took place a thousand years ago in his incitements for jihad. "The crusaders are still on their path of war to destroy Islam,"[2] keep repeating the al Qaeda masters, a message that is echoed widely around the Arab and Muslim world. In the minds of contemporary jihadists, Salafists' and Khumeinists' contemporary history is organically an extension of Islamic history and its wars and battles. In his speeches, bin Laden speaks of modern Westerners as the political successors of Richard the Lionheart, the German emperor Barbarossa, or the Byzantine emperor Constantine. As I have followed his speeches and the rhetoric of jihadists for 25 years, I fully understand the prism through which they think and operate.

History is a linear progression in the view of Wahabis, Salafis, and Khumeinists. All that has happened, or that they believe has happened, since the rise of Islam in Arabia in the seventh century to today is a single march toward a single goal—regardless of diverse historical experiences, political change, mutations, modernity, or new ideas. In the teachings of Jihadism, today's battles—terrorism, by international standards—are a continuation of past battles stretching over 13 centuries. Today's jihadists operate in the twenty-first century with the same mindset of the seventh, twelfth, and fifteenth centuries, as if no evolution has taken place in the Muslim world or the international community. These "universal" fighters are out of space and time. Salafism as a doctrine, reanimated by Abdel Wahab of Arabia and Hassan al Banna of Egypt, and deeply influenced by medieval chronicler Ibn Taymiya, is directly responsible for this state of mind. Its ideologues have convinced their followers that not only are they the representatives of the *umma*, but they also need to bring the *dar el Islam* back to what it was in the golden age of its conquests, somewhere between the first caliphs and the early Abbasid era. At that point, the borders of the empire stretched from Spain to China. Ironically, the ideologues of Jihadism consider the last stage in the history of the caliphate as the weakest: "The Ottomans have brought the *Khilafa* to its knees," say the radical clerics in the chat rooms. "The Turkish Sultanate has lost many Muslim territories to the infidels in Europe and other Muslim lands to European powers in North Africa. Worse, they've adopted reforms inspired by modernity, the most evil enemy of Allah's rulings."[3] (Astoundingly to many Westerners, who were hoping to engage the Islamists in dialogue, the modernizing but still religious Ottoman Empire was and is considered decadent.) Therefore, the Sunni jihadi movements want to go back centuries more to their ultimate model: an Arab caliphate preceding modernity, secularism, democracy, and the international political culture by more than a thousand years. From this perspective, the jihadi wars are aimed not only at defeating democracies and infidels, but also at dismantling centuries of human advancement and bringing the world back to what Salafists believe was their golden age—and their model for the future.

JIHADI SOLIDARITY: *UNSUR AKHAKA*

Democracies and Jihadism meet on yet another battlefield of ideas: international solidarity. Over the last century, the international community sculpted a very difficult agenda for justice, replacing the old intervention parameters centered on religious solidarity. For centuries across the globe, monarchs and empires launched massive military enterprises to rescue religious kin overseas or across borders. Powers would go to war to come to the rescue of "brothers in faith," even though the "brothers" might not be in jeopardy—or were in fact the aggressors: England's assistance to the Huguenots during France's Catholic-Protestant war; France's support to the German Catholics; Russia's

Balkan campaigns in favor of the Orthodox; the caliphate's wars in favor of Muslims under threat or engaged in conflicts with non-Muslims in the Mediterranean, India, and other regions; and France's interventions in Lebanon to save the Maronites in the nineteenth century are some of the many examples. This logic of international religious solidarity, mobilizing the military and political resources of a power to support or enhance the position of religious kin, regardless of the substance of the conflict, was about the identity of the assisted community, not the issue at hand.

This religiously based international solidarity has been slowly but systematically removed from the world political agenda, however. By the second half of the twentieth century, it was almost nonexistent. The right to intervene in a remote conflict is now confined under international law to assisting a population in self-determination, rescuing oppressed minorities or endangered civilians, giving humanitarian aid in the wake of disasters, and other related issues. Solidarity with ethnic and national kin didn't disappear as a justification, but it became an exception, acceptable only as long as it remained under the auspices of international principles. The United States and France in the last few decades, for example, didn't automatically side with Christian causes worldwide. Otherwise they would have supported the secession of the Christian Ibos of Biafra against predominantly Muslim Nigeria in the 1960s, the Christians of Lebanon during the Lebanese civil war of the 1970s, or the Christians of Southern Sudan when they were assaulted by the Islamic regime of Hassan Turabi in the 1990s. Instead, the United States and the Europeans supported Muslim Bosnia against Orthodox Bosnia and Muslim Kosovo against Christian Serbia in the 1990s.

Ethnic support remains a factor for individuals and communities in the Diaspora. Jews around the world support Israel and sometimes enlist in the Israeli forces for that purpose. Arab and Muslim lobbies stand for Palestine, and many individuals join the various Arab armies for that purpose. Armenians, Bosnians, anti-Communist Chinese, and a plethora of citizens from around the planet express their personal solidarity with motherlands and ethnic kin across continents and oceans. But though individuals have a right to support a struggle or join it, international society has agreed on a specific set of rules in modern times:

1. *States and non-state actors may not wage a war outside the norms of international relations.* They may not simply start military or terrorist activities

based on religious affiliation, either offensively or defensively. There must be a cause for any action or intervention other than mere affiliation with the religion of a nation-state. For example, Latin American governments would not have been permitted to send their military to support the Argentine military in 1982 during the Falklands/Malvinas Islands conflict just because the majority of the Argentine people happen to be Catholic, which is the majority religion in Latin America. And the United States, Australia, and Scandinavia weren't supposed to join Great Britain in its reclaiming of the islands just because of Protestant solidarity. Had the raw religious solidarity factor been accepted in modern international relations, then Russia should have been sending its divisions and nuclear assets to defend sister Orthodox Serbia against Muslim Bosnia and Kosovo, while France and Italy should have sided with Catholic Croatia, leaving the Muslims of Bosnia and Kosovo to be supported by their religious kin in Turkey, Saudi Arabia, and Egypt. Had the religious link been the engine of world politics, then the fledgling Lebanese Christians during the 1976 war would have been rescued by the U.S. Sixth Fleet and the French Army; the Southern Sudanese Christians battered by Khartoum's Islamist regime should have been protected by a Christian no-fly zone since the 1980s; the Muslims in the southern Philippines would have had the full support of Indonesia, Saudi Arabia, and Pakistan; and so on. But this whole vision of religious civilizations and empires doesn't have a space in contemporary political culture, even though Professor Samuel Huntington projects it as a possible future redeployment of nations.[4]

Feelings of belonging to larger religious cultures do exist, of course. In my first book, *Pluralism in the World (al Taadudiya fi al Aalam)*,[5] I established a chart for global civilizational blocs around the world. I showed how countries aggregate by religion and languages and engage in creating virtual and sometimes political gatherings in world assemblies, including at the United Nations. I made the case for how religions affect world politics sociologically and politically, even in modern times, and made the case clearly for obvious Muslim international solidarity, as well as for other, more timid expressions by Western and non-Western solidarities with kin connections. But the difference between an analysis of international behavior as it evolves in world affairs and positive law and conventional diplomacy is the real measurement. Nations and societies do have collective feelings and identify with sister societies in religion and culture; however, any action in favor of a kindred nation or group has to be based on universally accepted principles and international laws. Commonality of religion or culture is not enough. Even when Arab and Muslim countries side with a kindred state in the Middle East against Israel or any other country, they usually invoke a reason: occupation, invasion, or any related issue. But the fine line is too thin here—so thin that it has in fact become a main instrument in the War of Ideas. And here the jihadists, projecting a vision taken straight from the Middle Ages, flagrantly cross that line and shatter the international consensus on the most sensitive ingredient in war and peace: in short, the Islamists simply state that they wage war just based on the principle of supporting their kin.

2. *Religious ideologies cannot fit with international relations.* To explain where the jihadists are coming from, one sentence of Arabic political culture comes closest: "*Unsur Akhaka Zaaliman Kana am Mazluma,*" which translates as "Back up your brother, as an oppressor or as an oppressed." The concept is pretty self-explanatory. In premodern world affairs, all powers and empires practiced this, performing interventions to assist "brothers" on behalf of kings and sultans on both sides of the Mediterranean, within Christian Europe, or in the mostly Muslim Middle East. Almost all civilizations and nations rushed to side with religious kin, even if that kin was the aggressor in a conflict. That mode of behavior *was* international relations, as they existed before the development of more rationalized codes of behavior. The international community has moved away from the "brotherly" religious ties that produce "blind duties." But the jihadists are a cataclysmic exception to that international rule; they, more than any other ideological movement, expressly state that they are striking and will strike to support "brothers" wherever they are and for whatever reason. Sheikh Yussef al Qardawi has often advocated on al Jazeera the "often neglected duty of *Tadamun* [solidarity] with Muslims *Mahma Kaana el Amr* [for whatever reason]."[6] Bin Laden and his spokespersons for years invoked what they perceive as a religious duty "*Intisar lil Ikhwa al Muslimeen*" (to provide support to Muslim brothers). Overturning decades of political development by the international society, the jihadi Salafists and

Khumeinists engage in warfare or terrorism based on simple kinship in religion. The doctrine of *Unsur Akhaka* ("support your brother") is practically the spearhead of Jihadism.

All that jihadists need to do in order to wage a jihad is to declare the conflict to be a duty of *Unsur Akhaka*, and then all gates to holy war open magically. It suffices to frame any confrontation as being in support of religious kin for jihad to legitimize itself in the eyes of jihadis. It doesn't really matter if the kin in question are *Mazlum* (oppressed) or *Zalim* (oppressor); all that matters is that they are kin in faith.

The jihadi clerics furthermore secure the *Unsur Akhaka* doctrine with a lethal recipe: *Takfir*, rendering the enemy an infidel. As in the Middle Ages among all cultures, the enemy has to be demonized as an evil force to be destroyed. Christian Europe and the Muslim empires traded "infidel" labels with each other, as well as using the term within their own continents to justify internecine wars. The caliphs treated all their enemies as *kuffar*, while their Christian counterparts called them enemies of God. It sufficed in those ages to witness an infidel from any camp engaging a kin from the opposite camp to spur a group to rush into holy war. The jihadists of the twentieth and twenty-first centuries live mentally in the seventh to fifteenth centuries; their ideologues need only to cite two magical words and they will go to war. All that has to be said is that one's *akh* (brother) is in conflict with another who is *kafir* (infidel).

a.   Wherever you have brothers, you can engage in a *casus belli* with the other side, even if your *akh* doesn't really welcome that conflict or that type of rhetoric.

b.   Whoever is in a conflict with your brother is a *kafir*, regardless of what the conflict is about.

c.   Jihadi authority is able to declare a war in the name of brothers against the *kafir* without necessarily having the consent of these kin; worse, the jihadi can call on all brothers around the world to fight that particular *kafir* under his own timing, grounds, and laws.

Thus what the international community—including democracies—is facing in this century is a movement that can inflame conflicts anywhere and anytime; ignite international crises and fuel tensions; adopt or hijack ethnic and national confrontations, or create them; and move in and out of international relations with total impunity. The weapons used in this War of Ideas are powerful concepts that can send large segments of society hurtling into violence and battle, on the grounds of solidarity and survival.

THE "WAR ON ISLAM": *AL HARB ALA AL ISLAM*

In analyzing jihadi strategies against democracies, one can see a link between the way in which the Salafists and Khumeinists have depicted the so-called War on Terror since 9/11 and how they have taught global jihad for decades—since long before 9/11, in fact. In one chain of exegesis, stretching from Ibn Taymiya's apocalyptic teaching in the fourteenth century to al Jazeera's labeling of the twenty-first century's wars, one slogan stands out constantly: *al harb ala al Islam*, or the war on Islam. This one very short phrase summarizes the entire strategy of mobilization (*taabi'a*) and its various derivatives, depending on the geography of the conflict in question. In nearly every speech by bin Laden, Zawahiri, and other al Qaeda leaders and allies, from Indonesia to Britain and from Pakistan to Canada; in most speeches delivered by Imam Khumeini, Khamenei, and Ahmedinijad; and almost every five hours on al Jazeera and al Manar and constantly on the many Ansar web sites, this doctrine is spelled out with fervor and conviction. Tens of millions of apprentice jihadis on all continents, from Waziristan in Pakistan to Virginia in the United States, have been (and are) brainwashed that a real war is being conducted against Islam by Jews, Israel, America, Europe, Russia, India, and other *kufr* governments, targeting the Muslim religion and its followers.

The most explicit statements about this "War on Islam" are those of al Qaeda and its vast Salafist-Wahabi nebula around the world. In the bin Laden–Zawahiri stream of videotape and audiotape messages to the *umma*, the supreme chief and his commander, parroted by emirs and cadres online, repeatedly claim that the forces of *dar el harb* have been attacking Muslims around the world nonstop since the seventh century. They describe the entire 14 centuries of Islam as a constant struggle against the *a'daa' Allah* (enemies of God), during which Muslims and the caliphates have been subjected to invasions, oppression, assaults, and harassment in multiple shapes and forms. Instead of giving an objective analysis of the history of Muslim nations, as would be the case with Christian, Buddhist, Jewish, Zoroastrian, Taoist, and many other religions, the Islamic fundamentalists arrogate to themselves the unique and only explanation of Muslim history. They describe the series of events in terms of Muslim versus *kafir*—nothing else. And despite the scientific research provided by Muslim and other historians in modern times, the jihadi version of the story seems straight out of the medieval past. The rhetoric of al Qaeda and its affiliates doesn't even fit with the modern political rhetoric of the Arab and Muslim world; it sounds like an organic and linguistic continuation of medieval Muslim war literature. But more interesting is the fact that fragments of this jihadi speech are also used by modern intellectuals, editors, publishers, legislators, and sophisticated TV channels such as al Jazeera.

The jihadi political indoctrination machine teaches that the Soviet Union and the West have coalesced to invade Muslim lands and destroy Muslim culture. The ideologues claim that "by the will of Allah," the first enemy, Soviet Communism, was defeated at the hands of the mujahideen in Afghanistan. However, the story doesn't credit the Afghan national resistance for the victory against Russian occupation, but rather the world jihadist movement for bringing the wrath of Allah down on the Soviet *kuffar*. Victories are brought about only by Jihadism, and not by nationalism or democratic forces. The ideologues go on to explain that once the mujahideen won the war in Afghanistan, the West conspired to bring about internecine fighting among the various Muslim parties in the country, which compelled the purest of the groups, the Taliban, to take power in Kabul so that an emirate could be established in defense of Islam. This Afghan jihadi story is very telling: even when an Islamist force is on the offensive to establish a radical Islamist regime (including against other Muslims), it is portrayed as acting in defense and to withstand an infidel attack. This is the familiar refrain in every case explained by the jihadists.

"Islam is under attack everywhere in the world," argue Sheikhs al Qardawi and al Nufeisi on al Jazeera. "The forces of *kufr* want to dismantle the Muslim civilization and control its rich resources. They want to absorb the Muslim immigrant communities and eliminate their identity in the West; they want to dismember the Islamic nation in Sudan, Indonesia, Nigeria, Lebanon, Iraq, Central Asia, and elsewhere."[7] From Beirut's southern suburbs and Tehran, the Khumeinist alter egos fulminate in the voices of Iranian president Ahmedinijad and Hezbollah's secretary Nasrallah that the *Istikbar* (another appellation for infidels) wants to eliminate the capacity of the great Islamic Republic (Iran) to defend Islam against aggression. Al Ansar web chat rooms incite 24 hours a day, 7 days a week against the "enemies of Islam" everywhere in the world. "India is a dire enemy of Muslims," say the Salafi commentators, "It wants to take over Bengla Desh and Pakistan in coordination with Israel and America."[8] Moving on to Russia, they accuse Moscow—under Communism as well as after its collapse—of plotting to destroy the Muslim provinces inside the federation, starting with Chechnya. In Africa, the states of Kenya, Eritrea, Uganda (post–Idi Amin), and Chad are accused of "conspiring" to dismember Sudan by splitting the South and Darfur (although Muslim as well) from Khartoum's Islamic regime. Obviously, the Arab-Israeli conflict—an ethnic and territorial one in reality—is depicted as a "Zionist-Jewish conspiracy to devour Palestine and split the *Umma*."[9] Lebanon's war, another ethnic conflict, is described as "a beachhead for the world Infidels to build an isolationist *Kufr* mini state for the Maronites."[10] Similar interpretations are advanced for Syria, Iraq, Iran, and Pakistan.

But the al Jazeera panels and their counterparts online blast the mother of all *kuffar*, America, for being the force behind this "universal War on Islam." Dozens of fundamentalist and radical intellectuals, clerics, and politicians spout this rhetoric on a daily basis from all forums available. They accuse Washington of conspiring night and day against every single Muslim government, as well as the people and their resources. This jihadi "hallucination" about America and the West doesn't stop there; every Muslim who is in disagreement with the theory that Islam is under attack is also accused of being part of the attack. The Salafist-Khumeinist fantasy labels most of the Arab and Muslim governments around the world as "agents of their infidel masters and associates in destroying Islam." Not every regime that claims to follow Islam is really Islamic, the argument goes; dozens of leaders, and even moderate imams and clerics, are branded as being part of the conspiracy. The fever of this jihadi inquisition is boundless, endless, and relentless.

But the most methodical campaign of incitement targets Muslim dissidents and antifundamentalist intellectuals, academics, artists, writers, journalists, politicians, and other reformists, both within the Muslim world and living in the West. The most systematic "inquisition" aims at the delegitimization of Muslim voices of moderation who might criticize the radicals. Similar to the behavior of Nazis, Fascists, or Bolsheviks, the jihadis are lethal toward any opposition from the inside. Any Muslim who contradicts their vision of an Islam under siege is subject to immediate attack: examples abound, and I will cite a few of them later. Here it is important to note that one of the main reasons behind this jihadi hysteria toward critics is linked to the strategy of spreading fear. For if the jihadi story of Islam is undermined by Muslims who can testify otherwise, the whole edifice collapses. In other words, even if a normal debate were to occur about the jihadi ideology and put their tenets and doctrines in doubt, the whole structure would begin to shake and most likely crumble. In political-psychological terms, the jihadists have constructed an imaginary community (the *umma*) bound by fear of being aggressed by an imaginary, comprehensive plot executed by a historical enemy (the *kuffar*). But if Muslims from within that *umma* were to question the story and open the windows of that darkened cell built by the fundamentalists, the light would come in and shatter the jihadists' worldview. As such, this battle between radical Islamist Muslims and moderates within their own religion is perhaps the most critical juncture in the ongoing War of Ideas.

CHAPTER FIVE

THE ASSAULT ON PLURALISM

IN THE WAR OF IDEAS, SUPPORTERS OF JIHADISM AND THEIR ADVO-cates in the West claim that the various Islamic fundamentalist movements (including the Salafist and Khumeinist branches) are an expression of their rejection of authoritarianism and colonialism. The Western debate about the War on Terror has overlapped with the real War of Ideas to such an extent that distortions of fact have blurred the public's vision. The average person has a hard time distinguishing between the actual doctrines and ideologies of the jihadists and the explanations offered by the intellectual establishment. Politics is at the core of this campaign to confuse public understanding. As I will detail later in this book, some academic and economic elites, who either oppose the political systems in the West or profit from the oil-producing regimes in the East, have twisted the real essence of the jihadist agenda in an attempt to delegitimize the War on Terrorism or shift international relations back to the previous state of affairs that existed before 9/11. Jihadi strategists profit from this kind of obfuscation.

Stunningly, while radical Islamists publicize their deep antidemocratic statements and declarations in the open (mostly in Arabic), apologists for the jihadists within the Arab and Muslim world and their counterparts in the West argue that the violence displayed by the various Salafist and Khumein-ist groups is fueled by injustices, not by antidemocratic ideologies. The Western audience is fooled into assuming that if these injustices were ad-dressed, the jihadists would integrate with the democratic political process. I will argue otherwise. In this chapter, I show that in its essence, Jihadism is opposed to political pluralism and freedom of religion, the two pillars of democratic culture.

JIHADISM AND POLITICAL PLURALISM

The clearest antagonism between Jihadism and democracy is over political pluralism. Under the Islamist paradigm, there is simply no such thing as *al taadidiya*, or pluralism, neither political nor ideological. Jihadism and a multiplicity of opinions cannot coexist. This visibly perturbing reality is at the core of Salafism and Khumeinism. In a manner analogous to Bolshevism, Jihadism rejects the plurality of political parties and doctrines on an existential level, because this concept is in absolute conflict with the doctrinal beliefs of Islamic fundamentalism. *La taadud fil Islaam* (No plurality in Islam), argued Ibn Taymiya in the Middle Ages, in response to the many Muslim thinkers who attempted to find alternative explanations to the universe, life, religion, duties, and other aspects of civilization. These attempts were known as *Ijtihad* (interpretation) of previous dogma. Groups such as al Mu'tazila advocated multiple *madaaress* (schools of thought); other ancient reformists formed *Mazaaheb* (sects). In response, the followers of Ibn Taymiya (the ancestors of Salafism centuries later) harshly opposed sects, interpretations, reinterpretations, different schools of thought, different philosophies, and any other alternatives to the sole vision they promoted.[1]

It is important to make clear that during these times of obscurantism, reductionism and intolerance of diverse viewpoints were not peculiar to the Islamic world. Across the Mediterranean, Christian equivalents were present both inside the Church and even within learned communities. Rejection of pluralism was in fact prevalent in all civilizations, including in Asia, the Americas, and Africa. But here again, it is equally important to recognize that the most salient part of modern jihadist ideology is its direct connection and overt reference to the doctrines of these earlier Dark Ages. Indeed, when Islamic fundamentalists reject pluralism today, they do so with reference to the injunctions of thirteenth-century (some argue seventh-century) doctrinaires. Although it is true that the Marxist-Leninist paradigm of the twentieth century also banned democratic pluralism, this simply reinforces the assertion that Jihadism is as totalitarian as Bolshevik Communism.

Researchers or readers might ask the following question: Why is it that the vast literature of the modern West, particularly since the 1970s, denies the totalitarian nature of Jihadism? In other words, why have social scientists and Middle East and Islamic studies scholars avoided this theme altogether while debating the political centralism of Communism? In the early years of my scholarship and while I was researching the doctrines of Jihadism in Beirut, I was surprised to realize that Western academia didn't explain the phenomenon of Jihadism so that classrooms (and later on, newsrooms) could understand its essence. I found the explanation for that silence later, during the 1990s in the United States, when I came to understand that academic elites have avoided exposing the antidemocratic nature of Jihadism for a number of reasons, one of which was that funding for area studies related to the Arab and Muslim world was originating from regimes and private groups who believed in Jihadism. Hence, dramatically, Western and other democratic societies around the world weren't perceiving the movements and regimes that adhered to Islamic fundamentalism to be essentially in conflict with political pluralism—until the War on Terror opened a breach in that wall of misinformation.

THE PHILOSOPHICAL ARGUMENT

But why do the jihadists reject the idea of a multiplicity of opinions and the right of different political groups to organize and act? The first reason is universal to all totalitarian ideologies: it is about the projection of a unique "truth." Centuries ago, theological attitudes among all organized faiths also displayed this characteristic. It took centuries (and the Enlightenment, reforms, and revolutions) for a diversity of ideas and political philosophies to obtain recognition of their right to coexist. By the twentieth century, apart from the Communist bloc and a number of Islamist regimes, all other countries recognized pluralism as a fact of political life, protected by constitutions. Even authoritarian regimes simulated an acceptance of multiple political parties and currents, while they asserted their own absolute authority. From the industrialized world to the Third World, practice differed, but the principle of plurality was universally recognized, with one exception—the jihadists.

In fact, the Islamist ideology rejects a set of principles that is at the very foundation of international society. First, it refuses the idea that there are various philosophical and religious explanations of history, politics, and laws, which are in principle equal and are to be judged on rational grounds. "The Islamic explanation is perfect" ("*al tafseer al islami kamel*") state the radical clerics.[2] Therefore, there is no space for other explanations. Some ideologues go further, reminding their audiences or readers of the irreversible truth that

"*Allah, khalikul al malakut, la yujaadal*" ("One cannot argue with Allah, the creator").[3] The matter is thus closed by divine order, according to the fundamentalists, who hammer the Muslim liberals with their heaviest theological weapon: "Since Allah spoke directly into the Qu'ran," they theorize, "who from his creatures can say otherwise?"[4] Indeed, the Salafists and to some extent the Khumeinists have a massive advantage on their side, namely the divine nature of the laws they pretend they are protecting. Thus the circle is almost complete; short of Muslim reformists opposing this view, the fundamentalists have and will continue to have the upper ground in the intra-Muslim War of Ideas.

From this point on, the Islamists move forward with their implacable doctrinal logic. From the texts of Ibn Taymiya to the edicts and declarations of Abdel Wahab, Hassan Banna, Sayyid Qutb, al Maududi, Ibn al Uthaymeen, and al Albani, to the contemporary al Qardawi and al Nufeisi, a whole body of Islamist literature and ideological treatises has destroyed the concept of pluralism and the principles derived from it.[5] "If the Islamic truth is one," asserted Sheikh al Qardawi on al Jazeera several times, "how can there be more than one truth among Muslims?" The logic inescapably bears down on the multiplicity of ideologies and the plurality of political movements. "If there is no need for another vision of the world and society, why would there be a need to allow for other ideologies and political movements that would express the latter?" keep repeating the imams online on the Ansar web sites. "Creating explanations and actions other than Allah's own words," they conclude, "would be against the divine will and should be rejected."[6]

JIHADISM AND ALL OTHER IDEOLOGIES

One of the most stunning realizations liberal commentators and scholars would come to, if they would thoroughly research the premises of Islamism, is the attitude of jihadi ideologues and leaders toward all other doctrines, currents, and political parties: in short, jihadism is against all other viewpoints worldwide. However, the jihadi strategists play by the pragmatic norms of world politics. They develop layers of enemies: immediate, later, and long-term. Ideologically, the radical Islamists must suppress all other intellectuals; they are bound to do so, for if they don't, their doctrinal basis will collapse. The Islamic fundamentalists' raison d'être is their embodiment in the single and untouchable "truth." Any possibility of an alternative truth would crumble their whole edifice. Hence the jihadists are not quarreling with one or another policy, doctrine, or ideology on the grounds of specific points, actions, policies, or historical issues, as many Western thinkers have advanced in the past few decades. Instead, the Islamic fundamentalists are in an existential and nonnegotiable conflict with the idea of any other idea. Jihadism, by its own premises, cannot coexist with other Islamic schools of thought, let alone with socialism, liberalism, Marxism, capitalism, Christian democracy, social democracy, nationalism, environmentalism, Maoism, Hinduism, secularism, populism, revolutionary doctrines, and so on. Jihadism perceives itself as the sole bearer of what it calls *dar al Islam*, and everything else is *dar el harb*. Hence Islamism, in its main forms of Salafism and Khumeinism, is not one ideology clashing with the West, in parallel to other anti-Western ideologies, but in reality is an ideology clashing with all other ideologies, Western, non-Western, and anti-Western alike. Jihadism is neither an ally to progressive forces against the right wing, as it has cleverly projected itself when needed since the 1990s, nor a religious group allied with the conservatives against Marxism, a disguise it donned in the 1980s. It is a comprehensive ideology aimed at dominating the planet against all other forms of political thinking, which by definition must be suppressed.

JIHADISM AND POLITICAL PARTIES

The attitudes of the jihadists toward partisan pluralism derive from their initial position regarding other ideologies. But practical necessities and historical contexts play into the realpolitik of the Islamists. Observers and instructors in Middle East studies find it hard to distinguish the nuances and differences of the various Islamist movements. Thus scholarship and journalism often reach contradictory conclusions when it comes to explaining the position of Islamist movements vis-à-vis party pluralism. Indeed, the Western intelligentsia see different postures in different places and have a hard time developing a theory of Jihadism and political parties. Let's look at a few examples from reality:

- In Saudi Arabia, there are no political parties to start with. The problem is solved by laws. Wahabism doesn't tolerate the idea of a political party at all.

- Under the neo-Wahabi Taliban, other political parties were banned. Afghanistan was ruled by one party, which didn't consider itself a normal political party. In Sudan, a similar situation has occurred since 1989, when the National Islamic Front seized power and declared an Islamist state.
- In Algeria, the Islamist Front Islamique du Salut (FIS) ran for elections against other parties in 1991 and obtained more than 50 percent of the vote, then declared that it would eventually ban all non-Islamist parties after establishing a Sharia state in the country. Years later, offshoots from the FIS claiming a radical Salafist affiliation, such as the *Groupement Islamique Arme* (Armed Islamic Grouping, GIA) and the Salafi Group for Call and Combat, waged a genocidal war against the government and civil society, declaring that all political movements and parties had to be destroyed.[7]
- In Egypt, the once-banned Muslim Brotherhood ran for elections in 2006 and obtained dozens of seats in the Parliament. But its leaders refused to guarantee pluralism to other parties if they were to form a government in the future.
- In Pakistan, the Islamist parties tolerated the military government of President Musharraf for some time (before they began to struggle against it); but they have also stated that if they take power, they will ban the secular parties in the country. Similar positions were developed by Islamist parties in Bangladesh, Malaysia, Indonesia, and Nigeria.
- In Iraq, al Qaeda followers called for a boycott of the legislative elections, denouncing them as a product of the *kuffar* (infidels). But Sunni Islamists, practicing political "realism," participated in the elections and secured a number of seats. Among these politicians are supporters of Salafism, who state that eventually a Taliban regime will be established in Baghdad, where only Islamists will rule.
- In Somalia, the Islamic Court militia stated in 2006 that it served the elected government in the country before it waged a war for the control of Somalia and the establishment of a Sharia-based regime.[8]
- In Iran, the Islamic Revolution of Khumeini banned all non-Islamist parties after 1980 but kept the electoral system in place to "vote" for a parliament. However, the revolution controls the candidacy process. Iranians can vote for regime-authorized Islamist groups only. All or-

ganizations representing ethnic and other religious minorities were banned.

- In Lebanon, a pluralist democracy in the Arab world before 1975, the Syrian occupation (until 2005) installed a system of many parties, all supporting the Baathist-Hezbollah dominant coalition. Since the Syrian withdrawal, Hezbollah, which presents itself as a political party but is in fact a militia, has made sure during legislative elections that only its candidates represent the Shiia community.

- On a world scale, al Qaeda has several times (via the speeches of bin Laden and Zawahiri) condemned the principle of elections and the idea of political parties. "*Al intikhabat sharr, wal ahzab shar,*" keep repeating the jihadi ideologues: "Elections are evil and parties are evil."[9] The radical clerics, appearing on al Jazeera or sending letters throughout the Muslim world, use religious references to consolidate the jihadi rejection of the electoral idea. They argue that during the time of the Prophet Mohammed, there were too many *Ahzaab* (parties) in Mecca. They claim the Messenger of Allah disbanded these *Ahzaab* and created the one Islamic army, the defender of the one *umma*. On the Khumeinist side of Jihadism, an illustrative example is provided by Hezbollah. The creators of the group, Iran's Revolutionary Guards, called the organization the *Hezb* of Allah (hence Hezbollah), the Party of God. So if this is Allah's party, who can dare to form another?

Yet of course, there are many variations in Islamist attitudes and positions toward pluralism and political parties. Jihadists participate in elections in some cases, boycott them in others, ban parties sometimes, and form them other times. Does this mean that there are multiple schools of thought, or jihadists who reject party pluralism absolutely and others who use the process whenever they can? The answers are as complex as the jihadi movements themselves, but from a systematic observation of Islamist political tactics over a quarter of a century, I have developed an overall picture of their global logic. It is summarized as follows: if jihadis can secure power without the use of the political process, this they find preferable, but if they must use this process or segments of it, then that is permissible. This debate is not a secret one; it has been discussed on many occasions in chat rooms, by panels, and on televised shows. The ultimate objective of the jihadi movement is to

transform the institutions of the target countries into emirates and the emirates into a caliphate. In the Khumeinist realm, they have built the Islamic
Republic as a prelude to the imamate. Hence analysts must read the party
politics of the jihadists or Salafists from a tactical-strategic angle. In Saudi
Arabia, for example—and despite the fact that the nation is an ally of the
United States—Wahabism cannot tolerate political parties. But because the
country is a main producer of badly needed oil, international outrage over
the total lack of political pluralism is nil. Moreover, Wahabi oil money fi-
nances the top Middle East studies programs in America;[10] thus Western
elites are less likely to expose Saudi political realities. When jihadists control power, as in the case of the Taliban and in Sudan, other political parties
are banned. Ultimately, when these regimes stabilize, no political parties
should remain. The Salafists argue that the *Ahzaab* are detrimental to
Islam, and they must ultimately go. Therefore, in a perfect Islamist state,
there shouldn't be political parties or pluralism.

But as jihadists and political Islamists must often operate within democracies or transitional regimes, or under hostile authoritarian systems, they
manipulate the political and even democratic processes to advance their influence and power. In Egypt, the Muslim Brotherhood ran in elections
against what they described as an "authoritarian" government headed by
Mubarak, but they support the Saudi regime and other absolute monarchies
in the Gulf, which are every bit as authoritarian, while also extending their
support to Islamists around the world who seek a one-party Islamist system.
The so-called "Brotherhood" wants to establish a Sharia-based government
with no equal rights for the Christian Copts of Egypt and ultimately aims for
the creation of a Taliban-like state, on the road to a caliphate. On the one
hand, Western liberals (such as the Wahabi-influenced ones) are impressed
by the Brotherhood's decision to run and the number of seats they've collected in the national assembly, as though this were evidence of the embrace
of democracy. But the admiration stops short of looking at the larger picture,
which is the grand design of the *Ikhwan* (Brotherhoods) to eventually eradicate the very democratic pluralism that at present allows them to move forward inside the system. A comparison could be made to the National
Socialists winning seats in the German Republic of Weimar in the early
1930s. Western elites, under Wahabi influence, endorse the Islamists' participation in the democratic process but neglect to expose the latter's ultimate
goal of destroying that process.

The jihadists' use of elections to crumble democratic pluralism from the inside is part of an Islamist grand strategy. In Algeria, after decades of socialist authoritarianism, the Salafists won an electoral round in 1991 before being disbanded by an army-backed secular government. Western commentators saw this as an oppression of a democratic movement, while in reality it was a conflict between two authoritarian forces, one of which—the Salafists—rapidly embraced the most violent terror methods in the 1990s after their initial objective wasn't reached. In Palestine, Hamas won the legislative elections of 2006 but didn't change its charter, which calls for the dismantling of Israel. This jihadi doctrinal attitude contrasts even with the more secular position of the PLO, which, despite its conflict with the Israelis, concedes that ultimately there will be a two-state solution. (Even the more radical Palestinian nationalists have proposed a single country where Jews and Arabs could have their own political parties.) In Turkey, the soft Islamists of Prime Minister Najmedine Arbakan in the 1990s and Prime Minister Recep Tayyip Erdogan in the first decade of the current century have played fully by the rules of the Kemalist Republic. Elected as one party, they formed a majority cabinet and have respected the functioning of the secular institutions. But the president of Turkey, a hard-core anti-clerical, accused the Turkish Islamists of using executive branch powers to alter the country's educational system in order to sway the younger generations toward fundamentalism and hence reverse the institutional secularism of the country. The debate is raging in Turkey over the long-term goals of the *Fazila* (Virtue) Party: will it act constantly as one among other parties and play by the rules of pluralism, or is it setting the groundwork for a long-term reestablishment of an Islamist state in Turkey as a prelude to the return of the sultanate?

A thorough observation of the Islamists' political tactics worldwide reveals a progressive line of development in their strategy for achieving their ultimate goals.

If the jihadists are strong enough for an armed struggle against an outside power, they might resort to military uprisings and terrorism against the "infidel occupier" as a way to establish a power base and create an emirate, and thus bypass the necessity of political participation in the democratic process. Examples of this strategy can be seen in Afghanistan under the Taliban, Chechnya, Kashmir, southern Philippines, and southern Thailand.

Another variant of this model is for the Islamists to engage in a military-terrorist struggle against the "infidel" enemy, but then take advantage of an

election provided by the international community as part of the attempts to
solve the conflict. Winning an election secures a government base for the jihadi movement to reach the next stage, as in the cases of Hamas in Palestine
and Hezbollah in Lebanon.

A more advanced model is for the jihadi organization to play it both
ways. Jihadists engage in military and terror activities against the enemy as
well as opposition parties inside the country while at the same time running
for elections with the full backing of the guerrilla institutions. This is what
Hezbollah has done in Lebanon. This model is the most complex and also
the most successful, for while the militia controls large segments of the country and acts as a Taliban regime in those areas, it extracts the "representation"
provided by these militarily controlled areas in the Lebanese Parliament. International observers praise the political participation of Hezbollah in the
Lebanese multiparty system but fail to admit that it is the result of its de facto
control of south Lebanon and the Bekaa Valley, thanks to Iranian weapons
and money.

Finally, when jihadists form a government, seize power, and establish a
regime, regardless of how they got into power, they are determined to implement their doctrine of establishing an Islamist state, with a progression from
few political parties to one party and eventually to none at all.

In the War of Ideas, the jihadists attempt to take the best from democracies by using democratic elections and the pluralist setting to advance
their antipluralist and antidemocratic mission; ultimately they hope to use
this as a launch pad for their goal of establishing, by stages if necessary, the
emirate, imamate, or caliphate. At that point, pluralism will be swept
aside. But as long as they are participating in the pluralist system, the jihadists assert full respect for the democratic process, even abiding by the
rulings of the electoral institutions. Their use of the system is strategic,
not tactical. In most cases, they benefit from their participation even if
they don't win majorities, because they are able to penetrate the political
system, preparing for the next stage and also using the system to shield, or
cover, jihadi violent activities when needed. Often observers have noted
that democratically elected Islamists are the first to rush to the defense of
jihadi terrorists, using the fact that they are elected officials to defend the
legitimacy of jihadists engaged in terrorist acts or antidemocratic repression. Ironically, participation in democratic elections and pluralism by the
Islamists is ultimately converted into a vehicle for endorsing those ji-

hadists who, on the other flank of the attack, are brutally suppressing pluralism or openly trying to destroy democracies.

JIHADISM AND THE ROLE OF RELIGION

In addition to their rejection of political pluralism, the jihadists have an intransigent attitude toward religion. Again, this position would have qualified as mainstream during the first millennium AD/CE; most religious empires, kingdoms, and powers in the Middle Ages had an official state religion and suppressed other faiths. Religious persecution has accompanied civilization's history from the earliest times all the way up to the twentieth century. Many forms of oppression have taken place: a religion suppressing another religion, religion oppressing atheists, atheists suppressing religions, one sect within a religion persecuting another, and so on. Religious persecution existed until modern international law banned the suppression of individual and group rights to worship and practice freely. Although some states achieved religious freedom, it is universally acknowledged that religious freedoms are still under assault around the world. The UN Human Rights Reports and Freedom House annual evaluation are clear: persecution because of religious affiliation is still rampant in China, Vietnam, Korea, Cuba, Saudi Arabia, Iran, Sudan, Nigeria, and other countries.[11] Oppression of religious communities for actions beyond mere religious beliefs is also an international phenomenon, still occurring in many countries, particularly in the Third World. Here again the jihadist ideology stands out, for even as universal wisdom and multiple charters on international relations and human rights were gradually recognizing the rights for individuals and groups to worship freely and organize their religions and communities, only the jihadists were moving in exactly the opposite direction. It is not that religious intolerance is unique to Salafists or Khumeinists, but that these two groups distinguish themselves in openly maintaining official positions endorsing discrimination and practicing it.

It is important to make a distinction between the debate on Islam and other religions on the one hand and the question of jihadi intolerance on the other. The first question is one of theological interpretation and history, and it is still discussed within Islamic circles and among academics and intellectuals. Our focus here, rather, is on the specific attitude of the jihadi movement, as an ideological and political current, regarding the question of religion and relations with other religions. In this realm, the jihadists have developed a clear stance on how they perceive religion and how they see other faiths.

First, the radical Islamists advance a different framework for their definition of Islam, creating an ideological category separate from the rest of Islam. The construction of this special philosophical structure has different components. In most fundamentalist literature, including the writings of Ibn Taymiya, Hassan Banna, Abdel Wahab, Sayyid Qutb, and others, the concept of *"al Islam huwa deen wa dawla"* ("Islam is a religion and a state") guides all other definitions. From its inception, the radical Islamist paradigm has regarded Islam as different from all other religions in the sense that it encompasses a way of life, social organization, war and peace concepts, legal guidelines, and so on. In the eyes of the fundamentalists, Islam as a phenomenon cannot be equated with any other faith. It is larger than religion. Sheikh Yussef al Qardawi, in his ideological sermons on al Jazeera, often stated, *"Islam huwa awsa' minq al deen al Islami,"* a striking statement that could be translated as "Islam is wider than the Islamic religion." He goes on to explain that in his view, "it is a whole integrated system" (*"nazamon kamel wa mutakamel"*). Thus according to the Salafists, Islam cannot be contained within a superior system or even considered equal to another system, for it is the highest system. In political wording, the Islamists cannot view the global phenomenon of Islam as a subsystem inside or under a more overarching system, for if the Islamic revelation is made up of the direct words of Allah, what greater system can there be? This totalitarianizing logic is in fact at the core of jihadi thinking. Back in 1975, the director of Dar al Ifta' in Beirut, the highest Sunni authority in the country, wrote in the daily *as Safir* that "Muslims should only be ruled by Muslims."[12] From all of the above, the Islamist-jihadist attitude toward religion can be summed up thus:

- Jihadism considers Islam as a global phenomenon, wider than religion.
- Hence, according to the jihadists, Islam cannot be equated to any other faith in the hierarchy of the state.
- Furthermore, Muslims cannot be under the rule of non-Muslims in any fashion and must act whenever possible to establish Islamic rule.

Whereas in all other religions, civilizations, and philosophies, including moderate Islam, the issues of identification, theology, and afterlife are part of the debate and dialogue, the Islamists have no space for interactions with others, including reformist and progressive Muslims, on the matter of religion. In the lexicon of Salafists and Khumeinists, religion (and therefore truth) is cast in stone, nonnegotiable, and never to be reinterpreted. Thus jihadists have formed religion into a unitary, solid monolith, with no room for even the least modification or change.

JIHADI PRINCIPLE OF
INEQUALITY BETWEEN RELIGIONS

As with political philosophies and parties, the jihadists are firm on the principle of inequality between religions. The notion is not that they think their theological beliefs are the truest; all religions have the same confidence about their revelations. The notion of jihadi religious inequality, however, has political implications in the real world. Because, according to jihadi dogma, other faiths are wrong and untruthful, they cannot be granted equal rights in an Islamist state. Fundamentalists argue that their version of a purist state still grants those of other religions (mostly Christians and Jews) a range of rights. But they are granted by a higher authority to lesser entities, with no equality in essence. As we shall see, the Islamists have created special categories for other religions, based on the principle of voluntary discrimination. From this principle of separation between the only righteous and all other faiths, a variety of discriminatory regimes and situations have been established by Salafists and Khumeinists around the world.

- In Saudi Arabia—ironically, the most extreme example of zero tolerance with other religions—the matter has been reduced to its most compact dimension: no other religions are legal within the Wahabi state, period. Non-Islamic religious congregations, symbols, places of worship, books, audio-video materials, and even prayer in public are banned by law. During the Gulf War of 1991, U.S. and coalition personnel were not permitted to worship in the open. Building churches is illegal. Punishment for proselytizing is harsh, even up to death sentences.
- Under the Taliban, religious freedoms were nonexistent. Symbols of other religions were destroyed, such as the ancient Buddhist statues blown up with explosives.
- In Sudan, the Islamist regime of Khartoum imposed Sharia laws on non-Muslims in 1983, causing a civil war that led to more than a million

deaths, mostly among black Christians and Animists, and continued up to 2005.

- In Iran, the Islamic Republic of Ayatollah Ruhallah Khomeini severely restricted religious freedoms of Christians, Bahá'is, and Zoroastrians and waged a campaign of persecution against Protestants, assassinating leaders of that community in the 1990s.[13]
- In Egypt, the implementation of Sharia laws has suppressed the freedoms of the Christian Coptic community. Even with such institutional oppression in place, the jihadists have waged attacks against this religious minority for decades.
- In Indonesia, the Islamist Laskar Jihad organization waged war against non-Muslims, Christians and Chinese alike.

In these and many other cases, the jihadists have viewed their actions as theological duties, quoting from holy texts and traditions. The dangerous trend in these types of persecutions is that they are not confined to a mere religious tension or ethnic conflict with religious expression, but go to the core of the ideological attitude toward the "other" as manifested in religion. Wahabi and Khumeini doctrines classify other faiths as inferior almost in the same fashion that Nazism classified other races as lower. Jihadism is thus a supremacist ideology, which systematically categorizes other religions as inferior and unholy, and hence deserving of sanctions, aggressive action, and violence. Jihadism uses two pillars for this discriminatory attitude: the concepts of *kuffar* and *dhimmi*.

The Kuffar

The jihadist attitude toward the "other" is encompassed in one word: *kuffar*, generally translated as "infidels." But as I argued in *Future Jihad*, the translation is not totally accurate linguistically or semantically. *Kuffar*, the plural of *kafir*, comes from the root *kufr*, which in fact doesn't have an exact translation in non-Arabic languages. The closest sense, from theological and historical angles, is "aggression against the divine" (from *al kufr billah*); in other words, "sinning against Allah." Historians looking at the origin of the word find that it has been used to describe non-Muslims since the early seventh century. The *kuffar* as perceived since the early expansion of Islam and under the caliphates for centuries would be comparable, but not necessarily identical, to gentiles in the Jewish tradition and infidels in medieval Christian theology. Modern Western historians ascribed the meaning "infidels" to the Arabic term *kuffar*, assuming they were the same. In fact, both terms express how Muslim and Christian empires described the identity of the "other," with corresponding religious and politicomilitary injunctions against that "other."[14]

To pursue this discussion further would enter into the realm of comparative historical studies. Although the concept of *kafir* is found in ancient Islamic religious texts, modern jihadists have extracted it from the theological and historical context and molded it into an ideological and political weapon, regardless of the debate it may provoke in contemporary interfaith dialogue and international relations. By jihadi paradigm, *kufr* is the status assigned to individuals and communities who by not being Muslims—or in some cases, not being Muslim enough—automatically fall into a category that is legally punishable. *Kuffar* are therefore all those deemed by the jihadists to be impure. They can include non-Salafi Sunnis, Shiites, Christians, Jews, Buddhists, Hindus, atheists, and in fact all "others" around the world. Humanity is hence divided in two: the pure Islamists on the one hand, and all "others" on the other hand. This discrimination is the largest and most divisive in the world, on a scale with Nazi racial discrimination. In jihadi *aqida* (doctrine), it is not the actions of non-Muslim individuals or groups that transform them into *kuffar*; they are born under this status regardless of their actions. Among Muslim-born individuals, those who act "un-Islamically" are accused of practicing *kufr* and therefore becoming ones. But Jihadism's most lethal use of the concept of "infidels" is as a mechanism for rendering an individual or a group of people *kuffar*. For although the term is found in various religious texts and could be reinterpreted by modern reformists and humanist Muslims, the jihadi Salafists have gone one step further by establishing a mechanism for demonizing the "other." It is called *takfir*. This one word, a verb, means to render someone a *kafir*. It would be like a court sentence labeling someone as a sinner, evildoer, or criminal. The jihadists possess a doctrinal death ray that selects victims of their actions simply by branding them with the label; once marked, the recipients of *Takfirism* become legal prey to the action of Jihadism, from insult to execution, depending on the severity of the sentence or the strategy of the jihadists.

In real-world politics, jihadi movements or regimes cast the label of *kuffar* upon their projected enemies as a prelude to waging war on them. The most universal case in modern times is al Qaeda's declaration of war against the *kuffar* worldwide. By reading all the various statements and proclamations of jihadists around the planet, one can see a single overarching concept behind all other injunctions: the war on the *kuffar*. The conflict against the *kuffar*, in the minds of the jihadists, is a war against a concept, an idea, the very state of being "other."

The Dhimmi

From the global doctrine on the *kuffar*, the jihadists extracted a narrower concept of "special" infidels: the *dhimmi*, based on the original Arabic term *ahl al dhimma*. Islamist ideologues developed particular categories of infidels on historical and theological grounds. The term *ahl al dhimma* first appeared in religious texts in the seventh century. Linguistically, it translates into the "people under custody." The word meant those "populations who were at the discretion of [someone else]." Historically, the *ahl al dhimma*, or *dhimmi*, were essentially the Christian and Jewish populations who fell under the rule of the caliphate after the Islamic conquest of the Middle East. Although considered *kuffar* like all non-Muslims, Jews and Christians were granted a special status for a variety of historical reasons, the most important of which was the fact that Muslim theology projected itself as the heir of Judaic and Christian revelations, before the last Islamic revelation from Allah sealed the prophecies. In fact, religious perceptions of predecessor messages are not unique to Islam. Christian interpretation of Judaism, and later on Bahá'i interpretation of Islam, follow the same path and fall under interfaith dialogue. The concept emerged after Caliph Omar conquered Jerusalem in 638 AD/CE and declared the Omari Conditions (*al shurut al Umariya*), under which Christians and Jews were allowed to worship and live under the caliphate, provided that they would comply with political and socioeconomic measures; they were cast as second-class citizens but protected by the caliph.

The *dhimmi* category, in the contemporary debate, is perceived from two contradictory angles. Muslim scholars and many apologist Western academics state that Jews and Christians, also described as the *ahl al kitab* (people of the book), were made into a specially protected group under the Islamic state. But protected from whom? questioned Middle Eastern Christian and Jewish historians and thinkers such as Bat Ye'or, Fuad Afram Bustany, and Sami Fares.[15] This debate still continues worldwide within the intellectual community, but the jihadists have gone beyond a theological analysis: they've inserted the *dhimmi* status in their agenda for modern Islamic governments, when and if they come to power. On web sites and in articles, books, and declarations and discussions on al Jazeera and other media, the Salafist jihadis have been very clear about the fate of Jews and Christians in future Taliban-like states and eventually under the reestablished caliphate: they will have to comply with the Omarian Conditions—pay an additional tax called *Jizya* (penalty), dress differently, wear signs on their clothing, and be barred from a variety of offices within the state. In short, if jihadists establish an emirate or an Islamist state, they will erode the civil rights of any Christians and Jews who decide to remain in those territories.

As clearly stated and practiced by jihadists, the concepts of *kuffar* and *dhimmi* are in full contradiction to the basic norms of human rights and international law. This is yet further crystal-clear evidence that Jihadism is an ideology (regardless of its self-positioning in conflicts and foreign policies) that aims at crumbling the very foundation of the principle of democracy and the basis of civil rights in democratic societies.

CHAPTER SIX

DEMOCRACY'S PILLARS UNDER ATTACK

THE TWENTY-FIRST-CENTURY WAR OF IDEAS IS MARKED BY AN EVEN broader gulf between the consensus reached by international society and the rising tide of Jihadism—specifically over the foundations of democratic society. These pillars are secularism, human rights, national self-determination, the prevention of genocide, and relatively newer concepts such as women's rights and sexual freedom, among others. While there is certainly strong debate over these concepts between conservatives and liberals, reactionaries and progressives, religious and seculars, right- and left-wing parties, jihadists have developed their own, radically antidemocratic positions toward the same issues. Here I will take you to some of the main battlefields.

JIHAD JUSTICE OR NO JUSTICE

One of the most advanced achievements of the legal revolution in the West and many other regions around the world was the declaration of the independence of the justice system. The essence of the American and French Revolutions and the British constitutional reforms was about separating the judicial system from the executive power. Throughout the modern era, other nations, societies, and cultures have emulated this concept of separation of powers. Its essence is that the holder of power cannot also be the provider of justice. This principle divides modern times from the Middle Ages, political development from ancient regimes, and democracies from absolute government. Most legal cultures around the globe have established different norms for this separation: Romano-German law, with the Napoleonic Code at its center; the Anglo-Saxon Common Law; the socialist body of legal principles;

and Asian and other regional legal cultures have all converged on this universal paradigm. An overwhelming majority of Muslim countries (including Egypt, Tunisia, Iraq, and Jordan), especially during the mid-twentieth century, moved to adopt it in some form. The legal development in these countries was based on an attempt to balance secular laws and Islamic Sharia laws. In many transitional governments around the world, particularly in Latin America and Africa, crises developed over virtual constitutions and real implementation of stipulations regarding human rights and principles declared in their preambles. During the Cold War, Soviet-controlled countries announced the separation of powers, but Communist parties held the real control of all powers. Such is still the case in radical Marxist regimes, such as those in North Korea and Cuba, and to a lesser degree in China and Vietnam. In short, despite great ideological differences among the many legal cultures and regimes, the idea of an independent justice system is an accepted principle, though world political realities often create exceptions in implementation.

In the Muslim world, the general trend tilted toward a practical absorption of modern laws and the concept of an independent legal system, but with measures of Islamic law applied to such things as family status, inheritance, and marriage. Within the Muslim countries, however, extreme opposite concepts developed as well. For example, Turkey developed a Kemalist, fully secular legal culture, with zero application of the Sharia, whereas Saudi Arabia applied the strict Sharia code, leading to criticism by human rights organizations.

Toward the end of the last century, the common wisdom among democracies was to measure democratic governments by the independence of their judiciaries from executive power, even beyond the separation between the executive and legislative branches. The court system's ability to act outside the political and ideological order are what finalize the definition of a democracy as such. And the laws judiciaries apply must be the people's will, as enacted by elected lawmakers.

But it is against this universal agreement on the independence of the judiciary that twentieth-century jihadists warred in their violent return to the international scene after the Cold War. Both Salafists and Khumeinists reject the main pillars of the third branch of power: independence of the judiciary and the application of laws reflecting the will of the people. From different angles, Islamic fundamentalists of both Sunni and Shiia backgrounds oppose the Muslim reformers and progressive views that cleave to the world consensus on the independent justice system. The jihadists argue that the Western-inspired legal system is to be rejected on doctrinal (labeled as "religious") grounds. "*Qawaneen al kuffar marfudah*" ("The laws of the infidels are to be rejected"), repeat the ideologues of Jihadism.[1] On this deeply ideological basis, the various streams of Islamist militants build their arguments for why the separation of powers and secular legal systems are to be rejected.

JIHAD JUSTICE OUTSIDE THE PEOPLE

What binds all Islamists regardless of their various schools of thought is their opposition to the secular court system's most important feature: its independence. The basics of Salafist and Khumeinist teachings reject the notion that the people are either the source, or a source, of legislation or judicial decisions. By opposing the first principle of democratic political culture, the jihadists deny the public its right to participate in making laws, interpreting them, or having judges refer to the people and their representatives as the source of their authority and decisions. "It is in the name of Allah that we render justice, not in the name of humans" ("*Adalatuna hiya mina allah was laysat minal bashar*").[2] With this slogan, the ideologues and jurists of Salafism and Khumeinism justify their rejection of all secular justice, even if it is rendered by religious figures. In fact, such a theologically driven attitude is not so different from those of ancient theological monarchies and empires. Christian, Confucian, Hindu, Taoist, and Hebrew religious laws were state endorsed. So were the Sharia courts under the caliphate, which existed for 13 centuries. But the evolution of institutions and doctrines during the modern period produced a global acceptance of the principle of independence of the judiciary.

This is not to say that there have not been exceptions. Under authoritarian regimes, there were repeated breaches of these principles. Under Soviet and Communist systems, the courts were supposed to be separate from other powers, but in reality, the Communist Party controlled all three branches of power. In Third World populist regimes, such as under Peron in Argentina and the old PRI in Mexico, or paper democracies with authoritarian leaders, such as Venezuela under Chavez, tribunals are constitutionally sovereign but are actually under the influence of a powerful head of state. In some occupied countries, such as Lebanon under the Syrians, highly developed courts were in fact controlled by the intelligence services. These are significant exceptions to a worldwide move toward more judicial independence, both in reality and on paper.

But in contrast with these failures and exceptions, it is important to understand that the jihadi judicial system is a refutation and categorical rejection of the international consensus, not merely an exception to it. It is not some divergent version with points of contact with the global international view of justice that has developed over the centuries. Instead, it aims to overthrow that consensus. In short, under Islamic fundamentalism, there is no separation of power among branches of government in the sense that each branch is sovereign and reflects different democratic components. Since justice is perceived as *ilahi* (divine) only, those who serve it are legally not responsible to any other level of representation, neither to the people nor to such secular institutions as may exist. Under the caliphs, as the Islamists argue, the successor to the Prophet is the ultimate judge. He is not elected, and hence he doesn't bow to any other set of laws than the ones he interprets. Courts of Sharia *(Mahakem Shari'ya)* do not answer to any power in the civilian realm. They are directly connected to the caliph or his representatives (in the purest form of Salafism, at least). Attempts to actually implement these radical Islamist principles in modern times have been relatively few, but the cases are very revealing. In Saudi Arabia, there is no secular court system or civil law; courts are entirely subservient to the Wahabi institutions and ideology. Saudi Arabian monarchs and princes are attempting to modernize the technology of the court system but haven't been able to produce the reforms necessary for the rise of an independent judiciary. In Sudan, Sharia courts are the highest tribunals, but other courts exist as well. In other Arab and Muslim countries, odd situations emerge, particularly in Egypt, Qatar, and nations with similar governments, where civilian tribunals coexist with Sharia courts within a dual legal system. In moderate countries such as Jordan, Morocco, and Senegal, the trend is to have secular courts deal with general issues of contention, while religious courts are confined to issues of family status, inheritance, and related matters. Islamist political forces in these countries are putting pressure on the governments to diminish the secular and increase the religious component. But without doubt, the most striking model of drastic enforcement of self-defined religious laws by jihadists has been the Taliban regime in Afghanistan. Under the Islamist military rule, the courts were another form of judicial militia, with no shred of independence or balance. The *Mahakem Shari'ya* of the Taliban were the legal arm of the regime, alongside the military and security arms. They played a dominant role in the brutal oppression of the Afghan people until 2001.

The toppling of the Taliban regime does not mean that the model has been repudiated—far from it. In fact, jihadi-controlled religious courts worldwide are mushrooming, and one of the first items on the Islamist agenda in any battlefield is either to have those courts take over judicial control in areas dominated by Salafists (for example, in West Pakistan, some Indonesian islands, southern Philippines, northern Nigeria, and spots in Algeria) or Khumeinists (such as in southern Lebanon) or to pressure the governments to use them increasingly, as in Algeria, Egypt, Sudan, and Saudi Arabia (where they are exclusive). One of the most striking examples of the rise of jihadi-linked courts is the *Mahakem Islamiya* (Islamic tribunals) in Somalia. In this stunning case, the jihadi courts *are* the militia: a hybrid form of armed groups carrying out the sentences of alleged judicial courts formed by radical clerics—the arm and the head are one.

More relevant to the West now are the increasing demands by radical Islamists in Europe, North America, and Australia to allow and then impose Sharia laws within democracies. Jihadi-inspired pressure groups have been arguing that Islamic religious laws are a cultural and ethnic right for Muslim communities, and hence should be authorized within enclaves in the same way that other religious groups, such as Catholics and Protestants, have the right to practice religious marriages and baptisms. But the jihadi demands exceed the normal group right within a democratic pluralist society to call for separate courts to settle the civil, family, and some aspects of financial matters of Muslims living under secular systems. In cases in Canada and Great Britain, these courts were seriously considered. Under this agreement, Canadian, British, and other citizens would go to court on a country's soil but outside its laws. A Canadian woman, for example, is equal to a Canadian male under the secular laws of her country but will not be equal under the Sharia court of her ethnic group. These Western Taliban-like courts are now a beachhead from which the jihadists hope to increase the issues these courts can look into, and eventually to expand them within democracies, with all the attendant social, political, and security consequences.

SHARIA LAWS OR NO LAWS

The jihadist perception of the judicial branch is clear: it is an agency at the service of a higher authority, the caliphate or whoever represents it until it is reestablished. But what about the laws these tribunals use in their processes and sentencing? The answer seems very simple: Sharia laws, that is to say Islamic religious law. In fact, it is more complicated. Because the court system the radical Islamist wants to establish is at the discretion of the "just ruler" (meaning a caliph or an emir), and because this ruler is the highest authority above the civil servants or tribunal functionaries, the laws to be enacted or interpreted are also at the discretion of this nonjudicial authority. In simple words, not only is the content of the jihadi-promoted body of laws shielded from the sanction of the public (as in normal legal sources), but it also is at the mercy of the ruler of the Islamic state.

Civil society under the Taliban was ruled at the discretion of the judges interpreting the holy texts in the most restrictive ways. Even by classical Islamic standards, the Taliban's courts bypassed all norms of human rights and reasonable judgments. Women were brutally punished for minor breaches of a very severe code of conduct. They were executed without having any form of defense. Minorities were reduced to second- and third-class citizens. Taliban militiamen, executing orders by jihadi courts, destroyed ancient and precious Buddha statues with artillery shells and dynamite, because the Taliban's interpretation of Sharia law condemns any statue, picture, or depiction of humans in art and sculpture. Such an interpretation is not reflective of the global Muslim community's progress toward adapting religious laws inherited from centuries of practice by empires, emirates, and governorates. The jihadi justice system is based on the narrowest interpretation of the Sharia, which is an amalgamation of religious texts inherited from past centuries. Jihadism in this regard forces Muslims backward and obstructs a worldwide consensus on an egalitarian justice system reached after centuries of struggle. To the radical Islamists, it boils down to no laws other than the Sharia laws, and no Sharia laws except as interpreted by their ulemas and imams.

So what are the credentials of the religious authorities who are inspiring the radicals? To simplify, it depends on the two "trees" of Jihadism. To the Sunni fundamentalists, including Wahabis, the Muslim Brotherhood, Takfiris, and the like, the purest roots of Islamic law go back to those who saw their birth, the *salaf* (preceding founders). According to the Salafist ideologues, only the companions of the Prophet, their immediate successors, and those who succeeded them have the right knowledge of the divine set of laws contained in the Qu'ran, the Hadith, and the other sources. The caliphate was supposed to perpetuate these laws, but again (in Salafi interpretation), with the collapse of the Ottomans, the legitimate authority for the authentification and interpretation of all laws has fallen on the shoulders of the "real" Salafi scholars and Muftis. Hence today's Salafists and their affiliates have an open capacity in terms of claiming the entire body of Islamic laws as theirs and theirs only. From that holy code over which they assert exclusive authority, they can and have issued fatwa after fatwa, numbering in the thousands and covering all fields—from ordering massive strikes on the West, suicide attacks around the world, assassinations of opponents in the Arab world, and threats to leaders, to such mundane matters as marriages, divorces, financial agreements, and so on, all based on *Qadis* (judges) and imams who hold the code to be theirs. In many instances, for example, the Saudi government has put pressure on the state-funded clerics to contain the more extremist elements (*al mutatarrifun*), but to no avail. Mainstream imams in the Wahabi kingdom, such as Ibn al Uthaymeen, al Albani, and others, have gone to the extremes of Salafism themselves. Ironically, the difference between clerics within the Saudi monarchy has become that between radicals and more extreme radicals.

To top it off, most of the cleric-ideologues who formed the chain of scholars between Mohammed Abdel Wahab and the younger Salafists of the current century have passed away, and with them the potential of reforming. Dramatically, the younger clerics who endorse al Qaeda and the other jihadists proclaim that they have the code in their hands. Thus even when the Egyptian government of Hosni Mubarak, an ally of the United States, asks the official chief cleric Sheikh of al Azhar to moderate the Salafi stance on world politics or accept some aspects of modernity, al Azhar is accused by hardliners such as Sheikh Yussef al Qardawi (Egyptian himself) of playing the game of the infidels. The Sharia that the Salafi jihadists are dying and killing for has been boxed in tightly by clerics who are now dead and is controlled today by a younger generation who apply it and expand it boundlessly.

The other "tree" has also developed its own set of rulings and holy laws, away from the Salafi world, while awaiting divinely ordained catastrophic events set to happen in the future, including the return of the "missing imam"—a pillar of traditional Shiism. Indeed, the Khumeinist mullahs have for decades shaped their own theology out of the underground community that lived under Sunni rule for as long as Arab caliphates existed. But with the receding of Arab dynasties from Persia after the Crusades era and the transfer of the caliphate from Arab Abbasids in Baghdad to Turkic Ottomans in Istanbul, the Persian Shiia majority established its own dynasties. The Shiia version of the Sharia was officially one with the Sunnis'. But a more fundamentalist current of clerics arose in the second part of the twentieth century, most likely as a reaction to the rise of the Salafists. The surfacing of Wahabism and the Muslim Brotherhood among the Sunnis and their radicalization of the Sharia made an impact on many Shia clerics, particularly in Iran, who in turn brought about a parallel radicalization of their theology. It seemed as if the Shia jihadis engaged in a theological competition with the Sunni jihadis.

But Shia scholars have followed two different schools of interpretation. One is identified as the Quietist (*al Samita*), with Iraq as its base and Grand Ayatollah Sistani as its spiritual leader. The other, self-defined as *al mustad'afeen* (the oppressed), was represented by Grand Ayatollah Ruhallah Khomeini in Iran and Ayatollah Baqer al Sadr in Iraq. The new jihadi movement among the region's Shiia developed the political theology of *Vilayet e Faqih* (the mandate of the wise), which established a parallel line to the doctrine of the Salaf among Sunni Islamists. Thus the Khumeinists came up with a theology strategically comparable but not doctrinally identical to the Salafists'. The Shiia radicals looked at a strict implementation of the Sharia as a unique source of laws, but with Khumeinist long-term objectives. Practically, Khumeinist tribunals are fully linked to the Islamic Revolution of Iran and practice a radical form of Sharia injunctions.

NO CRITICISM OF RELIGION

Born of their rebellion against theological regimes, Western democracies have struggled hard to provide their societies with freedom from any coercion, including religious oppression. Jihadism comes from the absolute opposite direction: it strives to bring societies under absolute religious authority—Muslim communities first, to be followed by others. The question of freedom of religion, as explored in the previous chapter, has follow-on effects in the practice of democratic social rights: the freedom to talk about religion, analyze it, express an opinion about it, and even criticize one or all religions is a democratic right. But here as well, the War of Ideas is raging between the two camps. The position of democracies is ultimately that there is a freedom of expression in general, but that its practice should take into consideration emotional, historical, and social realities—in short, that it is limited. In democracies, conservatives, liberals, and progressives, from both religious and nonreligious backgrounds, are all in accord on the human end of the equation: people should not be punished if they express their views on any religion. But not only Christian and Jewish hierarchies oppose an earthly punishment for blasphemy; so do moderate Muslims. On many occasions when aspects of the Muslim faith have been criticized by either Muslims or non-Muslims, while the more militant and extremist camps have called for punishment including death sentences, moderates have argued that Allah is the only one to mete out retribution for these blasphemies, on *yam al day-nuna* (Muslim judgment day).

But individual radical Islamists are not the only ones who postulate severe punishments for what they consider blasphemy. In fact, a number of governments, including those in Saudi Arabia, Pakistan, and Egypt, continue to enforce public policies of punishing blasphemy. In Saudi Arabia, capital punishments have been and continue to be in effect for proselytizing: a number of non-Muslim residents and visitors have been arrested and punished for "insulting" or "criticizing" religion, some even being beheaded. Within the Wahabi kingdom, the *Mutawaa* religious police are endowed with a specific mission to look for any aspect of insult to, or criticism of, or breaches to religion.[3] In Pakistan and Egypt, punishment for converts from Islam to other religions and for those accused of blasphemy is carried out under the law. Although it is true that the full force of the law isn't applied because of international considerations, it is nevertheless a fact that insult or criticism of religion is punishable by the legal system. But in the jihadist sphere of influence, such as under the former Taliban regime or Islamist governments such as those of Sudan and Iran, or in areas controlled by jihadi militias in many spots around the world, direct and severe punishment was and is dispensed even for minor infractions. The divide between the jihadi realm and democracies is at its greatest in terms of the right to state an opinion contrary to the one of the dominant clerics on matters of religion. It is like the gulf between the twelfth and the twenty-first centuries. But why are the jihadists so extreme with regard to what they perceive as criticism of religion?

AL RIDDAH: RECONVERSION

The jihadists' harshness with Muslims or non-Muslims who insult religion or criticize it is rooted in their ideological fear of *al Riddah*, or what was known historically as reconversion of Muslims back to another religion. Here again, extremist contemporary behavior is dictated by doctrinaires who reenact past stages of history, a mechanism that has caused disasters in modern history, including the horrors inflicted under Fascism, Nazism, and extreme nationalism. Contemporary Islamist movements such as the Wahabis, Muslim Brotherhood, and Khumeinists, instructed by their doctrinal luminaries, borrow a principle applied in the early age of the Islamic state 13 centuries ago. In the first few decades of the Arab-Islamic conquests inside and outside the Arab peninsula, after the death of Prophet Mohammed, many tribes that had converted to the new religion decided to revert to a previous faith or abandon Islam. The caliphs waged relentless military campaigns against these tribes, which they called the *Riddah* wars. *Ridda* means "to go back to." The early Islamic state feared that a reconversion by tribes would disintegrate the whole army and the caliphate, for it was only religion at the time that kept the young empire together and ultimately growing. Although many religious scholars cite from the holy texts and preach that abandoning the *deen* (religion) is unacceptable and punishable by death, in reality what made the *riddah* injunction powerful and enforceable was the state's determination to head off any crumbling of the caliphate. So historically, even though it was prescribed theologically in the seventh century, the ban on reconversion had a raison d'état and continued to have one through the following centuries, albeit not with the same urgency, as the Islamic empire grew to be transcontinental.

Modern jihadists, because of their strict adherence to the *Salaf* (early founders of the state), apply the policy to the letter. Islamic governments apply it sometimes when pressured by fundamentalists. The circle is complete: the Islamists maintain pressure on all players, including on themselves, to physically eliminate any dissent, reconversion, and criticism. They see it as an all-or-nothing matter. Criticism or apostasy, and virtually any nibbling at the edges, they feel would disintegrate the whole edifice. The cultural dominance of the fundamentalists is so deeply rooted that even several years after the United States freed Afghanistan from the Taliban, a court under the government of President Karzai sentenced a *murtad* (convert from Islam) by the name of Abdel Rahman to a death sentence in 2006. The sentence wasn't carried out, and a legal solution was found to the case, but only because of Western intercession.

LA INTIQAD: NO CRITICISM

The radical Islamists do not tolerate the principle of *intiqad* (criticism), of any aspect of religion, from theology to practice. Because there is no concept of civil freedom in Salafi or Khumeinist thinking, religious critical thinking is nonexistent as well. Muslims and non-Muslims alike may not argue with the core beliefs of religion and would be sanctioned if they raised these matters. Such a "frozen" attitude of the jihadi dogma is reminiscent of the Christian Middle Ages. But ironically, back in the tenth century, Baghdad was illuminated not only with oil lamps, but also by Muslim minds looking forward and evolving their culture and sciences, in advance of the end of the Dark Ages in Europe (much like China's early superiority in technology). Surprisingly to many observers of the movement, twentieth-century jihadists chose to follow twelfth-century Ibn Taymiya's narrow thinking rather than the even earlier thinking of the Arab enlightenment of the ninth and tenth centuries. An analogy can be drawn with Fascism and national socialism, which opted for recent authoritarian ideologies rather than for previous (but weaker) democratic ideas. Insecure elites seeking power prefer totalitarian doctrines with intellectual rigidness over open thinking and its risky path toward pluralism. Thus a comprehensive analysis of the jihadist mind leads us to see in the Salafists and Khumeinists a move by formerly marginal segments of society who, thanks to their reviving of archaic models, have built their power base on a rigid ideology they are fully in control of. Their reliance on the purity of the doctrinal body ensures their power over it, hence their rejection of any form of criticism of their interpretation of religion. In other words, the rejection of criticism is not essentially about the core belief system as much as it is about their control of this system. The real battlefield for radicals is the tight control of the instrument of power—in this case, ideologically protected religious laws. From this perspective, the jihadists resemble more a sect, or even a cult, shielding a space in the name of the "community" they pretend they are defending, while in fact imprisoning all who lie within it.

But perhaps a more intriguing attitude is the obstruction of Western-based Islamist groups who have been attempting to create a firewall around the religious debate on Islam—amazingly, even inside Western democracies. For though it sounds historically understandable that radical Islamists would fight off reformism and criticism within the Arab and Muslim world, it is illogical that jihadist-inspired groups would break the democratic rules of engagement inside the realm of democracies. In the Arab and Muslim world, Salafists, Wahabis, *Ikhwan*, Takfiris, and Khumeinists often persecute Muslim liberals, reformists, or moderate conservatives for any attempt to criticize the dominant paradigm in theological affairs, and most certainly block efforts to contain the fundamentalist interpretation of Islam. Jihadi violence against Muslim critics of Islamism is now several decades old. Its examples are too abundant even to be compiled, but here are a few: In Egypt, *al Gamaa al Islamiya* used violence against liberals in the 1980s and 1990s, culminating with the stabbing of Nobel Peace Prize recipient Najib Mahfuz and the assassination of author Faraj Fouda. Intimidations and threats have been used against multitudes of intellectuals, including the world-renowned feminist Nawal Saadawi. In Algeria, the Groupement Islamique Arme and the Salafi Group for Call and Combat waged a holy war of terror against "secular affronts" to religion by moderate clerics, journalists, and writers, even killing a rock singer in the 1990s.[4] Similar violence against those who dared express their opinions or even criticize the fundamentalist version of the faith have taken place in Iraq (after liberation from Saddam Hussein), in Turkey with the assassination of a professor of political science in 2004, in Bangladesh against female author Talisma Nisrine, in Lebanon with the brutal killing of Muslim author Mustafa Jeha, and in many more incidents around the world. In Iran, the regime launched a systematic campaign for two decades against Muslim intellectuals who challenged the political theology of the ruling establishment. Among the most high-profile cases was that of Hashem Aghajari, a professor at Tehran Teachers Training University, who was prosecuted for a speech in June 2002 in which he urged people to question religious teachings, saying that the words of clerics should not be considered sacred simply because they were part of history. Aghajari was sentenced to four years in jail for criticizing the religious regime.[5] Ramin Jahanbegloo, a reformist and Khatami supporter, was also arrested. Moussavi-Khoiiniha, a religious nationalist, was arrested in June 2006 during a women's protest and released in September but is still being harassed. Last but not least, Canadian-Iranian journalist Zahra Kazemi was arrested, tortured, and killed.

But on a much larger scale, jihadi violence, both physical and psychological, was unleashed against non-Muslim intellectuals and social activists across the Greater Middle East and beyond. Christian editors, journalists, and students were and are threatened in Egypt, Lebanon, Sudan, Iran, Pakistan, Nigeria, and many other countries by the Islamists for "stating that persecutions have taken place under Islamist regimes" and in some cases for "lying about Islamic history."[6] Incredibly, jihadist ideologues consider it a criticism of religion if Christians, Jews, Hindus, or even reformist Muslims claim that centuries ago there "were military conquests at the hands of the Caliphate"[7]—even though they themselves celebrate these military victories in their chat rooms. The Islamists forbid contemporary historians to describe events as they took place a millennium ago in the region. Others cannot expose the past violence of the caliphate, because this would be considered an attack against the religion of Islam. And yet even more incredibly, the Islamists themselves brag about historical military achievements of the past in the name of Islam. Here again, it is clear that the jihadist movement wants to appropriate the exclusive privilege of speaking on behalf of all things Islamic, from historical accounts to dogma to politics. They have, so to speak, appropriated the right to express what is *Halal* (permissible Muslim food) in all realms. Any expression about Islam outside their authorization—from Muslims or not—is considered by the radical Islamists as a criticism of religion, punishable by death.

IHANATU AL DINE: THE INSULT TO RELIGION

In ancient times, insult to religion was a *casus belli* between nations and empires. In the Middle East, insulting one's faith is far graver than attacking one's race, culture, nationality, or family. Popular expressions in the Arab world are a living testament to how powerful insult to beliefs can be.[7] But while the rest of the world has reduced its reactions to such emotional matters, and as the West witnessed a surge of anticlericalism and began absorbing these attitudes under freedom of expression, the forces of Islamic fundamentalism haven't yielded an inch. Projecting their action as part of the greater package of infallibility and the sacredness of religion, Salafists and Khumeinists have kept the pressure on Muslim societies and governments to maintain the ban on offenses to religion as a capital crime. In the West and within democracies, insulting religion is not actionable unless it harms the social peace. Freedom is broad and limitations are very liberal. Insults to Catholicism, such as acerbic attacks against the personality of Jesus, have reached levels never tolerated by followers of Rome in history. Railing against the values dear to Protestants has also soared unchecked in North America. Christians and other religious communities have gradually accepted the new norms.

Muslims, especially those living in the West, have been fighting a more difficult battle to integrate with a more critical public culture. But the Islamists have drawn a line in the sand and fought back with virulence: East of the Atlantic and south of the Mediterranean, insult to religion "remains war" in the jihadi reading. Under Communism, religion was considered the "opium of the masses," and Lenin called for its elimination. The Wahabis and Khumeinists responded with a full war on Marxism-Leninism. Tens of thousands of Communists and Islamic militants died from Afghanistan to Iran in this war of ideologies over religion. In the West, attacking a person's religion is seen as inappropriate, but it is not illegal. In the Muslim world, radical powers have moved to transform the matter into a mobilization strategy. The most publicized case of the last century was the fatwa issued by Ayatollah Khamenei against British Muslim writer Salman Rushdie in reaction to his book *The Satanic Verses*. The Rushdie affair was not simple. In the eyes of the Islamic Republic and also of the Wahabi realm, the Indian-born author had insulted the very core of the religion that is the Qu'ran and its Prophet. By describing Mohammed in very offensive ways, according to fundamentalist parameters, Rushdie deserved radical punishment. This incident, still pending, was the first open and highly publicized clash of ideas between the jihadists and Western democracies. The latter couldn't tolerate a Sharia-based, transnational death sentence executed on a British citizen who had exercised his right as a free citizen to write a book. By Western standards, as long as no direct call for violence is made by an author, all content, however offensive it may be, is protected by law. The jihadist sees it otherwise. By touching upon the sacred, any author, regardless of the motives and context, is guilty and should be punished. The Islamists cannot afford a breach of their hold on the religious space. Moderate and modernist Muslims would feel insulted but would leave the sanction to Allah and, when possible legally, to the courts. The jihadists, in this matter as in others, have not accepted the reasoning of the modern age. The consequences can be grave.

Jihadists of all schools and movements are completely unified on the subject. The brutal killing of Muslim Lebanese writer Mustafa Jeha in the 1990s is highly symbolic. His brutal execution was in punishment for the publishing of a book entitled *Mihnat al aql fil Islam (The crisis of the mind in Islam)*, in which he dwelt on the struggle between rationalist and obscurantist thinking in Muslim history. Jeha argued that Muslim rationalism is possible and that criticism of religion is still Islamic; this put him in the crosshairs of the jihadists. Decades later, the radicals would take the battle to the West, spreading violence on the ground of offenses to religion. In Holland, filmmaker Theo Van Gogh was stabbed to death in 2004 by a radical Islamist because he produced a movie felt to insult the Qu'ran. A female member of the Dutch Parliament, Somalian-born Ayaan Hirsi Ali, was threatened with execution for offending religion. In Canada, gay and Muslim author Irshad Manji was also threatened for the publication of her bestseller, *What Is Wrong with Islam*. But the most explosive situation was that which followed the publication in Denmark in September 2005 of cartoons about the Prophet Mohammed. The affair led to a massive uproar and violent demonstrations by Islamists around the world, with a number of deaths and much destruction.

A more complex political battle has been taking place for the last few years inside the West, however, on the issue of "criticism, offense, and insults of religion." Using the media, lobbying efforts, and the legal route, Islamist pressure groups and militant organizations have been waging multiple campaigns to cease by law any insult of religion. Stunningly, jihadi sympathizers in Western Europe and North America, self-described as "civil rights" groups, are mobilizing to force democracies to make a concession on their main principle of freedom of thought: that is, to ban any criticism of Islam under the pretext of stopping offenses against religious values. The move, which is designed to put the definition of criticism and offense in the hands of Islamist lobbies, is very daring. It allows the jihadists to take the War of Ideas inside the West and use its laws to further shield the penetration of Islamist radicals within Western systems. This intertwined web of ideological thrusts shows clearly that Jihadism and democracies are now battling in each other's "zones." In the following chapters, I will analyze the War of Ideas as it rages on battlefields around the planet.

CHAPTER SEVEN

GENDER APARTHEID

HISTORICALLY, GENDER RELATIONS HAVE RARELY BEEN LINKED TO war and peace, and sexuality has seldom been a component of national security. But in the global War of Ideas, women's oppression and ideological marginalization are ingredients not to be ignored. For let's keep in mind that, from a sheer quantitative angle, females are just as if not more numerous than men in most societies, including in the countries engaged in the War on Terror and the underlying War of Ideas. Any shift in women's thinking and behaving, regardless of their status, can ultimately lead to groundswelling change. In addition, women's particular position with children and overseeing the very first steps of education gives them an incredible potential power to initiate and impact massive intellectual change. Moreover, as taboos about sexual relations are crumbling worldwide, the vivid contrast between mindsets in free societies and the Taliban-like attitude toward sexual freedom on the part of jihadists is playing a part in the psychological conditioning of jihadi violence. This book cannot deal comprehensively with the powerful subject of women's social history or with modern gender politics as a whole. (In terms of the study of the War of Ideas in general, this subject deserves a massive research effort, and one has been ongoing in recent decades.[1]) But the issue of women and sexuality, intertwined in its psychological dimension, has great significance for the jihadist ideology and must not be ignored.

In looking at this subject in detail, we are also examining the background of the conflict between the growing international consensus on democratic culture and diversity and the fundamentalists' diametrically opposed ideology. Simply put, while democracies attempt to equalize the rights of the sexes and support women in their quest for social justice, Jihadism has frozen their status—and indeed, even seeks to reverse their achievements, as it has done throughout history. This situation constitutes perhaps the most dramatic difference between the two camps. And it is a difference so deep that it could determine the future of the struggle between the two worlds of liberal pluralism and fundamentalist totalitarianism.

WOMEN AND FREEDOM

The role of women in Islam, as compared with that of their sisters in other cultures and religions, has long been debated. Theorists of gender and religious studies have often argued about the differences and similarities. The two sides have been divided into those trying to uncover and eventually expose the status of females under Sharia laws and in Muslim societies in general and those who defend the cultural legitimacy of that status in the eyes of religious women in that community. A mutual deafness has marred this exchange of accusations for decades: Marxism (in the Soviet Bloc and China) and secular anticlericalism (as in Turkey) have forced Muslim women to integrate themselves into an antireligious society for almost a century. Islamic fundamentalism has responded with extreme gender apartheid, as in Afghanistan, Iran, and Saudi Arabia, severely restricting or banning freedom of dress, movement, job access, and expression, in addition to imposing a whole set of other deprivations. In between, liberal democracy has been attempting to walk on eggshells, trying not to abandon women's long struggle toward liberation worldwide while also respecting the "understanding" of what the Islamic fundamentalists call intangible "religious values." This oddly intertwined relationship (including intellectual warfare) among the Marxist Left, liberals, anticlericals, moderate Muslims, and radical Islamists has forced Muslim women worldwide and in the West into an imbroglio that has isolated them from the global evolution toward gender equality. The ideological, social, and theological pressures surrounding this debate within the Muslim countries and diasporas have produced a peculiar "Muslim women's debate" within their own communities, and also with regard to the rest of their gender worldwide.

But this debate is not unique to Islam. Judaism, Christianity, Hinduism, Buddhism, and other religions have witnessed similar historical struggles. All religions and cultures have experienced their own gender tensions and evolutions, but twentieth-century Jihadism is an exception: in contrast with the global and natural development of societies, including Muslim ones, the radical fundamentalists have singled themselves out as unique oppressors of women. Moving beyond the parameters of the debate in most societies, jihadists have created a unique ideological system that separates women as a subjugated segment of society and legitimizes their oppression.

THE GENDER PREDICAMENT

Social scientists across the board would agree that it took long centuries for women to be granted basic rights equal to those of males. Anthropologists provide us with several reasons for this historical injustice around the globe; primarily, it has been through power economics that men have dominated. In a variety of social orders and institutionalized family relationships, females at different times and in various fashions have been subjected to the power of patriarchy. Matriarchal societies rapidly collapsed, much to the advantage of males; the social sciences are still researching the roots of the shift, which took place in prehistory and in later stages of civilization.[2] Recorded history, from antiquity to the Middle Ages and beyond, witnessed the consolidation of an almost absolute male power, from the highest stratum of the state to the lowest social stratum. In short, women in all cultures and civilizations, with or without religious endorsement, fell under the yoke of men.

The field of women's studies has shown how humiliating and devastating was the subjugation of women to raw male power. Their status was universally lower, regardless of the fate of the ethnic and racial groups they belonged to. For even with the defeat of their cultural community, the social pressures were never removed—in other words, even when the dominant males of their own society were crushed by other males from a different group, this didn't give rise to opportunities for oppressed females to obtain greater freedoms. Indeed, one of the first consequences of military-social defeat in the premodern era was the subjugation, uprooting, and rape of women belonging to the defeated community, in addition to the prevalent conquerors' war tradition of selling the women of the defeated group into slavery. For women, historical changes didn't translate into greater opportunity for many centuries. Even though we shouldn't generalize, the statistical record throughout centuries up to the early Enlightenment in Europe reveals that both the legal status and actual treatment of women were universally discriminatory and oppressive. Different civilizations, cultures, regions, and religions developed various experiments in women's advancement, however. During this developmental phase, the world witnessed a variety of leaps forward for women. In the nineteenth century, North American and European women of many countries had certainly achieved more rights than their counterparts in other regions of the world. In the twentieth century, women living in the Soviet Union had more social rights than women living in many Third World countries, but fewer than women in the West. Within the Arab and Muslim world, Egyptian and Iraqi women under socialism had more privileges than Saudi women, for instance. In the Middle East, women's rights developed in Israel first, followed by Lebanon and Turkey. Comparisons could be made based on different parameters, including socioeconomics, political culture, social values, and ideological activism. Swedish and Scandinavian women have reached the highest status worldwide, including the top political levels; women in Latin America have achieved constitutional recognition and are struggling for political empowerment; whereas most women in the Arab world are still lacking basic rights.

Many have argued, and with good reason, that religions have oppressed women in general or given preferential status to males. Just as many religious texts have perceived the people of their particular faiths as the best, the saved, and the most valuable, so have they awarded the same superior status to males. The Jewish Bible speaks of a "chosen people," the Christian New Testament speaks of the "church of God," and the Qu'ran speaks of the Arabs as the "best nation Allah has bestowed." These examples are not unique; other religions have also bestowed different levels of value on their believers and the rest of humanity. And indeed, philosophically, if not logically, this is what most organized religions are about: a new divine message that recruits or attracts people, hoping to bring all humans under one message or fulfill the mission of a particular faith. Inevitably, those who have joined the faith and those who have not are differentiated. The status of women in religions has followed the same path. Depending on faith, time, and context, religious perceptions of females have varied in their inequalities. In the Judeo-Christian traditions, many argue that women were not given full equality along with men. In marriage, man has been declared to be "the head of woman." Sociologists assert that such claims reflected the familial equation of the times. But females were in reality discriminated against in the Christian world for centuries, until a series of religious reformations and renewals, as well as social revolutions, rebalanced gender relations.

Looking at the Islamic world, many argue that from a social perspective, religious texts established clear discrimination here as well. And because Muslim theological texts have in addition a legal and sociopolitical force, as Islam is a *deen wa dawla* (religion and state), the status of women is—according to the texts themselves—*legally* inferior to males. The theological debate about women's status remains in the domain of theory, but the social and legal consequences of religious injunctions regarding women in Islam are significant. Because the theological references are numerous, the practical effects throughout history have been vast as well. In Muslim societies, women have fallen into a gender category with very specific roles, and their status vis-à-vis men is very clearly not equal. Some members of the faith—as in most religions—argue that this status is part of the divine order and is to be accepted by believers. Argumentation stops there; either you accept it or you don't. But social scientists and activists counter that for all religions, including Islam, such gender limitations are social, not theological. This means that although one is free to believe that women are second to males in the divine order, by the terms of social justice and international principles, all humans are equal, and therefore women aren't subsidiary or inferior to men. This debate pits religious zealots against social activists, and indeed history has been a battlefield between the two. Over the past three centuries at least, women have made advances in their gender status despite social, religious, and economic disparities. Today's feminists may not be satisfied fully with these achievements, but relatively massive leaps have been achieved, particularly in the West.

Although there are layers of differences reflecting regional, social, and economic variables, to put it simply, women in general want more freedom, struggle for it whenever and however they can, and have achieved better conditions in some regions than in others. It is equally true that women do not want to go backward. Naturally and logically, they do not wish to reverse the achievements they have made and the rights they have obtained. To argue otherwise is against human nature. Slaves do not want to be reenslaved, free nations do not wish to be re-colonized, and the middle classes do not seek pauperization. But the jihadists argue against this democratic logic. Obviously, in each category stricken by inequality, exceptions and opposing opinions exist for a variety of reasons. Hence there have been and continue to be women who accept these conditions or even justify and defend them. But the exceptions don't annul the principle of equality, just resist it.

JIHADISM AND GENDER APARTHEID

Against most schools of thought, civil and human rights declarations, international conventions on women's rights, constitutions, and the whole direction of global women's movements, the jihadists implacably oppose the tide of social history. Without any complex regard for political correctness or the international consensus on women's equality with men, Salafists and Khumeinists burst into the international arena to explode their doctrine on *al Imara'a* (the woman). In very direct statements made in books, speeches, articles, and radio addresses and on televised programs for more than half a century, the radical Islamists—bypassing the traditional Muslim debate on the matter—have said two things: first, there is a theological, unbridgeable gap between man and woman; second, whatever rights and status were granted to females in the twentieth century but not in accordance with their jihadist interpretation of the Sharia law must be taken back. Female advancement within the Muslim world, and eventually everywhere, argue the fundamentalists, must be reversed. Emerging from the three waves of radical Wahabism in Arabia, the Muslim Brotherhood in Egypt, and Khumeinism in Iran, along with South Asian Deobandism, the Islamists have declared war on the "infidel cultural penetration of society," which has been held responsible for the degeneration of what they perceive as "religious unchangeable and unchallengeable prescriptions for Muslim women."[3] As in other comparable fields of society, the Islamic fundamentalists use specific stipulations from Islamic scripture regarding women as rigidly as possible and mold these statements into an ideological code.

The strength of the Islamists resides in reformists' silence on these questions or their weakness in responding. The radical Islamists move forward armed with theological quotations, demanding that women be limited to the realm of homes, under male control. This entails that they be removed from public service and sent back to homemaking. The opposing camp states that it is in the community's interest for females to participate in societal activities outside their strict duty of attending to children and husbands. In general, the "pro-women" argument is limited to an act of mercy or a pleading of extenuating circumstances, instead of a frontal doctrinal response of scriptural reinterpretation or even a more daring answer based on civil society's norms and the international consensus on women's rights. Within the Muslim communities where the Salafists or Khumeinists operate, few progressive rebuttals are launched, and the core of the mainstream clerical and state order attempts just to calm down the radicals rather than move the debate away from their extreme demands and isolating extremism. In addition, many Islamists—though not all of them—have learned to adapt their agenda on women's issues to modern rhetoric, further confusing the women they have targeted and the Western intellectuals they seek to demobilize.[4]

In the War of Ideas waged by the Muslim Brotherhood and their allies, for example, including those within Western democracies, the argument that is made to legitimize hair covering, strict dress codes, the separation of genders, and a lessening of legal, social, and physical equality falls under the heading of "cultural relativism." Amazingly, a concept designed by Western intellectuals (including Arab-American author Edward Said) as a tool to combat the sequelae of colonialism and imperialism has been refashioned by radical fundamentalists into an identity issue related to the entire community, and hence part of a general defense against Westernization. In a very savvy way, Islamist intellectuals and their allies in the West have presented restricting women's freedoms in the Muslim world as resistance to foreign colonialism. Hence, practically speaking, the reduction of women's rights in the Greater Middle East, the Arab world, and even immigrant communities in the West has been described as a "protection" of their gender from the "outside forces that are threatening the community."[5] In fact, as can be easily demonstrated by political sociologists, male-dominated ideologies emanating from these regions have devised systems to restrain the female population from liberating themselves and moving up the ladder to social equality. For by achieving social emancipation, women in the Arab and Muslim world would not only break the male hold on power, as has occurred in other societies, but also dangerously cripple the male-promoting ideologies of Salafism and Khumeinism. Herein lies the core of the frenetic drive by the radical Islamists to crush women's liberation movements in the Middle East and North Africa. The essence of this drive is a doctrinal resistance to gender equality, inasmuch as it is a challenge to religious and social equality. A review of twentieth-century jihadi wars on women's rights reveals the big picture.

An early warning came after the collapse of the Ottoman Empire in the 1920s. The Turkish Caliphate was obviously a religious one, but some small steps were moving its women forward, albeit at a glacial pace, far too slow to catch up with contemporary League of Nations political culture or Western feminist advances. Out of the rubble of the sultanate emerged three trends: One was revolutionary, embodied in Turkey's Kemalist secularism. Turkish women were abruptly awarded full equality in the 1920s. Another trend was a mix of quasi modernism on the surface and underlying social-religious resistance to women's liberation. This was the case in most Arab and Muslim countries. Each regime embarked on its own experiment, ranging from spasms of liberalism, as in Lebanon, to socialism, as in Syria and Iraq, to strong conservatism, as in Morocco and Jordan. A third trend was fundamentalism, which can still be seen in Saudi Arabia, Sudan, Iran, and Afghanistan. The Sunni Islamists drove women backward with Salafi ideologies, while Shiia Islamists suppressed women with Khumeinist teachings. Sadly, as women in Latin America, Asia, and even Africa were moving forward toward emancipation, their sisters in the Arab and Muslim world were submitting gradually to a phased apartheid, year after year, blocking their development in some cases and even reversing their status in many others.

The most notorious example of obstruction of women's liberation based on the ancient caliphate's rules is Saudi Arabia since the 1920s. Wahabism in the absolute monarchy rejects basic rights for females (including the right to drive a car), while democratic political rights do not exist, period. The spokespersons for Wahabism in the region, and even in Saudi-funded institutions in the West, often state simply that "this is the culture of the country." This is an amazing argument, which obviously could also be used to say that slavery is a tradition in some countries, and therefore should be respected. After 1979, the Khumeini revolution set Iranian women's rights back decades. From modernizing and seeking socioeconomic enhancement, more than half of Iran's population had to revert to wearing chadors and living under the male dominance established in the Islamic Republic. Here again, the regime and its apologists have claimed that Iranian women actually prefer this new mode of life. Obviously, a free referendum is not allowed in Iran, and hence this Islamist treatment is not one option selected from among many, but the sole option. From Tehran to Beirut's southern suburbs in the late 1980s, the reversal of women's rights spread quickly, with Hezbollah importing the Khumeinist model for Lebanon's Shiia women. The Salafists, expanding from Saudi Arabia, Egypt, and Pakistan, rapidly "reconverted" women living under their zones of influence.

In general terms, fundamentalism diminished the status of women in many countries by forcing them to abandon various types of jobs, isolate themselves from open society on multiple levels, and miss out on advanced and equal education—all of this in addition to the general mistreatment by males as a result of the minimal protection females now had under such regimes. In their counterargument, the fundamentalists kept asserting that this was the implementation of religious prescriptions, and that pious women had willingly adopted this mode of life and its restrictions. In reality, the Islamists had constructed a virtual ghetto for women by extracting arguments as it suited them from theology and erecting a compulsory ideology. For, as liberal Muslims argue, there is a difference between Muslim women choosing to be pious and self-restrictive and being obligated to be so by a government, laws, or even a militant organization. As a result, the clash between democracies and Jihadism over women's rights is not about how the fundamentalists see women under their regimes or the restrictions they prescribe; the issue is Muslim women's choice. The Islamists can postulate what they wish, and they can refer to as many religious injunctions or interpretations as they like. But it remains true that they are imposing their doctrine on women instead of suggesting it. Women are not invited to revert to restrictive Islamist gender models; they are forced to do so.

Rulings against women's basic equality have been enshrined in law in Saudi Arabia, Sudan, and Iran. Restrictions are omnipresent in other countries of the region as well. More dramatic is the suppression of women's rights at the hands of violent militants, as has been the case since the 1990s in Algeria. Salafi terror groups have attacked many women as a way to either punish them or force them to comply with religious proscriptions. Tens of thousands of mothers, daughters, and liberal career women were killed and maimed during the 1990s as a result of the jihadi onslaught against the secular element of society in Algeria.[6] In Sudan, the National Islamic Front regime imposed the Sharia laws on females in 1989. And they were imposed not only on Arab Muslim women, but also on African Muslims, Christians, and animists. Hence women who followed different religions were forced to wear the Islamic fundamentalist–required clothing and were sanctioned under religious laws other than those of their own faith. In projecting these trends within the West, one can see years down the line the intentions of the fundamentalists to establish this status for women first within Sharia-enclaves, and, if the balance of power is reversed, across the lands.

But by all standards, the most lethal implementation of the jihadi doctrine on a female population was under the Taliban rule in Afghanistan after 1996. Taking the gender separation process to its most extreme in modern history, graduates of the Wahabi-funded madrassas split Afghan society in two and buried one segment at home. Women were subjected to the most severe system of social conduct, and the most inhuman punishments for any breach of it. In addition to imposing the burka on all females older than 12, the Taliban stripped all women of their fundamental rights to work, travel, and appear in male company uncovered or without escort by relatives. Many Muslim intellectuals argue that the Taliban wanted to copy regimes from the past, although even the most powerful caliphates didn't go that far in oppressing women. A woman under the Taliban couldn't chat with a male or even ask him a question. Confined to a closed space, women in Afghanistan were practically living under jihadi apartheid, but with one difference from South Africa's racist system: under white separation from blacks, African women still had more freedom within their separated society. Under Taliban gender discrimination, women had no space for freedom, even inside their own households. The jihadi suppression of women was so total that it simply has no equivalent anywhere.[7]

WESTERN FEMINIST ABANDONMENT

A disturbing aspect of the jihadi apartheid has been the response by Western women, for two decades at least. Naturally, North American, European, and Australian reactions to oppressive laws and actions against females anywhere in the world have been and continue to be energetic, principled, and relentless. This was the case regarding solidarity with women in Latin America, sub-Saharan Africa, and Asia. But, illogically, mainstream feminist outcry against the mistreatment and oppression of women under jihadi regimes didn't occur, or at least not with the same vigor. Indeed, throughout the 1970s and 1980s, the international women's movement, including the most influential feminist organizations, surprisingly turned their attention away from the status of their sisters in Saudi Arabia and later the enslaved women of Sudan.

Women's pressure groups were very successful in lobbying the United Nations and legislative branches around the world on behalf of females in various regions of the world and within the West, but they did very little for Muslim and Arab women, especially those suffering under radical regimes. Feminist literature and academic research in the West produced mountains of data and policy suggestions and received huge funding in liberal societies, but no collective action was ever seriously taken in support of millions of oppressed women under obligatory Sharia laws.[8]

But perhaps the greatest and most surprising abandonment by mainstream international feminism was regarding the systematic and almost unbelievable torture of women in Afghanistan between 1996 and 2001. Reporting on the elimination of women's role in public society was almost nonexistent within the powerful women's organizations on both sides of the Atlantic. Even when CNN and other networks began to show footage of Afghani women being hit with sticks and even murdered by the regime's militia toward the end of the 1990s, global and national conferences on feminism and women's issues had very little to say to their membership concerning this female genocide. On many Western campuses and in media forums, apologists for the Taliban (mostly Wahabis) argued simplistically in favor of the Taliban that "at least the religious police stopped rape in the street."[9] They claimed that prior to the Taliban, many women were raped by militias. But the Taliban's advocates failed to notice that the jihadi regime replaced the horrible rape experience of individual females with a system that substituted domestic rape for street rape. Once placed under the absolute control of their husbands, Afghani women lost the ability to report aggression and mistreatment. They were all imprisoned in what was figuratively a national jail.[10]

SEXUAL FREEDOM AND JIHADI SUPPRESSION

Below the layer of gender oppression under Salafism and Khumeinism, another, deeper layer indicates the psychological and intellectual trouble that jihadi doctrines and their implementation create: at the center of the fundamentalist suppression of women, Jihadism shows an almost inexplicable hatred of the sexual phenomenon itself, unless licensed through their excessively ideological regime. In short, the amalgam of Islamist views radically bans sexual and even free romantic relations, or any social behavior for that matter, if it exists outside the social and religious system they wish to establish. But more disturbing in the eyes of social analysts are the types of sanctions and the seriousness and primacy of sexual repression in jihadi authorities' ideology.

Again, the conflict over sexual freedom isn't unique to Islamic fundamentalism. But in this book, we're looking at the politicization of sex by an ideology that exercises totalitarian control over essential human characteristics, creating a mechanism of stick and carrot that can distort people's behavior, including that of youth. In past centuries, all cultures organized sexual relations in ways that would accommodate the dominant social order. In most cases, sex before marriage was proscribed, and sex was regulated through the marital institution. Virginity before marriage, the number of wives, the breakup of marriages, and the ethics of couple formation have impacted the evolution of humanity for thousands of years. Across all cultures, the drama was almost the same: to find a balance between love and sex. For long centuries, both of these components of life were severely, then less, suppressed. Reasons vary and are still debated. Some general trends can be observed. Conservatives around the world have usually clung to abstinence before marriage, whereas liberals have opened the question to personal choice. On the public policy level, liberal democracies have gradually opted for sexual freedom, but under the laws of the land. The debates are still raging within the West and worldwide, and extremist positions exist on both sides. The general idea is that basic freedom of sexual activity between adults should be protected, as long as those engaging in it do not break down the social order. Within society, it is up to religious and other moral authorities to provide the balance in behavior. However, at the extreme opposite end of the cultural and ideological debate, the jihadists oppose any discussion on the issue and impose a very strict order of behavior and an even stricter set of sanctions, including whipping and stoning to death.

Within the Muslim debate, the Salafists and Khumeinists take the issue to its extreme. It is not only about the morality and ethics of sex, but also about its relation to male dominance. Osama bin Laden's speeches, among a sea of books, articles, and chat room streams, have illustrated how the issue takes center stage and how jihadists politicize the precarious sexual freedom debate. In one of his interviews, bin Laden called U.S. female soldiers *"amerikiyat a'ahirat"* (American whores) just for being women in the military and assuming men's power roles.[11] In Tehran, the mullah regime's worst nightmare isn't Israel's nuclear power or Washington's policies; it is the growing trend among young Iranians, both boys and girls, to challenge the Islamic Republic by kissing in public places. Students, feeling the rage of the regime's guardians, blast the jihadi ideology by hugging, holding hands, and rushing away from the Pasdaran[12] when they come to suppress the activity. The matter of personal freedom is at the core of antifundamentalist attitudes among younger generations of the region. The jihadists thought that they had tapped into deep human needs when recruiting young male suicide bombers by convincing them that death will bring them an afterlife in which they will possess the famous 72 virgins. In other words, the jihadist ideologues, knowing all too well the power of love, sex, and emotion, thought they'd move these overwhelming feelings to the "other side," hoping to create a desire to follow among their recruits. This moving of sexuality itself into the spiritual or otherworldly realm is symbolic of the total repression that is central to the jihadist ideology. In Taliban and Khumeinist thinking, the issue isn't the modern debates over types of freedoms; it is that no debates are acceptable at all. Every question related to human needs is solidly handled by radical clerics, who would dispense with the pleasures and tensions of life, and in many cases even postpone them to the afterlife, for ideological reasons.

But here is where Jihadism collides with reality. As with any other type of freedom, the more you repress sexual freedom, the more it will attempt to liberate itself. The advantage of democracy is that it permits all views to coexist and all ways of life to survive, whether they are mainstream, subcultural, or marginal; needless to say, Jihadism does not.

CHAPTER EIGHT

JIHADISM WAITS OUT THE COLD WAR

The First War of Ideas,
1945–1990

ONE CAN TRACE THE BEGINNING OF THE WAR OF IDEAS IN ITS modern form to the period in which the international community agreed to adopt a series of international legal principles. This development coincided with, but was not necessarily closely linked to, the emergence of the United Nations as an organization and as a set of ideas, beginning with its founding in 1945. Before the UN Charter and the subsequent declarations were formulated, such as the Universal Declaration of Human Rights, world powers were already exploring new ideas of equality and self-determination—for example, the ideas embodied in the 14 points of Woodrow Wilson and the League of Nations after World War I. Prior to that war, absolute empires, such as Russia, Germany, and Austria, and religious ones, such as the Ottoman Empire and Imperial Japan, shared the international stage with transitional regimes, as in China and Latin America; republics, like the United States and France; and democratic constitutional monarchies, such as Great Britain. With few exceptions, both democracies and autocracies possessed colonies, which covered large areas of Africa and Asia. The Muslim world was divided among a central caliphate held by the Turkish Sultanate, autonomous dynasties and Khanates from Iran to central Asia, and dispersed provinces under European and Russian dominance. The nineteenth-century "cocktail" of regimes and ideas was shattered by the twentieth-century war that was supposed to "end all wars." The League of Nations was a direct product of the Allies' victory over the central empires and was meant to firm up the democratic principles and liberties of all nations, as declared by President Woodrow Wilson, the head of the new transatlantic world power.

But the shining humanist ideals weren't yet accepted by the extreme nationalist, totalitarian, and fundamentalist elites in the West and around the world. The new Leninist and Stalinist Soviet Union was eager to crush the capitalist bourgeoisie at home and expand geographically into communist imperialism beyond the state borders. Frustrated petite bourgeoisies in Germany, Italy, and Japan, shied away from liberalism and embraced fascism and racism. In the Muslim world, falling under new borders and colonialist regimes, intellectual elites clashed over opposing ideological futures: the anticlerical seculars of Turkey shocked the emerging Wahabis in Saudi Arabia by ending the Ottoman Caliphate; the Muslim Brotherhood of Egypt resisted the drive by modernist Arabs to reform; and similar ideological antagonisms erupted among south Asian Muslims, already at odds with a British-occupied multiethnic and democratizing India.

The period between 1920 and 1945 saw the first experiment in democratic ideas encountering reversals in Europe with the emergence of Nazi Germany, Fascist Italy, and Bolshevik Russia. The withdrawal of the United States from the League of Nations further weakened the very first universal organization to seek a sound coexistence among nation-states. Western Europe was facing the rise of Fascism and the totalitarian east, as well as juggling the weight of its own sizable colonies in Africa and south Asia; America was absenting itself through isolationism; East Asian tensions were building; Latin American development was isolated and struggling against the rise of populism and militarism; and Muslim identity conflicts were evolving. With all of these tensions in play, the world was heating up for a global conflict. And indeed, the international space for an exchange of ideas ceased to exist as of 1939.

World War II ended the ambiguity in world politics and, at least in the theoretical sphere, laid down clear, universally binding principles: no religious or racial wars, no colonialism, no cross-border aggressions, no genocides, and no massive suppression of civilian populations, especially when it would endanger world peace. Even if world realities didn't reflect these values in the following decades, most players, great and small, at least acknowledged these principles of international relations—in contrast with past religious fundamentalist and fascist powers, which had rejected outright the ideas of self-determination, human rights, and sovereignty. From 1945 on, a political "war" was waged over who better embodied and applied the progressive ideas. This first War of Ideas of the modern era, arbitrated by a virtual global society of nations embodied by the United Nations and shaped by intellectuals, writers, academics, and political leaders from all blocs, lasted for most of the second half of the twentieth century. From the end of World War II until the collapse of Soviet Communism, democracies, as doctrines and countries, and Jihadism, as ideologies and regimes, not only fought each other, but also others, in a triangular multilevel global battlefield. Liberal democracies had a dramatic priority: to defeat the Communist threat. The jihadist streams had their own priorities: to grow, penetrate their own societies, and, depending on their various geopolitical realities, defeat their most immediate enemies while preparing to do battle with more distant ones. Because of these different agendas, democracies and Jihadism crossed paths during the first War of Ideas but did not face off against each other overtly or systematically.

THE COLD WAR:
COMMUNISM VERSUS CAPITALISM

By 1947, an all-out confrontation between a U.S.-led NATO and a Soviet-led Warsaw Pact (soon to be joined by Communist China) would dominate the world's war of ideologies and politics. Without reviewing the details of this decades-long struggle between the supporters of free societies and Marxist-Leninists, one could almost reduce most regional wars, domestic tensions in the West, and the dissident crisis within the Eastern bloc to the liberal-versus-authoritarian conflict of ideas. And just as the first Berlin crisis of 1948–49, the Korean War of 1950–53, the second Berlin crisis of 1958–61, the Cuban missile crisis of 1962, and the Vietnam War of the 1960s and early 1970s were heating up the Cold War, a relentless intellectual and psychological war was raging in the media, academia, and public forums. Moscow's sophisticated propaganda, with the help of Communist parties around the world, delivered a massive attack behind enemy lines. Though Stalin and his successors, and Mao Zedong in China, relied on tanks and secret police to "persuade" public opinion at home of the righteousness of the Communist worldview, within democracies and the Third World more subtle but enormously powerful propaganda was deployed. This first War of Ideas raged from the Sorbonne in Paris to Aden in southern Yemen, from Berkeley in California to Bolivia in the Andes. The intellectual resistance to Marxism-

Leninism wasn't as uniform as the Communist ideological agenda. Anti-Soviets included the religious right, conservatives, nationalists, liberal democrats, social democrats, and humanistic socialists. Politically diverse and sometimes conflicting currents and forces aligned themselves against Moscow's Communists. American capitalists, European liberals, Christian Democrats, Latin American militarists, and Muslim conservatives found common ground against the "Red Menace." Thus a major current of Islamic fundamentalism found itself in the same trenches with anti-Communist "infidels." The Wahabi-inspired Salafi movement, encompassing the oil-producing Saudi regime and allied Muslim governments such as Pakistan and Indonesia, lined up with the *kafir* alliance led by the United States against the Soviets.

It should be noted that during the Cold War, the Arab and Muslim world split along the fault line of pro- and anti-Soviet, rather than pro- and anti-American. Conservative regimes such as Morocco, Jordan, pre-Nasser Egypt, and pre-Qadhafi Libya sided with the capitalists against the Marxists for logical reasons. But the Wahabis of Saudi Arabia and the region's Muslim Brotherhood sided against the Communists, striking a profitable alliance with an infidel power—the United States—that tolerated Islamist regimes in its struggle against a dangerous nuclear foe. Hence Salafi Jihadism converged momentarily with its future enemy, America, in the fight against the more lethal enemy of the moment, Communism. But state Wahabi clerics had to produce an *Ijtihad* (interpretation) for their followers to accept the idea of a convergence of interest *(Taqatuh Masaleh)* with the capitalist *kuffar* of the West against the irreconcilable *kuffar* of Marx and Lenin. The many clerics who signed off on this choice—such as Ibn el Uthaimeen and the Albani—invoked the concept of *darura* (necessity). "We needed the powers of America against the power of the Soviet Union. We had to choose between one *kafir* and the other," argued the sheikhs of Arabia when they were confronted two decades later by al Qaeda's leaders regarding this unnatural coalition with the Americans and their allies. "America wasn't atheist while Russia was. The West only cared about our oil and money while the Communists were attracting young Muslims around the Arab world and beyond," they countered. "We used the United States to resist and bring down the Soviet *Taghut* (oppressors)."[1] This Wahabi-*Ikhwan* (Muslim Brotherhood) "jurisprudence" restrained the Sunni Islamist movement from unleashing jihad against all infidels at the same time, whether Eastern or Western. While engaging the

Communists and the left within the Arab world, however, the Salafists spread a pure anti-Western doctrine in their madrassas, religious sites, and social institutions. From North Africa to Palestine, from Tripoli in Lebanon to Pakistan, the Islamic fundamentalists clashed with the Soviet influence head-on while digging trenches for the next War of Ideas with the West. It amazes researchers to discover that al Qaeda's masters in the 1990s were quoting from Salafi doctrinaires of the 1970s and 1980s, not to mention earlier waves of doctrinaires of the 1920s and 1930s.[2]

But the Islamists weren't yet the dominant power in the Arab and Muslim world, nor did they control (yet) the public discourse. In the Arab-speaking Middle East, the spiritual and ideological heart of the Muslim world, the most influential forces were on the leftist side. Facing the Saudis, the Brotherhoods, and the conservative monarchies, revolutionary currents ranging from Baathism to socialism to Pan-Arabism to Communism enjoyed various levels of control and influence. On paper, these Arab nationalists claimed some form of *Ishtirakiya* (socialism) and *a'lmaniyya* (secularism). In reality, after Arab liberals were eliminated from the picture through suppression and marginalization during the 1950s, the progressive Arab forces metamorphosed into a form of "historical jihadism," without claiming the official religious sanction of the fundamentalist doctrine.[3] Michel Aflaq, one of the Baath Party founders, said about the Pan-Arabist ideologies in the 1960s, "Islam is to Arabism what bones are to flesh."[4] Despite the socialist ingredient in Arab nationalism, the Islamic dimension gradually took over. To Baathists and followers of Pan-Arab leaders in the region, the history of the Islamic empires—their victories, leaders, and chronicles—merged with Arab nationalism. Baathists and other Pan-Arabists took pride in Saladin's jihad against the crusaders centuries before. With the exception of making Sharia laws the sole source for legislation and the legal structure, Arab nationalist ideologues adopted most of what Islamists would have prescribed themselves.

But instead of rallying the West, the Pan-Arabists lined up with the Soviet Union and the international left. Leading that trend, Gamal Abdel Nasser of Egypt suppressed the Muslim Brotherhoods, competed with the Saudis, and became an ally of the Reds. Ironically, the progressive regimes in the Arab world also contained the real Communist parties. Strangely, Nasser, Hafez Assad of Syria, Saddam Hussein of Iraq, and Muammar Qadhafi of Libya marginalized the Islamists and appropriated their historical slogans but did the same with the Communists, grabbing their left-wing slogans as well.

In sum, the Salafi Islamists chose to confront Communism and prepare for battle against the West; the Pan-Arabists chose to combine a "secular jihad" and a non-Marxist socialism, hoping to get the best of both: the sympathy of the Muslim masses and Soviet support. This was the path of Nasser, the Baath, and Yassir Arafat of the Palestine Liberation Organization (PLO). The real Arab Communists, though faithful followers of Moscow's campaign against the West, were deprived of power in the region (with the exception of southern Yemen). Last of all, the self-perceived liberals and democrats were persecuted by all of the above forces and the ruling regimes, and were eliminated from the political scene until the twenty-first century. Toward the end of the nineteenth century, Egypt emerged as a center for liberal press and intellectuals, under British control. In the early twentieth, liberal and reformist circles emerged, started political movements, and began publishing in Beirut, Damascus, and Baghdad. But with the rise of authoritarianism in the region, liberal politics receded and reformists were suppressed, with only one enclave surviving until 1975: Lebanon. This brief moment of reformist liberalism demonstrates that the experience is possible, but depends on regional and international conditions, in addition to the maturation of younger generations of democracy advocates.

THE NORTH-SOUTH TENSIONS

Juxtaposed with the Cold War, another axis of tensions arose between the industrial north and the Third World south beginning in the 1960s. The industrialist and democratic West was attacked ideologically by left-wing "revolutionary" forces claiming they weren't part of the Soviet influence, but a third bloc representing the poorer and less-developed countries. Initially, three leaders met to create the Non-Aligned Movement (NAM): democratic Nehru of India, Arab nationalist Nasser of Egypt, and Communist Tito of Yugoslavia. The idea was to develop another international alliance in between the two poles of the U.S.-led North Atlantic Treaty Organisation (NATO) and the Soviet-led Warsaw Pact. At the peak of the Cold War in the 1970s, many countries joined the NAM, each for its own political reasons. Yugoslavia wanted to distance itself from Moscow's Communism; China wanted to become the leader of the Third World; Cuba was to become Russia's enclave inside NAM. Egypt and a number of Arab progressive regimes hoped to gain momentum against Israel and the West through NAM, while

Nehru's India wanted to balance the influence of U.S.-backed Pakistan. Many African and Latin American countries simply wanted to flee alignment with either of the two superpowers. But as international relations came under increasing tensions because of the Cold War, the south shifted from non-alignment to outright opposition to the United States and the West. Many of its players in fact had strategic relations with the Soviets, such as Cuba; the so-called progressive Arab states of Syria, Iraq, and Egypt before 1977;[5] and Libya.

The War of Ideas waged by the south in fact targeted the "north-West" (the United States and Western Europe) but not the "north-East" (the USSR and its European bloc). The core of the southern bloc was in fact an international ally of the Warsaw Pact in a different guise. Democracies in the West and worldwide were attacked by both the Soviet Bloc and the Third World as *imperialist, colonialist, oppressive,* and *unjust.* These accusations came from a strange mix of currents: Communist dictatorships in the north, international extreme left-wing networks, and populist dictatorships in the south. With the exception of India, there were practically no democratic governments in this Third World bloc. Most of the political and doctrinal attacks were launched by totalitarian, fascistic, and extremist oppressive regimes: Sudan, for example, was suppressing its minorities and the democratic opposition, as were Iraq, Syria, Libya, Iran, Algeria, Uganda (under Idi Amin), Angola, and others. The Non-Aligned Movement mutated into another "southern front" against Western democracies, controlled mostly by regimes at odds with their own internal democratic opposition. The alliance between the Soviet Bloc and most of the authoritarian Third World regimes had a common rationale: containment of democratic dissidence. The axis, made up of the industrialized Communists of the northern part of the East and the Third World dictatorships of the south, feared the rise of liberal democracies, which they framed as "neocolonialism." Such an axis was convenient to many self-declared socialist regimes in the Arab world and their ideologues, as it allowed them to claim a nationalist "historical jihad"[6] while allying themselves with the anti-Western left wing, thus securing the widest scope of support to ensure the longevity of their regimes.

On the other hand, the Islamic fundamentalists situated themselves both inside and outside the Third World bloc during the Cold War. They devised an attractive slogan in these decades: *la sharqiya, la guarbiya, umma wahda Islamiya* (No East, no West, just a unified Islamic *umma*). Wahabis and Muslim

Brotherhoods also felt they could score best against all fronts: rejecting the Communists on the one hand, and rejecting the West but using its advantages on the other. Meanwhile, they called for a third Islamic goal: the caliphate. The Salafists used the Third World concept to further their own "third path": the reestablishment of a greater empire to defeat and replace the two infidel ones. The international anti-Western left wing supporting the southern bloc tolerated the Islamists as strategic partners as long as they denounced the Europeans and the North Americans as oppressors. But the socialist left failed to realize that, whereas pluralist democracies have the ability to accept all ideologies, including the left and the extreme left, Islamist regimes would crush all other ideologies, particularly the Marxists themselves.

Then, in 1979, the Islamic Revolution of Khumeini brought Shiia-inspired fundamentalism into Third World affairs. The Iranian Islamists, bolder than the mosaic of Salafist regimes and groups, blasted the Soviets and the United States equally, describing them both as "devils," along with the traditional "little devil," Israel. Tehran's doctrinaires chose to bolster the image of an Islamic republic leading the struggle against what they termed *Istikbar* (condescending powers), a Khumeinist homonym for Marxist "imperialism." Iran struggled to position itself as the international leader of the *Mustad'afeen* (disempowered), an Islamist version of "proletariat." Khumeini's mullahs fantasized about an Iran that would face off against the two superpowers, withstand them, and by doing so, unite and lead the Muslim world under a renewed imamate, which would in turn lead a disaffected Third World. Hence the north-south divide became a hodgepodge of competing ideologies, united against the West and the very essence of its political culture, pluralist democracy.[7] But the competition among Pan-Arabist socialists, Salafists, and Khumeinists over their Wars of Ideas against their enemies reached its epitome through the conflict that would marginalize all other conflicts, and set the agendas of all Arab and Islamic politics for decades: the conflict between Israel and the Arabs.

THE ARAB-ISRAELI CONFLICT: SUFFOCATION OF THE REGION'S DEBATE

No other conflict better served the long-term objectives of the Pan-Arabist–Salafist–Khumeinist trio than the multiple wars between Israel and the Arabs in general, and the Palestinians in particular. This half-century ethnic and territorial dispute was used, abused, and stretched by ideological agendas far beyond the question of the specific legal and political rights of the Palestinians. A quick overview of the trio's main arguments in the twentieth century reveals the picture. In 1947, United Nations Resolution 181 divided British-mandated Palestine into two states: Jewish and Arab. The Jews chose to call their entity Israel, accepting the UN decision. But on the other side, it was the Arab League, not Palestinian elected officials, who made the choice. Arab regimes, mostly influenced by or acting as Pan-Arabists, rejected the UN resolution and the emergence of a non-Arab—and non-Muslim—state on what they considered an Arab and Muslim land. What the regional elites strove to counter wasn't the actual shape of the state of Israel, or the borders it was allowed to have, but the sheer existence of a *kuffar* state in the region, especially if it was a Jewish state. By way of historical and regional comparison, however, the specific "Jewishness" of Israel is not the exclusive root of its rejection: it is rejected for its non-Arab and more particularly its non-Islamic identity. Herein lies the array of attitudes dividing Arab nationalists from Islamic fundamentalists regarding the past, present, and future of Israel.

The clearest ideological position against the existence of the Jewish state came from the Salafists, Wahabis, *Ikhwan*, and other *Takfiris*:[8] a Jewish sovereign entity (or any infidel entity, for that matter) such as Israel cannot exist, regardless of whether it existed in the past, and even if the Jewish presence predated Islam and the Arab conquest. To the Islamists, the whole debate about what land, which borders, when the Jews settled, and where is simply irrelevant. Any territory, affirmed the doctrinaires of fundamentalism from Najd to Cairo, that has been under the caliphate at any time not only cannot become a non-Muslim state, but also should revert to the future caliphate. The jihadi position is not about the unfairness of removing Palestinian populations and replacing them with Jewish ones; it is about an intangible *mabd'a aqa'idee* (doctrinal principle): land that was once ruled by the laws of Allah cannot be ruled by other laws afterward. This view doesn't stem from the events that created the undesirable reality (Israel), but from the mere fact that a non-Muslim entity was created within an Islamic space; its specific *kuffar* identity, Jewish or not, is immaterial. The same principle would apply elsewhere: French Algeria, Spain, Kashmir, China's Singkiang, Chechnya, Mount Lebanon, Bosnia, Kosovo, and beyond. Hence, ideologically, the conflict in Palestine is not unique, but is one in a series of similar causes in the greater Islamist global conflict with the infidels. The solution to this specific problem, according to jihadi teaching, is the eradication of the state of Israel, the removal of the Jewish population that has immigrated into Palestine since the collapse of the Ottoman Empire, and the reunification of the province of Palestine into a reestablished caliphate. From this perspective, the Arab-Israeli conflict isn't about the fate of the Palestinians, but the purification of Palestine as a Muslim land from invading *kuffar*, military and civilian. To the Islamists, the returning Jews and the invading Christian crusaders are one in nature. They are considered a reversal of *iradatullah* (the will of Allah) and must be removed from the lands, regardless of peace processes or any other arrangements under international law. This logic is implacable: even if Jews had legally purchased lands from Arabs in Palestine, those transactions would be illegal in the eyes of jihadists. Moreover, even if Muslim rulers strike deals or peace treaties with Israel, including the return of lands, these deals or treaties are not valid. The same is true of decisions by the international community under international law (such as the UN partition of Palestine).

What many intellectuals in the West have never been able to understand or explain to their public is the total, relentless, and irreversible attitude of Islamic fundamentalism regarding Israel and any other similar entity perceived as occupying lands in the middle of an area defined as Islamic by the jihadists. Hence the Wahabis, the Muslim Brotherhood, and Salafists in general have since day one rejected the very existence of the "Zionist entity." However, beyond the Israel question, a more daring claim is made about the jihad to take back Spain into the fold of the caliphate. The Iberian Peninsula is claimed by the Salafists as part of what was an Islamic land and should be returned to its fold.[9]

Later on, the radical Sunnis were joined by their Shiia counterparts, the Khumeinists. The Islamic Republic espoused the Salafi position toward Israel but also engaged in a direct and more confrontational style with the Jewish state. One decade after the Islamic Revolution, the entire multilayered jihadi movement was in a full-fledged war with Israel, bypassing the traditional radical regimes. How did the region's Islamists participate in the intense War of Ideas during the Cold War?

Interestingly, the Salafist ideologues produced the most radical stance on Israel but adopted a backseat approach to the conflict until the 1980s. Wahabis and the Brotherhoods made their views well known to their constituencies and to the Arab masses, but they preferred to concentrate on better preparedness against the "Jewish enemy." Their logic was that only a true Islamic power and its real jihadi forces could engage and defeat the enemy. In other words, "apostate regimes" such as the ones established or sought by the Baathists, socialists, Nasser followers, Marxists, or pro-Western monarchies such as the Hashemites of Jordan and the Moroccan Kingdom aren't the ones to defeat Zionism. Allah won't bless anything less than true jihad, they argued. Thus the Islamic fundamentalists, to the surprise of many, took a backseat in the first series of Arab-Israeli wars and let the Arab regimes and the PLO fight the battles, all of which were lost: 1948, 1956, 1967, 1973, and 1982. The Salafi priorities were to prepare for future global wars with the Zionists, offensives to be conducted by the real mujahideen, those formed by madrassas and ready to take on the enemy outside all international law and conventions. The Muslim Brotherhood produced Hamas and Islamic Jihad in the 1980s and 1990s, and the Wahabis funded and indoctrinated them. During most of the Cold War, the Pan-Arabists, mostly the Baathists and the pro-Soviet regimes of Egypt, Syria, Iraq, and Libya, would take up the "secular historical jihad" against Israel (with Jordan a part of the wars until 1967).

Nasser, Assad, Numeiri, Qadhafi, Saddam, and Arafat fought Israel as an "occupier" of Arab lands. Regardless of fiery speeches by Saddam and Qadhafi, the Arab nationalist position was one that evolved from rejecting Israel as a "colonialist" project in the 1940s to 1960s to an Arab League consensus as of the 1980s accepting a final settlement with the Jewish state—but with draconian conditions that made the endgame unacceptable for the Israelis, such as the demand for the return of all Palestinian refugees and their descendants to all of Palestine, including pre-1967 Israel. The ideological war from the Arab-Islamic side was waged on various political fronts simultaneously: the jihadi posture rejected the existence of Israel; the radical Pan-Arabist position reduced the Jewish state to a diminutive size; and peace agreements were made by Egypt (under Sadat) in return for the Sinai in 1979 and by Jordan in 1994. To complicate the matter further, Iran's Islamic Revolution joined the fray, with a total rejection of the "Zionist entity" and an alliance with Baathist Syria and Hezbollah in Lebanon in a drive to destroy the enemy. Thus the region's ideologues developed different objectives but made a single, major impression on the international community: they created the perception that the Arab-Israeli conflict dominated all debates and all issues in the region, and that no solution to any problem in any spot could be addressed before solving the crisis over Israel. But a careful unraveling of this situation leads to stunning realizations: it tells us, as readers of world politics half a century later, that the Arab-Israeli conflict was transformed by regimes and organizations into a "black hole" that overshadowed consideration of all other democratic transformations and human rights struggles in the region. These dominant establishments deliberately used the Arab-Israeli conflict as cover, behind which they suppressed civil rights and minorities' autonomies and, in the case of the Islamists, advanced the much larger goal of a restored caliphate.

Indeed, despite the differing agendas among dominant regimes and movements in the region, and regardless of the steps achieved by some parties in the direction of peace with Israel, the general ideological and public-relations attitude regarding the conflict elevated it over any other issue in the region. Although the Camp David Accords were signed in 1978, the Sinai was returned in 1979, and an Israeli acceptance of the principle of a Palestinian state (as well as a Palestinian recognition of an Israeli entity) was secured in 1993, the trio of the Baathists, Salafists, and Khumeinists subordinated all conflicts and crises in the Arab world to the Arab-Israeli debate, now dubbed the "Middle East conflict." And by doing so, they interdicted the discussion, debate, and attempts to solve problems affecting hundreds of millions of people, while the jihadists gradually fomented a clash of civilizations. Debates about democracy in the Arab and Islamic world were banned from public arenas and international forums. The causes of ethnic minorities such as Kurds, Berbers, Sudan's black Africans, Arabs in Iran, and so on, were suppressed. Investigations of religious persecution under most of the region's regimes, including those of Egypt, Saudi Arabia, Iran, and Sudan, were proscribed. Racial equality, women's freedoms, political opposition, and other democratic issues were all buried under the sacrosanct "Palestinian question"—to such an extent that even Saddam's oppression of the Shiia was overshadowed by the Arab-Israeli conflict. Syria's occupation of Lebanon was off the table of international debate as long as Hafez Assad was holding the line on the Golan Heights against the "Israeli occupiers."

This blanket thrown over the human rights and democracy crisis in the region became the focus of the War of Ideas as waged by the Middle East's regimes, elites, and later on, jihadi terror organizations. The dominant political establishment in the Arab world systematically shielded itself from criticism and pressure for social and political change by referring all questions to the "Middle East crisis." By packaging the fundamental and tragic problems of an entire region stretching over two continents, Asia and Africa, with at least 200 million people, into a single historical conflict (which, incidentally, was thereby frozen and left unsolved), the architects of future religious, ethnic, and civilizational wars succeeded in hijacking world attention away from peace and imposing their tunnel vision of modern history. The miniaturization of the Arab world's development crisis into a narrow Palestinian form, and the ideological deadlock over the Arab-Israeli conflict, have had cataclysmic consequences. The region's progressive energies have been cut off from the global community, while the radicals have obstructed the Palestinian issue's resolution. But as the first War of Ideas was unfolding (under the Cold War), an economic earthquake was sending shock waves across the Mediterranean and the Atlantic, planting the seeds for a second War of Ideas in the 1990s.

THE OIL SHOCK OF IDEAS

As a result of the Yom Kippur War in October 1973, the mostly Arab, oil producer governments of the Organization of the Petroleum Exporting Countries (OPEC) launched a petroleum boycott of world markets, which had a dramatic impact on Western economies. This political-economic shock transformed international relations for the rest of the century. Pictures of Dutch citizens biking and the long lines of large American cars in front of gas stations tell the whole story. Since the 1950s, Western democracies had relied heavily on OPEC and the flow of cheap oil to sustain the growth of their industries and economies. In reaction to what Saudi Arabia and the other oil producer regimes perceived as U.S. and Western support for Israel during the war, OPEC reduced its production dramatically, forcing America and its allies to alter their position and initiate diplomatic activities to mediate between the Arabs and Israel. An immediate effect was the shuttle diplomacy of U.S. secretary of state Henry Kissinger, who succeeded in negotiating a durable cease-fire between Jerusalem, Damascus, and Cairo. A second, ripple effect was to create strategic conditions for Egypt's president, Anwar Sadat, to reach a bilateral peace agreement with Israel under American auspices.

But the third consequence was a long-term one of a strategic nature and related to the War of Ideas. The impact of the oil crisis on Western societies,

particularly in Europe and North America, showed the Achilles heel of powerful democracies: economic reliance on crude oil. The United States and its
NATO allies had been able to strike a balance between using military power
to contain the Soviets and ensuring a comfortable level of economic development for their societies, in order to sustain the Cold War effort on the one
hand and shy away from Communism's ideological promises on the other. By
shutting down the golden flow of oil from the Arab world and the Middle
East, or reducing it to very low levels, the producers realized their incredible
hold on the Western economies, and therefore on the latter's policies toward
the region. The regimes and their allies within the West took advantage of
this discovery. The stunning results helped the oil regimes not only reshape
some components of the Middle East's multifaceted crisis, but also determine
the direction of the second War of Ideas, which would take place after the
end of the Cold War.

As of the mid-1970s, the oil regimes, particularly Saudi Arabia, but also
Iraq, Libya, and later on a number of Gulf states, began what would become
the oil-funded penetration of Western education. The "offensive" took place
on two tracks: either directly on behalf of the regimes themselves or via the
joint ventures of their financial associates with Western oil companies. The
two tracks united in a vast and steady stream of funding for academic and
think-tank projects within the United States and Europe related to Middle
East studies. U.S. and Western universities became the recipients of grants
from oil companies and foreign governments who then sought to "guide" the
academic and administrative leadership of these campuses toward establishing additional programs in the study of the region's countries, civilization, religion, and issues. In a decade and a half, by the end of the 1980s, multiple
institutions had developed a "new" teaching on Middle East and Islamic
studies within the United States and Europe. The funding of these programs
did not come without "policy direction." The oil regimes had a direct interest in defending their image and influence within the West. Hence the very
first "directive" was to brush aside human rights criticism of these regimes
and the others that they protected in the region.[10]

Ironically, as human rights monitoring of Latin America, Africa, and
East Asia was increasing in American academia, little attention was being
spent on the status of women in the Saudi kingdom, religious persecution in
the region, Sudan's genocide, minority questions, and related matters.
American academia, under the influence of oil-supported programs and

their scholars, turned a blind eye to the Middle East's myriad other problems. With oil financing of educational programs from coast to coast, Middle East studies fell under the influence of the funders. The off-campus power influenced the appointment of scholars evidently sympathetic to the funding parties overseas.[11]

The teachers and researchers, owing their funding and prominence to the donors, became the facilitators of political penetration by the Wahabis and other powers inside American academia. This move, getting a toehold inside the "factory" that forms the minds of Americans and Europeans, became the very first step in the War of Ideas launched against the United States. It would plant the seeds of global myopia within Western democracies that would last for more than three decades, up until 9/11. This chain of events was set in motion by the oil shock of 1973.[12]

THE SPREAD OF JIHADISM:
INNER AND OUTER

During the Cold War, the jihadist ideologies spread in all directions, mostly under the radar of the contending superpowers, but also sometimes in the open, especially after the 1979 Islamic Revolution in Iran. Deprived of state tools and favorable geopolitical conditions before World War II, the Wahabi and Muslim Brotherhood schools of thinking were confined to the Arabian Desert or urban areas in the still-colonized Arab Middle East. But with the departure of French, British, Italian, and other influences, Islamic fundamentalist networks began to develop in most Arab and neighboring countries. With the rise of oil politics and economics in the Arab peninsula, the dividends of oil began to be used for the export of ideology. The Wahabi state and clerics initiated a wide system of funding schools, the madrassas, and socioeconomic centers. Also, at the two holiest sites of Islam, Mecca and Medina, the greatest theological influence was focused on millions of pilgrims to have them carry the ideology back to their home countries around the world. The Wahabi-funded message was transported even further by Muslim Brotherhood cadres, but not always in harmony with the Saudi monarchy. On a larger scale, while the Cold War was raging between the superpowers, the Salafists were penetrating the Arab Middle East, North Africa, south Asia, central Asia, and Indonesia, powered by Wahabi support and Brotherhood, Tablighi, and Takfiri skills. Underneath ultranationalist regimes such as the Baathists and other Pan-Arabists, and while the Arab "big brothers" were busy fighting and losing wars with Israel and plotting against each other, the Islamists were extending their networks everywhere they could, from Sunni Iraq to Algeria and Morocco, in Lebanon's coastal cities, along the Nile valley into Sudan, and among the Palestinian communities of Gaza and the West Bank. Their colleagues were spreading in the sub-Indian continent and sub-Saharan Africa.

Ironically, these movements were portrayed by Western and American academic experts as those of "conservative Muslims" or "religious" currents, and not of jihadists penetrating Arab and Muslim societies. Such academic misreporting was certainly not surprising in view of the Wahabi preemptive strike inside Western academia. How could scholars, teachers, and experts blast the source of their grants and funding? Hence the spread of the jihadists deep inside the Greater Middle East took place without any reaction or concern by Western defense or security circles. This was not only because the U.S.-led West was focusing on the Soviet threat, but also because the expert pool serving as analysts of the region was minimizing these dramatic developments. Indeed, they even described the Salafi jihadists as potential allies in the war against the Communists. The Islamist grand propaganda scheme was working; not only weren't they checked by democracies as potential future foes, but incredibly, they were perceived as strategic allies in the confrontation with Communism. An underground alliance was growing between Western and American agencies and Islamic fundamentalists. Against Nasser of Egypt and later Assad of Syria and other Soviet client states, the CIA was said to have coordinated with the Muslim Brotherhood. Along with the Wahabis of Saudi Arabia and Pakistan's military, U.S. agencies were supporting the various mujahideen in Afghanistan's resistance against Soviet occupation. At the time, the choice was said to be limited: either support the mujahideen and defeat the Soviets, or refuse to support them and watch the Reds thrust through Baluchistan to the Indian Ocean. Strategically, by Cold War standards, the choice was sound—but its ideological underpinning was erroneous. With the Wahabi academic lobby influencing the U.S. foreign service with its analysis and its cadres, U.S. national security was thrown into confusion. National Security Advisor Zbigniew Brzezinski illustrated the line-crossing when he encouraged the mujahideen, still considered a national resistance, to "act on behalf of religion" and unleash a jihad against the Communists.[13]

Certainly, the U.S. government was badly advised in that a War of Ideas inside America led to the equating of Jihadism with spiritual conservatism, compelling U.S. leaders to endorse jihadist action against the Soviets, unaware that this move would return to haunt America later, from Beirut to Manhattan. Such a fog of confusion put the United States and the West even more at the mercy of the jihadists' strategic plans. In simple words, as long as they weren't on the national security radar screens of Western democracies, they had a "historical" opportunity and a strategic advantage that would enable them to launch waves of strikes in the 1990s, without significant responses. During the Cold War, the Salafi jihadists were progressing freely, despite warnings coming from different corners of the world, especially from liberal Muslims and targeted non-Muslims. But Washington had already been lulled to sleep, its mind culturally lobotomized on this issue.

The Iranian jihadists weren't waging a secret ideological war, however; just the opposite. After Ayatollah Khamenei took power, he unleashed an open ideological war with the West, particularly the United States. While the Salafists instructed their followers and madrassa pupils to focus the war against the infidels first on the Communists, deferring the war on the West, the Khumeinists of Iran (and after 1983 joined by Hezbollah) openly blasted all the "enemies of Islam." The Salafi ideological offensive was advancing underground, while the Khumeinist doctrinal campaign was being carried out in the open. Interestingly, the spread of Jihadism also progressed in the West as East-West tensions experienced ups and downs. Moving along with immigrants and travelers, radical clerics and Islamist cadres settled in Western Europe and North America in the late 1970s and early 1980s. Profiting from public preoccupation with the nuclear threat and the USSR, the first wave of militants and ideologues set foot on secure soil. The expert community was not eager to alert the public, nor was the latter duly informed about the upcoming post-Soviet threat to their societies. Thus Salafis, Wahabis, and other radicals freely settled in the West for a few years before the Soviet Union collapsed. This jihadi "settlement" would play an important role in the launching of the second War of Ideas in the 1990s.

THE FRAMING OF FREEDOM

One of the most powerful achievements of the first War of Ideas was the framing of freedom in international relations. This astounding victory for the

anti-Western currents worldwide and for the counterdemocracy forces in the
Greater Middle East rested on one intellectual pillar: the definition of freedom and its recipients. Indeed, the War of Ideas could be won when one of
the parties to the intellectual conflict succeeded in being the first to define
the war and its players, isolating the other side morally, politically, and
rhetorically. In the first War of Ideas, following World War II and the rise of
the United Nations and international principles of law, the anti-Western axis
was quick to win a number of battles of words, concepts, and terms. The
antidemocracy front put the West quickly on the defensive as it rapidly appropriated the new concepts on international affairs. In the Arab and Muslim
world, the pro-Soviets and Islamists fired separately at Western values and,
without merging their efforts, put liberal and democratic elements in the region on the defensive, often even silencing them. From legal-ideological
confrontations within the General Assembly of the United Nations to the
media and universities, the battle for the power to describe events and set the
terms of debate raged continuously. The battle over the framing of freedom
went somewhat in the favor of the anti-Western forces during the first War
of Ideas, although as soon as the Soviet masses were given the freedom to
choose, they opted clearly for Western-defined freedoms.

The international Communists and their allies advanced a Marxist notion
of freedom as socioeconomic equality regardless of individual liberties. The
power of the proletariat was equated with the collective freedom to acquire
the powers of production. Hence the Communists stood against the notion of
human rights and spiritual and religious freedoms *for the individual.* They ignored the pain and suffering of hundreds of millions of people around the
world, for under Communism, their feelings didn't fit the Marxist paradigm.
The followers of Lenin and Stalin would be proven wrong only after the
workers of Lech Walesa's movement, the dissidents of Eastern Europe, and
the Russian masses caused the Soviet power to implode when they began
seeking individual enhancement and personal and spiritual freedom. But during the Cold War, the Communists crushed these societies under their power.

The antidemocratic authoritarians of the Third World emulated the Soviets in suppressing debate in their societies, too. They argued that freedom
meant the power of nations to fight imperialism and colonialism, neglecting
to address the democracy crisis in their own countries. Perhaps the best way
to dodge these reform issues was the constant outward-focused struggle
against an imagined enemy—the Western version of Don Quixote. In the

Arab world, the argument regarding freedom was totally reversed by the ultranationalist rulers and the jihadists on the streets: it was "their freedom" that allowed them to force Pan-Arab Unity and fight the Zionists, the West, and secessionist minorities, and to create a grand power in the region. In reality, it also permitted them to suppress their own opposition movements, obstruct the full liberation of women, and resist opening up their societies to higher-level individual liberties. Hence the voices participating in the international exchange were those of the dominant elites, both in the Communist sphere of influence and in the multi-ideological Third World bloc. Facing them were the Western democracies and their allies around the world. These battles over words shaped the ongoing War of Ideas.

The key concepts at issue in the War of Ideas are these:

1. *Self-determination.* Recognized in Article 1, paragraph 2 of the UN Charter, this concept was accepted by the anti-Western alliance during the Cold War only when it meant the process of decolonization from European powers. Hence it was rejected when the people themselves called for independence from regional and local powers. The bias of the Arab League members was obvious when it refused to grant self-determination to the Kurds in Iraq, the Berbers in Algeria, and the Africans of Sudan, or even to consider autonomous community rights for the Copts of Egypt. But the League extended its support to Palestinian self-determination against Israel. The Islamic bloc (inspired by the Wahabis) called for, or was sympathetic to, the independence of the Muslim provinces of Pakistan and Bangladesh, and later self-determination for Kashmir from India, the Muslim provinces in the southern Philippines, Eritrea from Ethiopia, and Northern Cyprus from its south; but on the other hand, it rejected Biafra's freedom from Nigeria, Southern Sudan's secession, and East Timor's independence. The mathematics of self-determination are simple: it is granted by the Islamic bloc based on the identity of the group, not on its natural right. Beyond the actual diplomatic strategies, however, it was a fact that the anti-Western axis during the Cold War succeeded in appropriating the moral and political power to determine to whom self-determination is granted and when. However, the stunning position was that of the Western academics. Indeed, not only did the anti-Western axis succeed in discrediting many societies'

claims to self-determination, but Western elites also followed through and signed off on this issue. Rarely did the European and North American intellectual establishment, let alone their presses, legitimize the causes of Sudan, Kurdistan, or East Timor, as they did in the "mainstream" cases for decolonization. Iraq's Baath Party was praised for fighting against the British and Israel, but its Kurds were not acknowledged in their effort to attain decolonization from Arab imperialism. Sudan's Pan-Arabists (and later Islamists) were seen as anticolonialists, but not the blacks in the south and the west of the country when they claimed self-determination from the internal oppression of the state.

The general public in most democracies was supportive of the natural-right claim of peoples to separate or liberate themselves, but their governments measured out their support for freedom with an eye on the Cold War and economic interests. If self-determination would lead to the rise of a Communist ally, it wasn't supported, and if—after the 1973 oil crisis—such a claim of self-determination would alienate the oil-producing regimes, it also failed to achieve endorsement. On the other hand, the Islamist position, held mostly by Saudi Arabia and its allies, was based on Wahabism's view of the world. If a Muslim entity claimed self-determination, it would be supported; if a non-Muslim entity claimed it against a Muslim power, it would be opposed. And if the claim was made between two non-Muslim entities, then realpolitik would apply.

2. *National sovereignty.* Like self-determination, the concept of a nation's control of its own sovereignty and resources was applied first to the areas colonized by Western powers (those with mostly Europeans). But the idea that nations had also been colonized by non-Western powers of all sizes was quashed in the ongoing first War of Ideas. Examples abounded: While the former British, French, Dutch, and Portuguese colonies were granted sovereignty, the Central and Eastern European, as well as central Asian, nations were forced into Soviet domination and kept under military control, their resources serving the interests of the Soviet Communist Party. China backed Vietnam's Communists during the war against the south and its U.S. allies but smashed Tibet's and Lower Mongolia's sovereignties. Moreover, in the Arab world, the pick-and-choose method prevailed. Of course,

the question of Palestine was the first and only sovereignty question to be addressed. Meanwhile, the Syrian invasion and then occupation of Lebanon since June 1976, as well as the question of Western Sahara's and Southern Sudan's sovereignty, were off the table. Interestingly, concordances between sovereign regimes at odds with each other were achieved against nations seeking sovereignty from within their common borders. For example Iran, Turkey, Iraq, and Syria collaborated against Kurdish independence. In this area, democracies and jihadists applied the same parameters as for self-determination described above.

3. *Human rights.* This area was perhaps the most fought over in the first War of Ideas. The issue was, and remains in the twenty-first century, a major subject of verbal battles, mutual accusations, and exclusions among the international players. Since the Universal Declaration of Human Rights was produced by the General Assembly of the United Nations in 1948, the struggle over what rights and whose rights are to be recognized has never ended. The essence of the principles voted on at the United Nations was basic: human and democratic rights and freedoms as perceived by democracies in the mid-twentieth century. But the Communist bloc was quick to oppose what it described as Western, capitalist, and bourgeois human rights, instead pushing for social, economic, and class rights. Second to oppose the UN principles were the Third World regimes, which denied the international community access to investigate human rights abuses "inside" the sovereignty of these countries. Obviously, neither the Communist nor the authoritarian regimes had an interest in applying international norms to their societies: such a compliance with human rights and the enabling of their peoples to choose freely would have instantly caused these regimes to break down from the inside. The proof came with the fall of the Berlin Wall and the subsequent collapse of the Soviet-controlled regimes. Democracies supported the principles of human rights in general terms, but their governments were just as selective in recognizing human rights as they were with self-determination and sovereignty, depending on geopolitical realities. Although forceful toward the end of the Cold War with Latin American military regimes and dictatorships, openly supportive of the Eastern European dissidents, and firmly opposed to the South

African apartheid regime at the end of the 1980s, Western governments still turned a blind eye to human rights abuses across the board in the Arab world. The 1973 oil crisis and the rise of the Wahabi lobby and academic influence within the United States and Western Europe restrained policymakers from intervening in favor of large, oppressed segments of Middle Eastern societies. This Western laissez-faire attitude toward tens of millions of people in the Greater Middle East was the result of the oil regimes' pressure and a change in political education within the United States and other democracies as a result of the "oil-lobbying offensive" from the late 1970s on. In addition, Islamists of all ideological backgrounds, Pan-Arabists, Communists, authoritarian regimes, and various anti-Western intellectuals coalesced against Western liberal attempts to hook up with Middle Eastern, Arab, and Muslim dissidents and victims of abuse throughout the Cold War era, denying the region's oppressed communities significant access to international forums. The preemptive strike against the West by the antidemocracy forces was one of the most important strategies to keep Europe and North America from coming to the rescue of ethnic and religious minorities and oppressed political majorities alike in the region. Instead, escalating their War of Ideas against the West, the totalitarian ideologues counterattacked by accusing liberal democracies of being the most oppressive of all governments. This ideological blitzkrieg accused the West and liberal democracies around the world of using the issue of human rights in the Third World to "score economic advances." Hence, helping the Africans of Sudan, the Kurds, Christian minorities in the Middle East, women, students, democracy movements, or Muslim dissidents from the Atlantic to the Indian Ocean was described by regimes and radical organizations as a return of imperialism to the former "colonies."

But even more striking was the academic and intellectual backing these arguments found within the West. For the most virulent attacks against intervention on behalf of Middle Eastern human rights came from radical Western intellectuals and writers. From that War of Ideas perspective, Edward Said's book *Orientalism*[14] was about blocking the free societies in the West from reaching out to those abused in the East. Any other perspective than the one accusing Israel of violating the rights of Palestinians was politically incorrect. Although the Palestinians certainly deserved to recover their full rights via a peace process, tens of millions of other Arabs and Middle Eastern people were also suffering greatly, from Sudan to Kurdistan. Hundred of millions of women were stripped of their basic rights from Arabia to Iran, but their cause wasn't championed by the academic supporters of the oil lobby. Pressure and reporting by Western-based human rights watch groups were confined to the safe areas where the petroleum lobbies still had no interests, such as Latin America, sub-Saharan Africa, and the Caribbean. In short, the war for controlling the international human rights issue was raging throughout the Cold War between two main camps: democracies and totalitarians of every stripe. The former were selective in their support as a result of oil lobbying after 1973 and their governments' confrontation with the Soviets and sensitivity to economic pressure. The other camp displayed an aggressive approach: the Soviets and other Communists waged a preemptive war of words against the West in order to dodge their own domestic rejection of human rights. Meanwhile, the authoritarian regimes of the south met with fierce resistance any effort toward international investigation of the human rights abuses within their own societies.

The first War of Ideas evolved while the Cold War was moving from one stage to another. In this conflict of ideologies, two major trends clashed and struggled: communism and democracy. Eventually the Soviet collapse would free many peoples and relatively increase the influence of democracies worldwide. But under the screen of the Cold War, the seeds of the next War of Ideas were being planted and growing steadily. While democracies were preoccupied with containing Marxism-Leninism, Jihadism was spreading to what would become the battlefields of the future. The Salafi madrassas and the Khumeinist regime of the 1970s and 1980s were preparing the wave of strikes that would shock democracies in the 1990s.

CHAPTER NINE

BATTLES OVER MINDS

The Second War of Ideas, 1990–2001

WITH THE COLLAPSE OF THE SOVIET UNION, A WORLDWIDE tremor shook the foundations of politics and international relations. An ocean of literature has been produced about these changes; researchers, academics, politicians, and journalists, particularly in the West, rushed to re-arrange the concepts, ideas, perceptions, and rhetoric into a new world order. For any person involved in public and international affairs at the end of the Cold War, not to see the Soviet Union in the news anymore was a major shock. The community of newsmakers and commentators had to scramble to revise the issues and ideas that would drive world affairs now that Communism was bankrupt. Two major arenas had to be reshaped: the balance of power, as the East-West struggle wound down, and the principles of international relations, as the Communist-totalitarian offensive receded. What ideologies would now confront the international consensus on democratic principles and human rights? At first sight, many in the West and indeed the world hurried to congratulate the United States and its allies for winning not only the strategic conflict, but also the War of Ideas—or so they thought. In the immediate wake of the collapse of Eastern and Central European regimes, followed by the astonishing crumbling of the Soviet giant, viewers around the world were in total disbelief: the mighty superpower, with all its nuclear arms, had been brought down by Polish workers, Czech writers, East German rockers, frustrated Russian soldiers and their moms, and marginalized political dissidents.

In 1982, as Lech Walesa was still defying the Soviet power in the Gdansk shipyards, I was publishing a weekly newspaper out of Beirut. The Cold War seemed to be eternal, and few projected that the Red Empire would eventually come to an end. But that year I wrote in *Sawt el Mashreq* (*Voice of the East*) that a crack had started forming in Gdansk among those Catholic workers. "The crack will reach Moscow someday," I wrote in Arabic. "It is ineluctable, once the idea is born and accepted by a few minds and hearts, it can't be killed. It will find its way to wider and wider circles." That was my first published comment on the War of Ideas then in progress. The year before, in 1981, Jesuit scholar Jean Aucagne prefaced my first booklet in French by likening my writings to those of Russian dissident writer Andre Amalrik, who had predicted in the 1960s that the Soviet Union would begin crumbling by the mid-1980s. He was almost right—Gorbachev's *perestroika* emerged in 1986. Nevertheless, actually seeing the empire collapse was something else. It reminded me of the words of my late grandfather, who saw the four-century-old Ottoman empire vanish in 1919. So it is possible that grand edifices from history can simply crumble, not just as a result of wars and conflicts, but also simply because people living under their regimes adopt other ideas and move forward.

As the Scorpions played "Winds of Change" and the Berlin Wall fell to masses of German youth in October 1989 (200 years after the fall of the Bastille), millions of people in the Middle East, including me, followed with stupefaction the collapse of the Communist-controlled governments from Prague to Warsaw. What questions immediately leaped to mind? The most powerful totalitarian regime in history was crumbling before our eyes; the most rigid doctrine of power, Bolshevik Communism, had been broken down from the inside by Mikhail Gorbachev, Boris Yeltsin, and the Russian mothers. This democratic revolution had been made possible by the ideas of Andrei Sakharov, Alexander Solzhenitsyn, Václav Havel, and thousands of dissidents and exiles. It took them half a century of sacrifices, but the Eastern Europeans had broken their chains. We had to wonder, "If it happened there, under Marxist dictatorships, why can't it happen here, under these totalitarian regimes and radical organizations?" The elites dominating the Arab world and Greater Middle East weren't as powerful as those behind them who had armed their militaries and trained their secret police. But what escaped many observers worldwide was the deeply rooted radicalism inside the region's political establishments.

Compared with extreme nationalists such as the Baathists and the radical jihadists, the European Marxist-Leninists were in fact much weaker, we realized. But it would take the West another decade to understand the types of political cultures that dominated the Middle East at the time of the Soviet collapse. The logic of freedom versus oppression is eternal, but the time factor varies. It took waves of dissidence to create the cracks within the Communist strata. When the USSR finally succumbed, the Middle Eastern and Arab dissidents weren't even on the radar screen of the international community. Very few knew of their existence; worse, Western elites had convinced their publics in Europe, North America, and the rest of the Free World that the region's peoples were upset not with their own governments, but rather with the remnant of colonialism, Israel, and the new Western imperialism. Although during the Cold War the Eastern European dissidents (including Russians) were admired from Paris to New York, their Middle Eastern counterparts were unknown to Western social elites. Now, being abandoned is bad, being ignored is very bad, but being unknown is even worse. This was the condition of supporters of democracy in the Muslim and Arab region. The end of the Cold War only confirmed this peculiar but dramatic reality. The West rushed to press Latin America's dictatorships to change. It openly praised the dissidents of the Soviet Bloc and stood by them. It condemned the apartheid regime of South Africa until it faded away. It opposed China's human rights abuses, at least with words, if not action. With the end of the Cold War, a wind of change was blowing around the planet—but not all of it: the Arab-Muslim world was excluded from Western mercy and compassion. Why?

I was reflecting upon this question on the day I saw Soviet-made Syrian tanks rolling over the last enclave of resistance in Lebanon. How was it possible that the Russian tanks were leaving Eastern Europe and Baathist tanks were thrusting into East Beirut on the same day? Why was the Soviet Air Force being repatriated from East Germany to Siberia while Antonov bombers were dropping napalm on Southern Sudan during the same week? And finally, why was it that nationalities of the former Soviet Union were forming their own independent republics while Middle Eastern minorities were being gassed and massacred in Iraqi Kurdistan and among the Berbers of the Atlas mountain range? The first War of Ideas was coming to end, but the second was already raging.

With the collapse of the East, a race began to inherit the Soviet sphere of influence and redesign the Middle East's equations. China saw a straightforward task: Learning from Moscow's Marxist developmental disaster, China's Communists decided to transform the country into a secure economic superpower. Learning from the USSR's mistakes, the Chinese regime saw that it was important first to ensure survival as a solid economy before getting busy with the "shining" future of the world proletariat. Hence Leninist and Maoist militancy were off Beijing's agenda for the moment. Meanwhile, sub-Saharan Africa stagnated in its eternal crisis, awaiting the international community's help as the Cold War seemed to free the industrialized economies to aid the weaker societies trailing behind—at least, that was the African hope immediately after the Cold War. Latin America witnessed its authoritarian regimes gradually recede as East-West tensions faded away. With the United States no longer fearing the Soviet challenge in Europe, military regimes in Argentina, Brazil, Chile, and elsewhere were demoted in importance. On the left, the Sandinistas were voted out in Nicaragua. Only the Castro regime remained as an ideological island burdened with Spanish-speaking Bolshevism. But as freedom or relative rationality was sweeping the continents, one big "black hole" remained, defiant to the global political evolution: the Arab and Muslim world, especially its Middle Eastern core.

THE FOUNDATIONS OF
THE SECOND WAR OF IDEAS

The reason why the region didn't or wasn't allowed to celebrate the fall of the Berlin Wall or follow through with its own democratic revolutions was the great race for control among all the region's ideological and political forces. As soon as world geopolitics changed abruptly, the dominant regimes and ideological forces of the Arab world rushed to assert the region's identity, take control of its resources, establish its legitimacy, and, above all, define its future. Far from imitating the worldwide democracy movement, a wave of military attacks swept the region. Saddam invaded Kuwait, Assad invaded Lebanon, Turabi invaded Southern Sudan, Northern Yemen invaded Aden, Morocco kept its troops in the Western Sahara, and the Algerian forces deployed in the Kabyles Mountains. Many regimes hurried to secure themselves, as they watched Ceausescu being executed by the people, fearing the dangerous democratic idea might tempt native revolutionaries. And to consolidate their power against the risk of democracy, almost all contending ideological camps agreed on one thing: keep the West out and freedoms down.

Baathists, Pan-Arabists, dictatorships, Islamist regimes and organizations were still leaping at each other's throats, but with one voice shouting to the outside world: "This is a family matter, there are no grounds for you to intervene in our business." In other words, while the regions' authoritarian forces clashed with one another, they were allied in keeping the international community at bay. "Our culture is different," kept claiming the spokespersons of the Arab League and Iran when asked about post–Cold War concerns about human rights abuses in the region. "We will solve all issues among ourselves in our region, even though there are disagreements among brotherly states and peoples." Under this formula—suppression of democracy and pluralism on the inside, and rejection of the international community on the outside—the region's totalitarian forces launched the second War of Ideas to preempt the rise of democracy in the Middle East, shield the regimes from a fate similar to the USSR's, and in the case of the jihadists, eventually establish the caliphate or imamate. In the following sections, I explore the foundations of the this second War of Ideas, which began around 1990 with the collapse of Soviet totalitarianism and the wave of democracy movements that swept the globe—except for the Arab and Muslim world.

Authoritarian Solidarity

Most of the authoritarian regimes in the Greater Middle East, regardless of their differences, realized that the Soviet collapse had revealed the startling truth that freedom from totalitarianism is possible. That principle, witnessed by the whole world when dissidents, youths, mothers, and ordinary people overthrew the most powerful totalitarian state of all time, obviously threatened the majority of regimes in the Arab and Muslim countries, and the most authoritarian ones in particular. The perpetrators of the most bloody repressions, such as Saddam's and Hafez Assad's Baath Parties, Iran's Ayatollahs, and Sudan's National Islamic Front (NIF), feared bloody retaliation by their former victims. The Iraqi dictator had gassed the Kurds and assassinated Shiia and Sunni opponents for a decade. Any democratization was out of the question. His alter ego, Assad of Syria, had massacred a large segment of the population of the Sunni city of Hama in 1982. In addition, his regime had tortured, killed, jailed, and massacred many opponents in both Syria and Syrian-occupied Lebanon. How could he relinquish power to an opposition? Didn't he see on TV the rapid execution of Ceausescu and his wife? Ayatollah

Khamenei had ordered the massacre of thousands of opponents from all walks of life: Communists, left-wing Muslims, liberals, and minority leaders. How could his elite accept any *perestroika* à la Gorbachev? Hadn't they seen how the KGB and other Communist officials were dragged to jail in Moscow? Hassan Turabi and Omar al Bashir of Sudan were sending militias to ethnically cleanse Southern Sudan of its blacks and allow the *difaa shaabi* (popular defense) thugs to enslave Africans, even as Nelson Mandela was being freed in Pretoria. What would the reaction in Africa be if the Islamist Party in power relinquished its brutal repression of Africans in Southern Sudan? On the other hand, the Saudis and Qadhafi, despite their different outlooks, were also not ready to allow political parties to be formed. And to some extent the Mubarak, bin Ali, and Qatari regimes, for example, weren't ready to surrender power to their opposition. The big picture here is dramatically simple: the region's regimes had been involved in so much violence against their peoples and the opposition that ceding any power to an alternative establishment (especially if elected), was practically impossible.

This explains the regimes' rejection of the post–Cold War era and its values. Dictatorships and ruling elites in the Greater Middle East and their counterparts in many other Third World countries had long taken advantage of the global competition between the United States and the Soviet Union. If one superpower put pressure on them, the other superpower would open up the gates to support. Hence Western chancelleries, and particularly the American foreign policy establishment, were keen during the Cold War not to disturb the relationships with those regimes that chose the West as their protector. Let us even add "at any price." Thus even if Saudi Arabia, Iran's shah, or the Arabian principalities wouldn't allow human rights on their national agendas, that didn't affect their relations with Washington. But as soon as the East came apart, almost all regimes in the region feared the monopolar world based on Western values, especially when led by the remaining superpower, the United States of America. In short, with fears of the Soviets gone, American support was expected to shift from the so-called stability of the Cold War—in other words, maintaining the balance of power—to the promotion of democracy. And so, ironically, the region's authoritarian elites divined what the shape of the new world order would be after the end of Soviet Communism even before American elites figured it out. Hence as the Berlin Wall was crumbling, another wall was about to be erected in the Greater Middle East—one that would separate the peoples of this region, particularly the oppressed, from the potential new and democratic direction of the international community. Even though local conflicts would continue, along with political competitions, jealousies, and interests, a regional understanding would remain in effect: keep the West at bay, mollify the United States' potential policies toward civil societies, and play all cards possible to delay democratization. These cards included oil influence, the mantra of so-called "stability," and fear of international terrorism. If necessary, small concessions could be made on issues important to the West without exposing the whole region to democratic penetration. In this post–Cold War convergence of interests among the ruling elites, and despite their confrontation with each other, it was fundamental to manipulate the Western vision of the region's realities. Thus the previously mentioned tunnel vision concerning the "real" issues in the Middle East was constructed and solidified in the 1990s by the ensemble of ruling establishments.

PALESTINE FIRST AND ONLY. To the American and European establishments, as well as to other democracies worldwide, maintaining the centrality of the Palestinian-Israeli question was the top priority. "The Arab world won't enter any other discussion on any issues before solving the Palestinian question," repeated presidents, prime ministers, monarchs, and a nebulous collection of state officials and legislators, as well as a majority of academics, intellectuals, and politicians, all in favor of the consensus against Western intervention on behalf of democracy in any issue except Palestine. Thus no one from across the Mediterranean or the Atlantic would investigate any other question regarding governance, self-determination, human rights, or related matters before the Arab-Israeli conflict was solved. And that meant the authoritarian regimes in the region would be safe for many, many years.

HUMAN RIGHTS ARE A DOMESTIC MATTER. This was a strategy to rebut Western and international intervention in Arab and Middle Eastern affairs. This answer to any investigation by the international community into allegations of mass abuse, such as in Sudan, Iraq, Lebanon, Afghanistan, or Iran, was part of the post-Soviet "wall" constructed by the region's elites and regimes.

AN OFFICIAL VERSION OF THE MIDDLE EAST. This third pillar built by the authoritarians in their solidarity in the War of Ideas was uniquely sophisticated. Not only did the dominant political elites of the region forge their own presentation of what should or shouldn't be part of the Greater Middle Eastern agenda in international forums, but they also moved to impose this agenda on the democracies' plans regarding the Middle East. Perhaps the most powerful component of all three strategies was the oil-backed Middle Eastern regimes' offensive against the center of Western political thinking. As I will detail later, the petrodollars collected by ruling elites in Arabia would determine how young students would be taught the history and politics of the Middle East, thus shaping future policymakers in America and Europe, who would in turn shape the future of the world and the Middle East.

Pan-Arab Ultranationalists

The second dynamic of the post-Soviet War of Ideas was generated by Pan-Arab, ultranationalist elites, who refused to follow the model of *perestroika* and *glasnost* and instead continued their oppression of ethnic and national minorities. Arab ultranationalism, as well as all other dominant extreme-nationalist ideologies promoted by a radical petite bourgeoisie with fascist tendencies, opposed the ideas of liberal patriotism[1] exercised in the modern West and the "reformed" nationalism that allowed the Soviet republics to exit the Communist Federation. Arab Baathist leaders in Iraq and Syria, observing the disintegration of the Soviet Union in 1990–91, not only rejected the model, but also pressed to the limit their own military capabilities. Saddam Hussein, seeing his allies in Moscow relinquishing control over their former clients of the Warsaw Pact in 1990, sent his armies on August 2 of that year to invade Kuwait. Meanwhile, Hafez Assad, observing with great concern the decline of Soviet power, ordered his armed forces to complete the invasion of Lebanon's last free areas in October 1990.

The attachment of Baathist dictatorships to the Soviet totalitarian giant had always been strategic. When Communist leaders staged a coup against Gorbachev in August 1991 and reconstituted the old USSR for a few days, the very first message of congratulations and support came from Saddam Hussein, followed by a number of Pan-Arabist leaders in the region. The ultranationalists feared a decomposition of their own regimes, and the vanishing of the dreamed-of "Arab unity" to come, because of the collapse of their main weapons supplier. They worried that their ideology, Pan-Arabism, would collapse as well. But more important, Baathists and other irredentists feared that they would lose control of acquired territories (Syria's occupation of Lebanon, for example), or that the rise of ethnic minorities would be assisted by the West. Saddam didn't want to let the Kurds and the Assyrians go; Bashir and Turabi of Sudan worried about secession by the African south and west; Iran feared its Kurds, Azeris, Arabs, and other minorities; and even Algeria wasn't ready to extend self-determination to its Berber minority.

But in political reality, the Arab ultranationalist elites also feared for their accumulated power in Damascus, Baghdad, Yemen, and Libya; within the political and intellectual establishment in West Beirut, Sanaa, and Cairo; and among their enclaves overseas. If Arab nationalism collapsed as an idea, it would crumble as an ideology, and with it decades of elite control over political affairs and the media. Additionally, the Pan-Arabist logic overlapped with the regimes' interest in suppressing democratic empowerment in the region. Put simply, the Pan-Arabist ideology, like the Pan-German and Pan-Italian ideologies, had allowed waves of middle-class elites to rise against the older feudal class of the Ottomans. But instead of promoting democratic ideals, they took the fascistic route, denying all national minorities their rights. Then, to dodge the inescapable debate about liberation, they dumped the entire problem of nationalities in the Arab world on, of course, the Arab-Israeli conflict and the only cause ever allowed in view, Palestine.

As for the authoritarian regimes in general, the Pan-Arabist movement immediately adopted post–Cold War prescriptions to protect its prominence in the region. Its participation in the second War of Ideas would follow almost the same tracks: opposition to freeing Middle Eastern minorities, particularly the non-Arab ones; opposition to political pluralism; opposition to UN or Western intervention in the region to promote "multiethnic constitutions"; and the imposition of their version of the Middle Eastern and Arab international agenda in both regional and international arenas. Thus, despite the end of the Cold War, the defeat of Saddam Hussein in Kuwait, and the advances made in the Arab-Israeli peace process of 1992–93, the Pan-Arabist agenda didn't move forward to catch up with the rest of the world, but instead moved backward, isolating the civil societies of the region from the wider international community. In order to do so, the radical nationalists, along with the fundamentalists in Iran, shut the doors on all public matters except the Israeli occupation of the West Bank and Gaza—an issue the United States and the West were trying to solve through the peace process.

But Assad, Saddam, Arafat, Khomeini, Turabi, Qadhafi, and their supporters in the region ignored the millions of oppressed within their own borders and refused to address the region's crises in social and political development; instead, they concentrated solely on amassing weapons of all sorts (including unconventional weapons) and waging terror across the land, while also preparing for the "wars to come." Gigantic resources (among them oil revenues) were dedicated to setting the agenda of the international community and distorting the Western "reading" of Middle Eastern developments.

Using many public-relations companies and consultants based in the West, and welcoming journalists and academics with largesse, the radical regimes and their spokespersons in the West launched campaign after campaign to influence the minds and hearts of decision makers on both sides of the Atlantic. In the next sections, I will analyze the various levels and procedures of this War of Ideas waged against democracies by the Arab power elites and their allies.

ISLAMISTS AND JIHADISTS

In addition to the authoritarian regimes and the Pan-Arab radical nationalists, the third "army" in the post-Soviet War of Ideas was made up of all Islamist and jihadist regimes and organizations combined. But one can distinguish between the two major "trees" of Islamic fundamentalism: the Salafi Wahabis on the one hand and the Khumeinists on the other. Each developed its own brand of ideological warfare against the West, depending on its strategic objectives.

Iranian-Controlled Warfare

The Iranian-controlled warfare used the state resources of the regime, including oil money and intelligence, to further its objectives. Beyond its borders, Tehran backed Hezbollah to wage a Lebanon-based war of media and intelligence. After a series of terror attacks against the U.S. and French military and diplomats in Lebanon during the 1980s, Hezbollah abruptly stopped the direct and systematic terrorism against Western targets and focused on organizing its political influence in Syrian-occupied Lebanon. With the exceptions of terrorist strikes in al Khubar in Saudi Arabia in June 1996[2] and against Israeli (1992) and Jewish (1994) targets in Argentina,[3] Hezbollah diverted all military efforts to Israeli and Lebanese objectives in south Lebanon throughout the 1990s. But the bigger political war was pursued through media and psychological warfare with a global scope: a satellite TV station, al Manar, and radio channels to broadcast Hezbollah's propaganda into the Arab and Muslim world. The aim of this campaign was double: to project Hezbollah's image in the West as a resistance movement instead of a terrorist organization and to plant the seeds of anti-Semitism and anti-Americanism in the minds of youth in the East.

The Salafi "Tree"

The Salafists in the 1990s launched an even greater War of Ideas, with a gigantic scope of operations ranging from state-funded propaganda to Internet-based militancy. Unlike Iran's continuous political warfare since the 1980s, the engagement of the Wahabis, Muslim Brotherhood, Deobandis, and other Takfiris in an ideological war within the Arab and Muslim world and against the West resulted from a change in strategic position. As noted previously, the radical Sunni Islamists clashed mostly with the Communists and sporadically with local governments during the first War of Ideas (1945–90), while preparing their constituencies for a future assault against the West after the Soviet collapse. And as soon as Moscow's international arsenal of operatives, institutions, literature, and activists disintegrated, a Salafi army of propagandists rose to launch a second War of Ideas against established democracies and the seeds of democracy growing in the Arab and Muslim world. By the beginning of the 1990s, there were several Salafist forces of ideological warfare.

THE WAHABI REGIME IN SAUDI ARABIA. During the first War of Ideas, and particularly after the 1973 oil shock, the state policy of the kingdom undertook "soft" worldwide operations with Islamist investments. In the Arab and Muslim world, the Saudis funded or founded large numbers of madrassas, mosques and other religious sites, programs in public schools, orphanages, socioeconomic institutions, and newspapers, and also contributed to agencies and ministries under Muslim governments. This sizable amount of "foreign aid" was linked to spreading the teachings of Wahabism within the Muslim world. It was carefully designed not to appear bellicose toward the local governments or to the United States—the Saudis' ally against the Soviets. The

"Wahabization" of Muslim institutions across the Muslim world over two decades by the power of petro-revenues was culturally devastating: thousands of people were converted to a more radical brand of religion in many countries, from Indonesia to Algeria. This pool of theologically reeducated men would serve as the reserves for the second War of Ideas.

From the kingdom and its "religious settlements" around the globe, Wahabi cadres were recruited to lead the further radicalization of the 1990s; join al Qaeda and other jihadist groups in that decade and beyond; and travel to the West to manage the Wahabi investments inside Western democracies. Indeed, the oil power had already "invested" in Western Europe and North America under the Cold War. Targeting the main institutions of Muslim émigrés as well, royal and clerical funds laid the foundations for fundamentalist enclaves within many of the Muslim communities inside the West by the early 1990s. And it is from these islands of Islamist thinking that the cadres of the second War of Ideas would rise. By early in the decade, the rulers of the kingdom had mobilized their resources to spread their ideology inside the West. In order to secure protection and shield their regime from domestic criticism, the Saudi strategists had recourse to American and European "associates." Companies, pressure groups, and lobbies were mobilized to implant a benign image of the country and its activities. From media to academia, the penetration proceeded throughout the decade. But it should be noted that Riyadh's rulers have always planned that Wahabi gains, both in the Muslim world and within the West, would be theirs and theirs only. However, the Saudi-led Wahabis would soon witness the rise of post-Wahabi jihadi Islamists and of neo-Wahabis as well. The peninsular Wahabis had opened the bottle of Jihadism, but more than one jinni got out of it.

MUSLIM BROTHERHOOD AND AL JAZEERA. The Wahabis weren't the only internationalist Islamists of the 1990s. Competing with them were the Muslim Brotherhood and their various surrogates in the region's regimes and oppositions. The *Ikhwan*, remnants of the old networks of Egyptian Hassan al Banna, grew wider and more mature. With a history of harsh experiences under secular and Pan-Arabist regimes, the "Brothers" were able to infiltrate many governments, bureaucracies, media, and academic entities. In fact, the *Ikhwan* were already in their second generation after the 1920s. Profiting from the Wahabi funding of numerous institutions in the Muslim world and the West, their cadres had a tremendous advantage over other Muslims: they had the know-how, literary skills, and "underground" experience needed to penetrate and weaken the resolve of the enemy—basic needs in a psychological war of information. Soon the *Ikhwan* and their disciples found themselves hired by Wahabi-funded projects around the world. From there, many were rehired—thanks to the worldwide influence and endorsement of the oil companies working in the Gulf—by media agencies to use their talents in Arabic; these included the BBC and Monte Carlo, but also Voice of America and others.[4] Gradually, the message about the Arab world transmitted by Western information agencies took on an anti-Western slant.[5]

But the internationally trained Muslim Brotherhood media cadre soon married their skills with an unexpected offer for "media jihad" from an unusual party: Qatar's emir. Competing with the House of Saoud, the Qatari regime embarked on one of the most powerful and efficient projects of the three Wars of Ideas combined: the al Jazeera TV channel. Some trace the decision by the Qatar elite to fund al Jazeera to a mere quarrel between this small emirate and the powerful Wahabi kingdom; others believe that al Jazeera represented an opportunity for the Muslim Brotherhood to lead the Salafi jihadists internationally; but more likely, the launching of al Jazeera was a result of a combination of all these motives.[6]

Regardless of the reasons, al Jazeera emerged as the first Islamist media outlet in the world in 1996. Backed financially by Qatar's oil, gas, banking, and other related industries, the new "Jihad TV" was extremely successful under the leadership of the Muslim Brotherhood's best ideological and media strategists.[7]

The Islamist side of the War of Ideas had now equipped itself with top-of-the-line weaponry.

THE JIHADI SALAFI NETWORK. The Wahabi regime, emirs, and clerics jointly pushed for the radical Islamist agenda internationally under the Cold War, mostly to fight the ideological conflict against Communism, but also to spread their own interpretation of Islam. But intentionally or not, the classical Wahabis engendered a more lethal brand of their own doctrines: the Neo-Wahabis. Salafis by indoctrination, Wahabi by tradition, and jihadists by involvement in battlefields, especially in Afghanistan, the Neo-Wahabis had cultivated their own extreme Islamism, which went even beyond the realism of state Wahabism. Led by Abdallah Azzam first, then by Osama bin

Laden and Ayman Zawahiri, these neo-Wahabis finally formed al Qaeda as an ultimate international network. Al Qaeda per se leaped beyond the classical Wahabis and the Muslim Brotherhood's pragmatic approach, creating their own discourse based on fatwas and fiery declarations publicized throughout the 1990s. They, too, from their own extreme angle, engaged in the second global War of Ideas all the way up to 2001.

PRO-JIHADIST LOBBIES IN THE WEST

Unexpected allies of the region's authoritarian regimes and radical ideological groups in the post-Soviet War of Ideas were interest groups, both financial and intellectual, linked to oil influence. The region's regimes had since 1973 consolidated their grip on the multinational companies and their Western associates, and as soon as the Cold War ended, they rushed to plant their influence deep inside European and American society. From the Middle Eastern power centers situated in poorly educated societies, they launched one of the most formidable politicocultural invasions in the history of democracy. The objectives were to control Western thinking about and action toward the Arab and Muslim world and to create a remote or long-range defense of the region's regimes, ideologies, and status quo. The ultimate goal of this massive, authoritarian War of Ideas was to take control of media, academic, and political "messages" regarding the governance and development of the region and the correct approach to it. This remote-controlled machinery would define how American and European students should understand the political cultures of the Middle East, how journalists should report events (or ignore them), and how security officials should interpret and prioritize threats. The most sensitive element of the process was the formation of specific perceptions. Ironically, while jihadist clerics took responsibility for fostering the dangerous beliefs and perceptions of young Arabs and Muslims, the apologist scholars of the West were seemingly unwilling even to acknowledge the parallel operation that they were performing on the collective mindset of American and European students.

The oil powers and their financial tentacles within the West used the 1990s to massively fund Middle East studies and other social sciences programs, as well as institutes and think tanks, in order to create an entity that would have control over education (managed by administrators and professors), grants, and business interests, so that academia would continue to support the lobby. Dozens of American, Canadian, European, and other universities were "assaulted" financially by "donors" who imposed their ideological will on the funded programs. In the 1990s, jihadi oil dollars were responsible for the West's collective misunderstanding of Middle Eastern events and politics, including its blindness to the rise of the jihadist menace. This "Western front" opened by the Eastern totalitarian powers was at the heart of the War of Ideas—a war they won against the basic intellectual defenses of Western societies. It was precisely because of the blurring of the collective vision of Americans and Europeans that a question as incredible as, "Why do they hate us?" was even possible the day after September 11, and still is asked to today. The fact that such a question arose at such a time shows the stunning success of the oil-funded Wahabi propaganda campaign against the West in the preceding years. Indeed, the Wahabi political success worldwide is embodied in this implacable chain of strategic achievements: oil revenues funded madrassas around the Muslim world; the madrassas produced Islamic fundamentalists who controlled most of the Muslims' discourse; oil revenue also funded academic strongholds in the West, which produced apologists for the Islamists. One Wahabi hand was clapping with another Wahabi hand. The Islamists rose in the East, and the apologists covered up for them in the West. Had Osama not hastened the inevitable clash in 2001, the silent invasion would still be spreading.

TACTICAL OBJECTIVES

The War of Ideas just described resembled a lobotomy: it removed from the collective international mind the ability to learn what was really happening in the Arab and Muslim world and to form a correct vision of history, facts, objectives, and the real attitudes of these radical forces. Following are what we might call the marching orders in this war:

- *Denial of other identities.* The radicals' first message, conveyed through both Arab and Western education, was to deny the existence of identities in the region other than the national and religious ones that Arabists and jihadists were aiming to control. National and ethnic groups, such as the Kurds, Berbers, Africans, and Aramaics as native peoples, were erased from the international curriculum. The region was portrayed as purely Arab and Muslim by both Eastern elites and Western

academics. Such a "cultural cleansing" of diversity was used subse-
quently by intellectuals and politicians who stated that the region as a
whole had a global identity, which they claimed to represent. One has
only to recall how often commentators, spokespersons, journalists,
and scholars attacked U.S. and Western policies on the grounds of the
policies' "total rejection by the region."[8]

- *Denial of political opposition.* The radicals' second message was to deny
  the existence of comprehensive, serious, and struggling opposition to
  their regimes and ideologies, and particularly to reject any insinuation
  that the majorities in the region's various countries weren't satisfied
  with their rulers, elites, and political systems. The War of Ideas waged
  in the West rejected the claims by Middle Eastern dissidents that oppression was endemic and systematic, especially against liberal and
  democratic elements and collectivities. The authoritarians' apologists
  in the West denied that the masses and human rights activists were
  calling for democratization and insisted that the region's "culture" was
  satisfied with the state of affairs. The UN Charter and its Universal
  Declaration on Human Rights states that there are basic universal
  human aspirations to self-determination, freedom, and individual liberties. The Wahabi, Khumeinist, and authoritarian brainwashing promoted the idea that Arabs and Muslims are "just different," not
  "wired" for individual freedom, self-expression, etc., but (in a figura-
  tive comparison), like the Borg in Star Trek, happy being little cogs in
  a great machine. The jihadist claim of "relativism" in a sense dehu-
  manized the peoples of the region by affirming that, unlike everybody
  else, they didn't want the freedoms embodied in the Universal Declaration of Human Rights. The advocates of the "one big frustrated
  Middle East" wanted to impose the image of a frustration directed
  only against the United States and the West, mainly because of Israel.
- *Denial of women's oppression.* The third message of the ideological war of
  the 1990s was to deny that, on the whole, women under Islamist
  regimes were suffering injustices. This most daring denial was close to
  delusional, as the most visible and obvious of all oppressions in the
  Greater Middle East were and still are the various forms of gender
  abuse. They range from the very basic inequalities that women in many
  other countries and regions still suffer, such as legal, social, and psychological discrimination, to the excessive discrimination against women in

Iran, Sudan, and Saudi Arabia. But the most striking denial was the dodging of the issue of the brutal oppression of women under the Taliban from the mid-1990s on. Academics and commentators, not to mention Wahabi activists in America and Europe, argued during that decade that "women under the Taliban were immersed in their cultural traditions" and that their treatment shouldn't be held to the standards of the West. Advocacy groups and scholars have attempted to convince the stunned citizens of the West that women under the Islamist and jihadist regimes are as happy as their counterparts worldwide.[9]

• *Denial of human rights abuses.* Perhaps the most widespread "shielding" practiced by the authoritarian lobbies was the suppression of human rights reports regarding political prisoners and the kidnappings, assassinations, mass jailings, and intimidation of Arab and Middle Eastern men and women. The first line of attack was to focus all or most public attention on the "Israeli abuse of Palestinians." Although certainly this problem existed, it was proportionally just a segment of the global abuse of human rights in the region. Quantitatively, by comparison, there were as many political prisoners or "disappeared" individuals in the Arab world and Iran in the 1990s as the entire population living in Gaza—that is to say, one million people.[10] The apologist elite in the West, and increasingly the globalized radical media from the region, systematically omitted the hundreds of thousands of abused prisoners in Iranian, Iraqi, Syrian, Sudanese, Libyan, and Lebanese jails, focusing on Israel and the United States and "abuse linked to pro-American regimes in the region."[11] The imbalance was so flagrant that prominent journalistic and audiovisual media in Europe and North America often refused to publish or air reports sent in by dissidents and opposition groups if they didn't toe the party line of the lobbies.

• *Denial of Slavery and Genocide.* The most unethical denial of all was the suppression, by the oil-supported elites on both sides of the Atlantic and the Mediterranean, of reports accusing regimes and organizations of mass humiliation and murder, plunging these countless victims into a "black hole" of international relations. Between 1991 and 2001, the mainstream media and major academic institutions in the West dodged the question of black slavery in Sudan at the hands of the National Islamic Front of Turabi. High-level officials, wrongly briefed by their advisors and subalterns, and college professors reading from militant literature, entirely suppressed the issue of slavery until freed slaves hit the podiums in America and the West. "We were slaves of militias waging jihad against our villages," testified runaways from the bushes of Sudan in front of Congress and classrooms toward the end of the 1990s, to the astonishment of legislators and students.[12] "How can such undeniable truth about the horrors of slavery have been brushed away," lamented Samuel Cotton, one of the leading African American intellectuals who fought back against what he called a "war of deception by Oil lobbyists."[13] But the highest point in mass deception engineered by the architects of that War of Ideas was the hermetic isolation of the international public from the several genocides under way in the Middle East. In Algeria, a series of massacres by Salafists during the 1990s took the lives of more than 120,000 women, children, and elderly, as well as journalists, singers, artists, and others. In the United States and Europe, academics were presenting the Algerian jihadists as "alternative political forces to open dialogue with."[14] In Iran, tens of thousands of citizens, including reformers and right- and left-wing activists, were assassinated; in the West, the "experts" advised governments to talk to the Iranian regime as it allegedly "made progress toward reform." And the mother of all denials for more than a decade was the refusal to admit that genocide was taking place in Sudan throughout the 1990s. "It's an intratribal warfare," stated both the progovernment lobby of Khartoum and Middle East studies scholars in America.[15]

- *Denial of jihadi menace.* Last but not least, the denial of all denials, nothing caused Western democracies and civil societies in the Middle East more suffering than the denial of the jihadi menace. This highly strategic deception, aimed at blurring the vision of the foe and blunting future resistance to the authoritarians of the Middle East and the jihadists themselves, is at the ideological core of the War of Ideas. It is based on the assumption that by depriving the enemy (infidels, West, democracies) of the ability to understand who its enemy is (the jihadists and their allies), what they want to achieve, what their ideological beliefs are, how they recruit, and how they can be identified, then that enemy can eventually be destroyed, even in spite of its superior technology and power. The most lethal (and intelligent) tactic devised by the Wahabis, Salafists, Khumeinists, and their allies to subvert the "infidels" was to blind them from seeing jihad as a threat, even while actually executing a jihadi war against them! Such a subversive tactic has no equivalent in modern times. Some would argue that Marxist-Leninists lured societies into Communism while denying they were Marxists until the opportune time. This probably was the closest that previous totalitarians came to what I would call the jihadi deception doctrine. But in fact, even the Communist subversive methods didn't go so far in camouflaging Marxism-Leninism as something it wasn't. Communist tacticians hid the fact that they were Communists as long as necessary to gain the trust of their adversaries or until the balance of power shifted. But the jihadists went further even than the comparable classical *Taqiya* warfare deception. For instead of simply hiding that they were jihadists, they were even able to hide what jihad itself was.[16]

Already in operation as of the 1980s, the denial of the jihadi menace took center stage for the entire lobbying machinery within the West, beginning in the early 1990s. Ironically, while the Salafi jihadists were launching their wars in Chechnya, Kashmir, Sudan, Afghanistan, Algeria, and beyond, and while al Qaeda was beginning its salvos against the United States and issuing its fatwas in 1996 and 1998, both the Islamist cadres in the West and their allies in the intellectual establishment—from the most prestigious universities to the most modest colleges—were screaming one unified slogan: "Jihad is not holy war. Jihad is essentially a spiritual experience."[17] The 1990s witnessed the most focused War of Ideas against the international perception of Jihadism. In almost every single book, article, research project, and encyclopedia that mainstream academia was able to impact, the term *jihad* was explained as a "religious duty" to all Muslims but "not necessarily violent." The logic of deconstructing jihad was as follows:

—Linguistically, *jihad* means "effort" or "struggle," and therefore it doesn't mean "war."
—Throughout Islamic history, it was mainly used to promote a personal inner cleansing, not to call for war.
—Most propagation of Islam was by peaceful conversions; violent jihad rarely took place—and if it did, it was in a defensive mode.
—In modern times, some pious Muslims decided to revive this ancient tradition and engage in spiritual renaissance.

—The contemporary jihadists, Salafists, or Khumeinists are just "re-formers" who wish to abide by Islamic traditions and laws.

—Describing jihad as a war and jihadists as terrorists will insult Muslims because Jihad touches on a religious duty.

Evidently, in the absence of an alternative explanation in the West, the general understanding by opinion leaders drifted away from the real historical meaning of jihad—regardless of its validity in modern times—and obstructed learning about who the jihadists are and what they want. The denial of the jihadi menace not only was silent on historical realities and modern developments, but it also constructed parallel interpretations of the war doctrine followed by the radical Islamists since the 1920s. A "Kafka-esque" situation developed rapidly. Incredibly, while the Salafi Islamists were disseminating Jihadism, decade after decade, Wahabi lobbies in the West were camouflaging the nature of jihad. The Islamists preached "real" jihad to their recruits worldwide, and the "protectors" of the Islamists in the West tranquilized the public as to the spiritual nature of jihad. A possible comparison would be to the rise of Nazism in Germany. Imagine apologists in Western Europe and North America arguing that "real Nazism" is just nationalism. Western eyes would have been watching the Nuremberg hate fests and the rise of Hitler while academics would have been describing this sight as not really racism.

With all the above tactics, the Islamist chain of propaganda production and its tools within the West waged the most comprehensive and systematic campaign of mind control ever achieved in the democratic world. From subverting teaching, research, hiring, and publishing, to crushing dissidents, manipulating interfaith dialogue, and influencing policy and national security decision making, the campaign kept replicating itself and penetrating further and further inside society.

THE ACADEMIC JIHAD

From the early 1990s, considerable Wahabi money was made available for the "academic jihad." Both government and independent emirs offered money to be invested in the West to "teach about Islam, correct the image of it, and better explain the real problems in the Middle East." These benign initial offers couldn't be refused by academic institutions and think tanks hungry to better educate students and better inform the public about this complex region of the world, from which many civilizations emerged. At first sight, the "nice," philanthropic packaging of these "grants," in an environment stripped of the capacity to see through the ruse, enabled the subtle assault to penetrate defenses smoothly. From coast to coast in North America, and from the Mediterranean to the North Sea, a wave of oil funding hit university after university, college after college, and research center after research center, as well as public libraries, museums, and other places of learning. The offers were coated as strictly "academic"—neutral, balanced, and inclusive. On the donor end, however, the objectives were fully ideological: further the cause of Islam as they envisioned it, support the Palestinian cause as the sole issue in the Middle East, and plant the seeds of the concept of an illegitimate West. This real agenda by the donors merged with the anti-American, anti-Western, and in some cases anti-Semitic elements of the extreme left and extreme right in America and other Western societies. The grand axis between the jihadists and the Western radicals was formed in the wake of the Soviet collapse.[18]

The roots of this "unholy" alliance certainly deserve wider research, but for the purposes of this book, I shall limit the analysis to the jihadi lobby, the factory of the academic jihad. Funding of the programs led to the penetration of school systems; from there, the "chain" branched outward.

- *Teaching.* Because of the funding and its derivatives, teachers couldn't expose the ideology of the donors. Middle East studies and history professors were conditioned to teach a sanitized version imposed by the oil lobby. American and Western classrooms in the 1990s weren't trained to understand the region and its ideology as they really were, but through the lenses of the Wahabi donors and their American partners.

- *Research.* To be considered teaching material, the "research subjects" (i.e., the fields, titles) had to follow the guidelines of the teachers. Most research themes relevant to the subject that denied the disinformation described above were eliminated. In the 1990s, textbooks didn't contain chapters explaining the real crisis of ethnic conflict, minorities, Jihadism, terrorism, and gender discrimination. The students were betrayed intellectually by most of their specialized teachers in the field.

- *Graduation.* Students who graduated in Middle East studies and related subjects were conditioned by the material and teaching restric-

tions on taboo subjects applied by the instructors. Graduates thus
replicated the "knowledge" offered in the classrooms and academic
conferences. This cloning perpetuated the indoctrination.

- *Hiring*. After graduation, the students would seek jobs in the fields of
international relations and comparative politics, with a concentration
in Middle East studies with language skills. Many graduates trained by
"Arabist" and Wahabi-funded teachers were likely to end up in the real
world of entities influencing the public and actual decision makers.
That is, these indoctrinated graduates would get into offices and positions responsible for analysis and recommendations regarding national
security, as well as jobs in the media and academia itself. The "class"
that was graduated by the Wahabi-funded establishment would spread
its worldview—including the intentionally induced ignorance of significant parts of the worldview itself—into the public sphere. Decision
makers, readers, viewers, and other consumers of "academic expert
knowledge" would hence be at the mercy of the worldview of the graduates of these colleges. The circle would almost be complete. Since the
teachers graded students on their content and conditioned them to
make certain interpretations, the hiring process in these fields would
also require the same type of worldview. From the *New York Times* to
the State Department, from getting a job on a campus to *Le Monde*, the
Guardian, Oxford, and the Sorbonne, those responsible for educating
and informing democracies on Jihadism were doomed to fail.

THE CLOSED GATES

Until September 11, 2001, the gates of knowledge about Jihadism and its
branches, tactics, and strategies were closed. In one decade, the capacity of
average citizens in North America and Europe, as well as most other
democracies in the world, to develop an understanding of who the enemy
was, let alone have a basic comprehension of Middle Eastern realities, had
been reduced to almost nil. The perception of the politics and ideologies of
the Arab and Muslim world was shaped by the funding power that penetrated academia, and through it media and government. The ordinary social science graduate of U.S. and European schools had been indoctrinated
by this War of Ideas. In my 14 years of teaching at the undergraduate and
graduate levels, I have observed with amazement American students

stripped of their basic rights to be educated accurately about the main geopolitical and ideological threats to their homeland. Instead of using classroom time to profoundly analyze the rise of what would become al Qaeda or the Khomeini regime's long-range strategies, we professors had to "clean up" the diseducating process that blurred the intellectual vision of a whole generation. They needed to understand the real ethnoreligious makeup of that crucial region, its history, its conflicts, its actual ideological currents, and so on. Only at the end of the semester were students able to see the big picture, and hence comprehend the world they were in after the end of the Cold War. Influenced by such works as Fukuyama's *End of History* and Esposito's *Myth of Islamism*,[19] American students across the nation thought the world was heading toward the ultimate democratic experience and the nirvana of universal society. Viewers of CNN, BBC, and other Western outlets saw O. J. Simpson and Monica Lewinsky as the greatest stories of the decade; readers of *USA Today* and *La Stampa* in Italy thought terrorism to be a last spasm from the previous century's Cold War.

In reality, Jihadism was on the march, camouflaged by a systematic shield. Presented as a "spiritual yoga," the movement that was responsible for the 1993 Twin Towers attacks, the Khobar strikes, the takeover by the Taliban in Afghanistan, the bombings of the U.S. embassies in East Africa, the USS *Cole* attack, and other terror conspiracies was developing, mutating, closing in, and spreading—all in the midst of a collective, engineered blindness. Audiences in the West were rendered unable to connect the dots between the attacks and the ideologies at work in Chechnya, Algeria, Sudan, Kashmir, Israel, Egypt, and the Philippines. "These are all resistance movements struggling against authoritarian regimes," asserted the Wahabi-influenced establishment in the West.[20] Maybe a number of these regimes, such as Egypt and Algeria, were indeed ruled by oppressive elites, but what was the alternative regime the jihadists wished to impose? In 1996, the Islamists provided the model: Afghanistan's Taliban. Indeed, the coming to power of the ultrajihadists in Kabul by itself should have been a powerful wake-up call to the international community. But to no avail; scholars at Harvard presented the turbaned mullahs as "elements of stability."[21] And if the most prominent academics in the nation disregarded the menace and dismissed it as mere "conservatism-revivalism," why would the average Joe, or even an analyst in the CIA, contradict the "masters" on the subject?

By the time the psychological and indoctrinational offensives had blanketed the bulk of America and Western centers of learning and information, defense and security analysts, journalists, government advisers, and international organizations, the collective perception had been damaged. One could even have come back in history from the future, as in *Star Gate*, and shared the information about 9/11 and the subsequent events with the public, and it wouldn't have had any real impact. *Alea jacta est:* the die was cast, the second War of Ideas had been won by the jihadists and their sympathizers, and as a result America's vision was blurred, its ears blocked, and its mind taken hostage by the enemy.

CHAPTER TEN

THE CLASH OF FUTURES

The Third War of Ideas, 2001–2006

ON THE MORNING OF SEPTEMBER 11, 2001, OSAMA BIN LADEN'S 19 suicide jihadists blasted the Twin Towers in New York and the Pentagon in Washington and struggled with civilian resistance in the skies over Pennsylvania. By American standards, this was the beginning of the War on Terror, triggered by al Qaeda. By jihadist standards, this was the eleventh year into their "holy war" on infidel America. But to both camps, that tragic day would mark the beginning of the third War of Ideas, an ideological, intellectual, and political conflict between the U.S.-led democracies and the jihadi-led agglomeration of anti-Western forces. The third War of Ideas is still raging, and it would be difficult to determine who is winning it; however, it is interesting to observe that its beginning wasn't planned systematically by either side. As noted in previous chapters, the democracies—systematically blinded by the jihadist-Wahabist propaganda campaign—weren't foreseeing a terror war, nor even the 1990s War of Ideas. Yet on the other side, not all of the jihadi-authoritarian camp was ready for this new war. Historians may discover that, with the exception of al Qaeda, the jihadi network, and its media, most players were caught off guard by 9/11. This leads to the question, Why were al Qaeda and the international Salafists ready for the third War of Ideas, whereas the bulk of Wahabis and Khumeinists, not to mention the Baathists and other authoritarians, were not? A first answer is provided by the facts: bin Laden and his team, although at war with America and the *kuffar*, had worked on their plans in secrecy to ensure their success, and hence other jihadists were not privy to them. But a second answer, more strategic and historical, is also warranted: not all

jihadists and totalitarians were in agreement on the timing of the grand offensive against America and the West.

THE JIHADISTS' STRATEGIC DISAGREEMENT

As I detailed in *Future Jihad* and other writings, interviews, and lectures, bin
Laden's decision to strike America in 2001 preempted a much larger global,
political, and ideological war already under way. The debates that followed
the September 11 *Ghazwas* (raids), including on al Jazeera and online,
showed differences between al Qaeda and other Islamist centers around the
world. Bin Laden's nebula, which had been operating worldwide since the
early 1990s, had reached the historic and strategic conclusion by the end of
that decade that, like the Soviet Union in the previous decade, the United
States and its allies could be destroyed. Hence they decided to launch a massive mainland strike, expecting it would break the American giant's political
will. Such a conclusion proves that al Qaeda per se, although part of the ideological warfare of the 1990s, wasn't the global director of the War of Ideas
against America and the West; inasmuch as it was a conglomerate, it shared
goals with others, but it didn't lead. So who were the "armies" of the ideological war prior to 2001?

The forces engaged in psychological warfare, within both the Muslim
world and the West, were more of a hydra with multiple heads than a single
organization directed by one person (bin Laden). There were the Wahabi
power out of Saudi Arabia, with its own internal influences within the kingdom and its vast financial and educational networks internationally; the international Muslim Brotherhood organizations, with their influences within
Arab and Muslim governments, NGOs, and international groups such as the
Organization of Islamic States, as well as their ideological dominance of al
Jazeera through their impact on Qatar's regime;[1] the Sudanese Islamist regime
of Hassan Turabi and Omar Bashir; Iran's regime and its extension in
Lebanon via Hezbollah and its alliance with the Syrian Baathist regime; Saddam Hussein's Baathist regime and its limited influence in some quarters of
the Arab world; and finally, the vast constellation of Salafists, Deobandis, neo-
Wahabis, and Takfiris. The "world jihadics" (a new term I am coining) are the
sum of all the competing streams of ideological and political Jihadism. The international Salafi jihadists are a cobweb of radical groups led by al Qaeda,
forming part of the world jihadis but not abiding by their global strategies of

engagement with the West. To simplify, the planetary jihadians were conducting a massive effort, at a deliberate pace, to penetrate, weaken, delegitimize,
and then defeat democracies. Al Qaeda broke away from this consensus and
leaped forward to attack the dormant giant immediately. The initial reaction
of the international anti-American axis was frustration with bin Laden's "early
and reckless"[2] raids against a foe that was slowly being bled and subverted.
"The al Qaeda and the Taliban blew it up," complained many architects of the
anti-West warfare.[3] "The guys of the Afghani jihad did global jihad more
harm than ever," argued intellectuals and strategists on al Jazeera and in the
dailies, Lebanese *al Safir*, Saudi *al Hayat*, Syrian *Teshreen*, and Egyptian *al
Ahram*, in the weeks following the tragedy in New York. But for a moment, a
very short one, barely 48 hours after the attacks, a hesitation in expressing the
world jihadis' position betrayed a deep feeling inside these quarters. "What if
bin Laden succeeds?" The frontal attack against the "blind animal," which was
how the jihadists perceived the United States at the time, might have a chance
to succeed, fantasized the dictators and ideologues of the region. What if
America had fallen into confusion, its will to fight shattered? What if Washington had reacted as Madrid did later, in 2004? Had this happened, al Qaeda
might have obtained a stunning victory, but it would have had many partners
in this *Nasr* (victory): the entire anti-American, antidemocracy axis worldwide
from Tehran to Khartoum, from Damascus to Baghdad.

That fantasy was short-lived, but American political surrender to the jihadist blitzkrieg was at least theoretically possible. The possibility of surrender was proportional to the national inability to understand what happened
on that September morning, and thus also to the enemy's progress in the
second War of Ideas. An illustrative image of the moment was the photo of
President Bush flying back from Florida to Washington, looking through
the plane window. Regardless of partisan and domestic politics, the picture
represented what the overwhelming majority of Americans were going
through. Unlike with Pearl Harbor in 1941, to which 9/11 was immediately
compared, Americans didn't know who the enemy was and so didn't understand "why they hate us." Had the second War of Ideas been given more
time, perhaps just a few more years, the collective will of Americans might
have been so undermined that their national security would indeed have collapsed on that day.

In short, on September 11, 2001, America wasn't as ripe as the planetary jihadians wished her to be. Al Qaeda's decision to strike had arisen

from theological ideology, overconfident assessments by its intellectuals, and the inspiration of its leaders. In the midst of an unfinished War of Ideas, bin Laden measured his enemies wrongly and failed to kill with one blow; thousands of individuals tragically lost their lives, but his larger target was not destroyed. Instead, the attacks awakened America and propelled it into the War on Terror. The "rational" jihadists, those who knew the actual level of penetration and mollification of America and the West that had been achieved, realized how premature 9/11 was. They saw years of investment in ideological and indoctrinational propaganda crumbling with the New York towers. "Al Qaeda spoiled it," they felt. Hence a third War of Ideas was launched. A global offensive by all the enemies of the United States and other democracies was focused on stopping the United States from demolishing the totalitarian fortresses overseas and building public support for the war with the jihadists at home. Al Qaeda, still a renegade in terms of the "wiser" and more realistic global jihadists, was to be dislodged from its real estate in Afghanistan in December 2001. But from that moment on, as I will describe, all jihadists and anti-Americans would reposition themselves in different quarters, different capacities, and different settings and alliances, to deliver the mother of all Wars of Ideas—one that would make or break the U.S.-led War on Terror and reshape the history of humanity for the century.

THE CONSEQUENCES OF THE SECOND WAR OF IDEAS

The post-9/11 War of Ideas between Jihadism and democracy was initially determined by the consequences of the second War of Ideas of the 1990s. The most salient achievements of the jihadi offensive up to September 11 were its success in framing international relations, its presentation of the jihadi view of dissidents and opponents to their goals, and its victory in the battle of definitions. On all these fronts, the Islamists, Baathists, Pan-Arabists, and Western radical left and right wings scored multiple victories over democracies. Following is a summary of the main successes.

Framing of International Relations

Whoever controls the rhetoric of international relations dominates world politics. During the Cold War, the diplomatic language was split in two: Soviet Communist and Western democratic. But in the 1990s, things changed. After a few months of American and international jubilance over the collapse of the USSR and the images of happy masses in the streets of Eastern Europe, the First Persian Gulf War strengthened Western cohesion for a few more months, opening the path to what became the Madrid talks of 1991 and the peace accords between Arabs and Israelis signed in 1993. But that was the high-water mark for the post-Soviet ideological cohesion. Quickly, the forces of Jihadism and authoritarianism regrouped and refocused the international debate, from academia to media, as follows[4]:

- The "new enemy to peace" was reframed by the radical neo-Marxists as the United States, the G7, and globalization. In view of the rapid media success of these slogans, anti-Americans and authoritarians, although emanating from fascist and repressive backgrounds diametrically opposed to the Marxist sociopolitical agenda, rushed to join under the umbrella of the extreme left-wing policies. The Islamists, although religious fundamentalists, worked side by side with the atheists, as long as the enemy was the Free West.

- Operating on another track, the militant Islamists played the "interfaith dialogue" gambit as a way to direct criticism against the United States, Israel, and the claims by Christian minorities that they were persecuted and deserved autonomy in the Third World. Hence, ironically, some mainstream Christian churches in the West aligned themselves with Muslim activists against the struggle by Christians in Indonesia, Africa, the Arab world, and Iran. Here, too, the Islamists scored points by delegitimizing the claims of the persecuted. The interfaith enterprise was transformed into a pressure group directed against any potential American rescue of minorities in jeopardy. In other words the dialogue was coated in a relativist rhetoric such as "all religions are one in essence," a discourse that tends to smooth over differences and suppress questions such as a theological comparison of war and peace; basically, this either legitimized Jihadism or simply cut it out of the picture.

- Which causes are "kosher and halal"—in other words, politically correct and acceptable in the international context? In this regard, the authoritarians and Islamists imposed their views on almost all issues. They set the media and diplomatic agenda for when ethnic cleansing is recognized and when it isn't, when genocide is condemned and when it is not. The secession of the southern Philippines is legitimate, but the independence of East Timor wasn't. Interventions in Yugoslavia on behalf of Bosnia and Kosovo were acceptable, but Sudan's genocide wasn't recognized, and the international community was not allowed to intervene there. The Palestinians as a national entity were recognized, but not the Kurds. The Shia Hezbollah was considered a "resistance movement," but the Shiites of Iraq were forgotten. Israeli occupation of Gaza was raised, but not the Syrian occupation of Lebanon. In addition, the framing of international relations imposed the idea that there is one Arab world, one Middle East, and one Islamic world with one position on all matters related to culture, identity, and world politics, relegating diversity, pluralism, and differences to other regions. Often the phrase "the Arab World thinks," or the "Muslim world refuses," or other similar slogans are used by militants to lump all nations, minorities, regions, and political trends into one basket of so-called Westernism. In recent years, particularly since 9/11, many Arab and Muslim intellectuals have rejected the political culture of the "we the Arabs or Muslims," and have argued that Muslim civilization and the Arab world are as diverse as other civilizations, if less free at the moment.[5]

Framing of Dissidents and Reformers

Another victory for authoritarians and jihadists in the 1990s was obstructing the rise of dissidence in the Greater Middle East. The crisis of dissidents in the Arab world is at the core of its political underdevelopment. The rejection of opposition to regimes and ideologies is comprehensive. In Iran, Afghanistan, Syria, Sudan, Iraq, and Libya, for example, opponents of the regime were not only violently oppressed, tortured, and eliminated, but also systematically accused of being Israeli agents and Zionists. Even ethnically based activism is thrown into the catchall category of "Zionism." A jungle dweller in Southern Sudan, a Berber mountain peasant, an Algerian rock singer, a Coptic fellah in Egypt, a Christian or Druze of Mount Lebanon, a Kurd or Assyrian in Mesopotamia, a Shiite in the south of Iraq, a student in Iran, a woman in Afghanistan, a Sunni journalist in Syria, a writer in Libya—all are projected as "Zionists" in the eyes of the dominant establishment. From a Western perspective, the question is about how pervasive anti-Semitism is in the Arab and Muslim world. Throughout the 1990s, not only were reformers in the Middle East framed as "Zionists" by these regimes and organizations, but also, astoundingly, those dissidents in exile in the West were intellectually harassed by many Western elites as "American or Israeli stooges."

Also troubling were the demonization campaigns directed at authors, researchers, experts, and academics within the West, and particularly in the United States, who exposed the jihadi War of Ideas against democracies. The systematic verbal attacks against scholars such as Daniel Pipes in the United States and Bat Yeor in Europe, journalist Steven Emerson, and many others by Wahabi lobbies such as Council on American Islamic Relations (CAIR) are examples of the ideological intimidation that accompanied the terrorist attacks in the 1990s, and which some believe precipitated the terror war launched in 2001. The jihadi persecution of intellectuals operated by Western-based converts such as Ismael Royer of CAIR is a high-profile case of the "psy-ops" conducted by the political arm of Jihadism. Royer's harassment of writers and human rights leaders included attacks on, among others, antislavery pioneer Charles Jacobs, Daniel Pipes, and me as well. In 1999, the jihadi operative unleashed Internet attacks against my advocacy for liberating Lebanon from Syrian occupation and raising the profile of oppressed minorities in the Middle East. To tarnish my profile, for example, he attempted to portray me as a person linked to Lebanon's civil war. Later, a number of jihadi secular sympathizers, such as Professors As'ad AbuKhalil and Juan Cole, picked up Royer's initial canards in their blogs. But in 2004, Ismael Royer was sentenced to prison for terrorist activities, including "training with a terrorist cell in Virginia" known as the Paintball Gang. This example illustrates the link between terrorism and the ideological war in the 1990s. The jihadi terrorists did not limit themselves to preparing bombs and hijacking airplanes. They also acted under the camouflage of journalists, scholars, and advocacy groups to demonize their targets. Once they accomplished that first stage of villification, they or others would accomplish the subsequent terror acts against intellectuals. In Holland, Theo Van Gogh was heavily demonized by militants before he was attacked by a terrorist.

But the campaign was even more intense against Muslim dissidents, such as author Ibn Warraq, an Indian Muslim exile who criticized Jihadism. He was threatened into hiding and changing his name.

Last but not least, the "psychological offensive" against dissidents and reformers exiled in the West reached the court system, where jihadi operatives and their allies were able to attack asylum seekers from the Middle East and attempt to influence courts to reject their claims. Sympathizers of both Salafism and Hezbollah, penetrating the system in the United States and Canada as translators or "experts," were often successful in derailing the cases of persecuted Middle Easterners—who, once rejected, were returned to their home countries, to be arrested and tortured by either regimes or terrorist organizations.[6]

The consequences of this War of Ideas were enormous: the average citizens in North America lost track of the struggle for freedom in the Greater Middle East; they didn't know that Middle Eastern peoples were oppressed, but thought that they "naturally" disliked America and democracy. Joe and Jane Doe never heard the voices of Arab and Middle Eastern dissent, which had been suppressed by the regimes in the East and the elites in the West. The Western public never was exposed to the true histories of the Arab world or made aware of the mounting threat of Jihadism. On September 11, 2001, the workers entering the two towers in Manhattan had no idea that, for a whole decade, their vision and that of their society had been obstructed, even subverted.

9/11: START OF THE THIRD WAR OF IDEAS

"Why do they hate us?" This was the most asked question at the onset of the War on Terror. While jihadists and their allies on both sides of the Atlantic had been campaigning energetically for a decade, average Americans were asking the most basic of questions. In testimony to the U.S. Congress five years after 9/11, I described the balance of power at that time as an Islamist offensive against democracies before 2001, followed by an uphill U.S. counteroffensive on the jihadists ever since.[7] In a wider assessment, one would perceive the watershed of the third War of Ideas as a tectonic clash between global Jihadist networks and a dormant enemy, the United States. The latter was awoken by a terrorist act of large dimensions. September 11 had the effect of awakening the sleeping giant; future historians will no doubt note that the initial American and Western responses were confused and partial, but began to resolve into focused rhetoric over the ensuing years.

The question "Why do they hate us?" shows a dramatic hole in the public understanding of the enemy and its agenda. The American people, and citizens of other societies of the Free World, had been submitted to a War of Ideas by the international Jihadi propagandists and their allies within the West. On September 11, 2001, the score in the ideological war was 10 to 0, to the advantage of the world jihadists. The U.S. public and its government were woefully unready to understand and react to the assault. This shows the effect of conditioning by the Islamists, their oil-producing allies, and the academic arm on the collective thinking of most Americans at that moment. Still, the al Qaeda terrorist assault on America awakened the collective sense of resistance among officials, legislators, and more importantly, citizens. After dozens of documentaries, hundreds of books, thousands of articles and lectures, and endless press releases, emails, and other forms of intellectual obfuscation, the collective consciousness of the American people was stunned by the planes hitting the towers, and yet decided to survive. Each one of us in America and other democracies experienced the "moment" in that crush of images.

Had the 1990s War of Ideas matured enough, and ideological subversion penetrated deeper and wider in the minds of the public, the first collective response wouldn't have been "Why do they hate us?" but "How bad we are to deserve this?" This psychological reaction is very close to that of the Spanish public to the March 11, 2004, attacks in Madrid. The Spaniards, victimized by both their terrorist enemy and a segment of their intelligentsia and media, collapsed psychologically. The War of Ideas worked on Spain, but it didn't work on America. It was close, however; very close.

THE WAR ON TERROR:
BATTLES OVER DEFINITIONS

In the first hours, days, and weeks after the massacres, a decisive battle of ideas took place in America and worldwide over the definition and explanation of the 9/11 attacks. Average citizens didn't know it occurred precisely because they were conditioned not to. As soon as the buildings in Manhattan were down, and the smoke over the Pentagon and Pennsylvania's crash site had dissipated, the jihadi propaganda machine unleashed its most determined offensive in history. On al Jazeera's powerful airwaves and on the websites of the global jihadists everywhere in America, the West, and around the world, material was churned out to explain the incidents. While most Americans were still struggling with the "Why do they hate us?" question, world jihad was producing the definitions. Amazingly, al Jazeera ran a news item for few hours stating that an unknown group had assumed responsibility for the attacks as retaliation for Hiroshima and Nagasaki. I remember vividly the rapid evolution of the description. In the following few hours, another release spoke of revenge by the American Indians. The next day, as the U.S. government was confirming the possibility of Middle Eastern–related terrorism, thousands of emails sent from U.S. campuses submerged media and student web accounts, introducing another interpretation: "It is a response to American foreign policy." This campaign rapidly widened, and in a few days, from al Jazeera to the Internet, the whole drama was linked to U.S. support for Israel, sanctions on Iraq, and military presence in Arabia. Strangely, these same arguments were used by Osama bin Laden weeks later when he appeared in his first video aired by al Jazeera. This leads to the inescapable conclusion that the ideological battle plan against America and democracies was shaped long ago, honed in academic warfare, and then launched more broadly when 9/11 took place.[8] One cannot help but realize that the "political ammunition" had already been prepared for an opportune moment, but it had to be used earlier than expected because of bin Laden's hasty decision to strike the "bear" before it had completely drifted off to sleep.

AMERICAN AWAKENING

The sum of all Islamists, jihadists, radical left and right, and even rogue regimes all jumped on America, hoping to shatter its capacity to understand the motives of al Qaeda and to resist. The worst fear among the jihadist propagandists before 9/11 was that democracies would suddenly open their eyes and understand who the real enemy was. Had the world jihadists had the capacity to stop bin Laden from striking in 2001, they would have, for their preparatory work wasn't finished yet: America wasn't Europe and Washington wasn't Madrid at the time. The sophisticated anti-American strategists well integrated inside the United States and Europe needed more time to mollify and confuse the public of the most powerful democracy on earth. Independent thinking was still alive in America, and a shock of such magnitude risked reawakening the body. When this in fact happened, the jihadist propaganda machine had no choice but to engage in a third War of Ideas. With the United States awakened, the new goal was to "kill" the American awakening before it deepened, widened, and turned to action.[9]

A strategic concern of the apologists for Jihadism and its derivatives was the exposition of their low-intensity War of Ideas by the striking, naked, and virulent statements made by bin Laden, his spokesperson Abu Ghais, and Zawahiri, and later on by other jihadists around the world, including al Muhajirun of Britain, and eventually, years later, by Iraqi al Qaeda leader Abu Masa'ab al Zarqawi and Iranian president Mahmoud Ahmedinijad. These statements forced men and women to ask more and more questions about what the terrorists were talking about. Hence the apologists and the jihadi propaganda machine had to move fast and act firmly to defuse what was for them the most dangerous part of the War of Ideas: What would happen if Americans and democracies around the world began to ask questions about jihad, Jihadism, the caliphate, *kufr, kuffar, dar el harb, dar el Islam,* and other crucial matters? They might suddenly understand that an ideology is growing inside the Muslim world, one that was previously misexplained within the West, and as a result there would be a crack in the wall. Someone would have to respond to bin Laden's speeches. "What is he talking about?" Americans would ask. "You've told us in the classrooms and in the newsrooms that jihad is a spiritual business only."

The irony of history is that without 9/11, the public would have remained unaware of the "debate," and the propagation of the camouflaged ideology would have remained unchecked. Conversely, 9/11 created a breach in the wall that the jihadists wanted to close, but that was no longer easy, for as soon as it became clear, as of October 7, 2001, that a War on Terror had been declared by the U.S. president—supported by the British prime minister and the Europeans, endorsed by moderate Arab governments, and not opposed by the Russians and Chinese—the Islamists and their radical left- and right-wing allies had to shift their line of attack to slowing the War on Terror, confusing its objectives, driving wedges among its partners, and continuing with their subversive tactics to blur the Western vision. Indeed, the third War of Ideas is far more complex, intense, and dangerous than the second one. Back in the 1990s, the jihadists and their Western advocates had free rein, and few opposed them. All they needed was more time. But after the fall of 2001, when the United States opted for confrontation and resistance, the third War of Ideas became a more balanced one, simply because it now was being fought by two parties, unlike during the 1990s, when America was somnolent.

ESCALATION OF ARGUMENTS

From the fall of 2001 on, conflict escalated over the type of war the United States and other democracies were involved in. On both sides of the Atlantic, the idea of a Global War on Terror (GWOT) was being firmed up by presidents and prime ministers. But on the other side, jihadi media and elites were arguing that this war was illegitimate. The Islamists accused the United States of waging a "War on Islam" (*al harb al Islam*), and the radicals in the West (both extreme left and right) made conflicting and contradicting arguments accusing Washington of waging a political war. The radical left called it a war for oil, but the radical right identified it as a war inspired by the Jewish and Israeli lobby. In the president's January 29, 2002, State of the Union address, the War on Terror was directed against an "axis of evil" comprising Iran, Iraq, and North Korea, along with three main terrorist groups (in addition to al Qaeda): Hamas, Islamic Jihad, and Hezbollah. The U.S.-led War on Terror was gradually moving forward and identifying the enemy, entity by entity. But the public was trailing behind, moving one step at a time, now asking the next question after having failed to find an answer to its first question, "Why?" The new question became, "But who are they?" Amazingly, as the leadership was moving forward in naming regimes and organizations, and as the jihadi-apologist machine was waging a counterwar of confusion, the masses in the middle were moving slowly to grasp the essence of the war.

The psychological guerrilla warfare conducted by the radical Islamists aimed at slowing the identification of the enemy as much as possible. Throughout 2001–2002, the lines of attack concentrated on trying to fool both the Muslim and Western masses. To the Arab and Muslim audiences, some al Jazeera commentators still claimed that those who attacked the Twin Towers weren't even Arab or Muslims, creating confusion in the minds of viewers. But another set of arguments was also released, stating that even if they were Arabs and Muslims, it was the fault of the United States. This last argument remained the official one used by al Jazeera and other global jihadists until 2006. In the West, pro-Islamists and radical (left and right) intellectuals, activists, and academics adopted the al Jazeera argument that the attacks were America's fault. A whole literature produced by American and Western European elites explained the War on Terror as a reaction to U.S. foreign policy. The objective of this thesis was to deflect the attention of the public away from the overwhelming fact that Jihadism is a modern ideology that has existed since the beginning of the twentieth century, inspired by much older doctrines and possessing its own strategies. Were this known by the public living in the democracies, they could win the War of Ideas and thereafter change the course of the War on Terrorism, which in fact is a conflict with Jihadism. All it takes for Americans and other democracies to defeat their foes is to understand who that foe is and what it wants to do. The overwhelming power of the Free World, if well directed politically, economically, diplomatically, and militarily when needed, could reverse the tide against the jihadists and the authoritarians and unleash the power of civil societies in the Greater Middle East, leading to an isolation and marginalization of the radicals.

That equation was fully understood by the jihadists and their allies; it was also absorbed by the dissident democratic forces persecuted by Islamist fascism and authoritarianism in the region and overseas, and increasingly perceived by the partners in the U.S.-led coalition against terrorism. It needed to be explained to the masses in all these democratic countries, however, so that the balance of forces would shift against the jihadists and their axis. Hence the main objectives in the War of Ideas against the U.S.-led coalition were, and remain, to blur the vision of the public, undermine popular support for the efforts in the War on Terror, split the coalition when possible, and destabilize the allies of the coalition, while on another front eliminating the rising tide of Middle Eastern support for the international campaign against terrorism. And in essence, this is what terrorists, ideologues, and their advocates and sympathizers on all continents have been attempting to achieve since 9/11 and the collapse of the Taliban.

AFTER TORA BORA:
THE HISTORIC CHOICES

The more dramatic choice to be made by the international community, the West, and more particularly the United States came after the defeat of the Taliban in Tora Bora in December 2001. The United Nations, the European community, and the other major powers such as Russia and China did not oppose removing the Taliban from Kabul as a regime. The taking down of the regime was licensed as a "legitimate response to 9/11," especially given that the Taliban didn't dissociate themselves from al Qaeda. Only al Jazeera and Islamists worldwide, in addition to a few radical professors at Berkeley and Columbia in the United States, opposed the invasion of Afghanistan. Saddam Hussein, Iran, Syria, and the Sudanese regime blamed the crisis on U.S. arrogance and imperialism before 9/11 but knew that opposition to the Afghan war was futile. The rest of the world was standing firmly with the international campaign to remove the "terrorists" from Kabul. The real question, however, arose immediately after the defeat of the Taliban. The global jihadists expected that the war would stop there, enabling them to mount a counterattack within one or two years. Now that the wall of cover-up had been breached and the public in the West had begun its long process of awakening to Jihadism, and now that bin Laden and his cohorts had blurted out the real message and agenda, it was a priority to escalate the War of Ideas so that a shield would cover the region from future Western action that might lead to regime change. The removal of an Islamist power by a Western force committed to pursuing the terrorists wherever they were hiding left an impact in the region. The American promise to remove regimes that harbored terrorists, enabled terrorism, or were engaged in mass persecution emboldened dissidents and human rights activists, who rushed to seek support from Washington. The U.S. president, in his speech to Congress that year, spoke of a free Middle East, ending decades of neutrality regarding democracy and pluralism. He went as far as exposing the ideology of al Qaeda (without naming "Jihadism" yet) as an oppressor of Jews, Christians, and moderate Muslims. To the authoritarians and jihadists in the region, such statements were too close to shattering the worldview they had carefully constructed over the years. The battles over words, political culture, and history would now rage under unfriendly skies. The debate in Washington shaped the fate of the next step after the removal of the Taliban. Had the War on Terror halted there, and had a mere capture of al Qaeda's leaders ended the conflict and brought back the United States and the international community to September 10, a Third War of Ideas would have receded and the previous one would have resumed. The reasons why a Third Conflict of Ideas existed independent of the fall of the Taliban or the capture of bin Laden were in the speeches delivered by Osama on al Jazeera during the fall of 2001. Had he, or his deputy Abu Ghais, spoken only of local conflicts such as the Arab-Israeli one, there wouldn't have been a Global War on Terror as we know it, but a campaign to eradicate al Qaeda, as was the case before 9/11. But when the leaders of that movement spoke of worldviews and of jihad as a global confrontation with the *kuffar*, they transformed the military objectives from seeking revenge and justice to a war against an international threat. It was the words uttered on al Jazeera, and later on the web, that triggered the Global War on Terror and the Third War of Ideas. The American, and, later on, the international public had "discovered" an ideology and a movement that gave a new, dramatic, and terrifying dimension to 9/11. The masses, regardless of the speeches of their own leaders and the explanations by their own intellectuals, realized that those who were behind the Manhattan massacre had much bigger and more dangerous plans on their minds. The people wanted to know what those minds were projecting into the future.

Many schools of thought clashed over the future of the War on Terror. Following are the main ones:

1. Still operating mainly from their on-campus pockets, the extreme-left and ultra right intellectuals, with specific goals in mind, allied themselves with the radical Islamist activists and shouted against the War on Terror as a concept. Each group for its own reasons—a salad bowl of jihadists, Neo-Marxists (a mix of post-Maoists, surviving Trotskyites, and anarchists), Neo-Nazis, and isolationists—rejected the idea that terrorism was bad or existed.[10]

   They inundated their own enclaves as well as the Internet with many contradictory arguments, one conflicting with another. But gradually, the jihadist operatives on American and Western campuses advanced the most cohesive agenda, dragging behind them those who would constitute the "mercenary army" formed in the midst of the infidels. A hodgepodge of irreconcilable ideologies and militant movements were assembled and led by the Western-based Salafists, and mounted massive opposition to any form of resistance to terrorism. This was one of the ongoing successes of the radical Islamists in the West: to bring radical feminists, extreme environmentalists, Marxists, and Neo-Nazis to fight in one trench against the liberation of women and progressive, free societies in the Middle East. This was a strategic result of the second War of Ideas of the 1990s, when an obstruction of knowledge on campuses reinforced the ignorance of many students who were seeking revolutionary change for domestic reasons. They ended up being manipulated by activists who supported the most oppressive forms of government in the Arab and Muslim world. This "school" rejected all considerations of national security. It produced, for example, surrealistic professors who called for "a million Mogadishus" and claimed al Qaeda as their "savior."[11]

2. The second school of thought, more conservative in its international agenda but situated mostly on the moderate left, and with significant support from the conservatives' isolationist wing, called for an international police operation and cooperation among the world's governments to find the terrorists, specifically al Qaeda, and bring them to justice. This school, including many politicians, academics, and the media, described itself as mainstream and mostly liberal, with some conservative support. Its central thesis was that terrorism is a way for radicals to harm international and national security and should be fought as such. They believed that terrorism and violence are bred in poor socioeconomic conditions. Improve these conditions, and terrorism will vanish, the argument went. This school, which dominated the public and foreign policies of the 1990s, thought that by sending VCRs to Gaza, Hamas would be isolated; by recognizing Hezbollah as a "resistance movement," they would convince it to drop its weapons; and by inviting Taliban scholars to Harvard, they would learn from the Taliban's wisdom, as was about to happen in the summer of 2001. This pragmatic school in world politics recommended dialoguing with jihadi and radical regimes and choosing stability over political change in the Greater Middle East. It was this school that was in charge of international relations during the second War of Ideas and oversaw the crushing defeat of democracies in the West at the hands of terrorism. It also abandoned the democracy movements, dissidents, and minorities—Kurds, Shiia, Sudanese, Lebanese, and women—to their tragic fate under the authoritarians. This school recommended halting the geopolitical offensives in Afghanistan and metamorphosing them into police campaigns.[12] It advanced many sound ideas, such as creating the largest coalitions possible against the terrorists, but didn't clarify its strategic grounds—other than "getting the bad guys,"

knowing that "bad" as a concept is relative in each country and under different regimes.

3. A third school was formed of several streams coming together from different political backgrounds: in the majority, those famously (or infamously, to the jihadists) called neoconservatives, generally coming from conservative circles but breaking with the old isolationist trends; those who came from the left and were identified as neoliberals but agreed with the neoconservatives on the War on Terror; and to a much lesser degree, those who had participated in human rights activism against the Soviet Union, flanked by the Middle Eastern dissidents against Jihadism. This school, while it advocated the relentless pursuit of the terrorists as prescribed by the second school, advanced further the theory of freedom versus terrorism and sought victory in the War on Terror via spreading democracy in the areas that were breeding radical ideologies. This new set of doctrines was influenced by a number of factors and developments. First was the successful experiment in democracy after the collapse of the Soviet Union, as the masses of Eastern Europe showed the world that oppressed people weren't necessarily represented by the dominant ideological statements made by elites and regimes. The comparison was made with the Greater Middle East when dissidents from the region, in their writings, statements, and testimony to Congress, informed legislators and American leaders that "civil societies" under oppression were ready to move against the oppressors. Second was a conviction that the region's peoples were not different from other cultures, in that as soon as freedom reached them, they would reach out to it. This school became attractive to many Americans, despite the dominance of the second school, simply because it proposed a new vision of the world after 9/11 and a path to follow. The second school was more pragmatic and basically said, "We can't and won't do much to change the world. We will just find the troublemakers when they come after us." But the public, horrified at the sight of the cataclysmic events in New York, wasn't satisfied with the wait-and-see attitude. Mothers wanted a real protection of the "home." Besides, when al Qaeda declared during the fall of 2001 that "four million Americans should die,"[13] even as the ashes of Ground Zero were still warm, a silent majority shifted to the "do-something-about-it"

school. The thesis of "resistance to terrorism, wherever it is" attracted a large segment of the Christian public, as argued by pollsters on the left, but only because a large majority of Americans happen to be of a Christian affiliation. A large segment of the Jewish community supported this attitude as well, and logically so, because of the strident threats made against all Jews by the jihadists. In short, as a significant public supported the forward strategy advanced by this school (itself well implanted in the administration and Congress), the next choice after Afghanistan was the Iraq option, a path that led to the second geopolitical conflict in the GWOT and inflamed the War of Ideas to its highest levels.

WAR OF IDEAS IN THE COURTS

The debate about the next stage in the War of Ideas leaked into the most sensitive segment of government: the court system. At the onset, the first War of Ideas in the 1990s had damaged the capacity of the public and the educational establishment to recognize the history, ideology, and strategies of America's enemies. As indicated earlier, graduates from Middle East studies, political science, and history classrooms were not given a solid and accurate knowledge of the Greater Middle East and its main conflicts, including the rise of Islamic fundamentalism and its aims. Many of these graduates wound up in law schools and later in the courts, working as lawyers, prosecutors, and judges. And facing them were other graduates from high schools or colleges who occupied the jury benches. It was in this setting that terrorism had to be addressed. Most players in American and European courts (with the exception of the suspects and some of their defense lawyers) didn't know much about the jihadists. If they hadn't been educated about Jihadism in school, or had been badly educated about it, they would not necessarily understand its analysis inside the courtroom. And that's how the global jihadists assisted in defeating many U.S. and European prosecutions in the years after 9/11. American law enforcement, with good instincts, would apprehend suspects—albeit in many cases with excesses of zeal and unfairness—and bring them to justice. And because the War on Terror in its early stages wasn't directed at a movement and an ideology by the administration and Congress, the prosecution, court, and juries had to understand these as simple criminal cases and not as enemy acts. Inside the U.S. and European courts, there was no consideration of a War on Terror. No laws prescribed the judges to regard it as such, and hence they dealt with such cases as violent crimes or incitements to them. And this is where the confrontation with the jihadists failed. Because Jihadism was an ongoing operation to prepare for the final stage, that is, the actual terror strike, 90 percent of its war preparations were below the level of criminality, including spreading the ideology that prescribes killing and violence. And because the main players, other than the indicted terrorists, weren't immersed in the ideology of terror, here entered the "experts."

Both sides, of course, had their own. Numerically, it was 1,000 to 20 or so. The Middle East studies programs, mostly funded by the Wahabis, had graduated hundreds of "specialists" under the leading masters in the field, themselves mostly sympathetic to the funding sources of their research and projects. Hence the overwhelming majority of academic expertise in the field of Islamic and Middle East studies wasn't in the middle of the debate, but at its pro-jihadi end. It would have been difficult to extract from most "specialists" a statement explaining that the jihadists are actually an ideological movement aiming at creating a world caliphate, or that the Khumeinists hope to build a regional nuclear power with jihadi world visions. The majority of experts, and all of those hired by the defense, obviously tilted toward covering up the ideology as a basis for indicting the suspects in alleged terror acts. It all boiled down to the "experts' opinion," and the balance was heavily on the side of the detainees. Unlike the cases of Soviet agents, Neo-Nazis, white supremacists, or black separatists, all radicals and some with foreign ties, the jihadists did not fall into a recognizable terror or criminal category. And that was because the 1990s War of Ideas had done a good job of obliterating the ideological identity of Jihadism. Hence juries after 2001, as well as judges, weren't able to see the "big picture." There was either a smoking gun or nothing. But given that the artillery the jihadists had put together was ideological, it wasn't visible in court. The context of why the terrorists were perpetrating their acts was interpreted by the defense lawyers as relating to mishaps in their personal lives, ignoring the power of indoctrination. Their experts, when the evidence of Jihadism was overwhelming, sanitized the ideology as "mere spiritual experience." Watching the match between defense and prosecution experts, citizens deprived of a good education on the subject were lost as they instinctively tried to determine the most balanced and fair sentence. Thus between 2002 and 2006, as a result of a lack of education in the 1990s, America's courts weren't able to sentence jihadist activities as such, even though Congress, the president, and both parties had condemned what they described as an "ideology of hate." One of the most serious consequences was to encourage more jihadists to move forward, because if the courts could not recognize the root cause of the action, they couldn't impose effective deterrents and the activity could spread wider without fear of proper prosecution.

If the legislative branch doesn't develop a new and comprehensive body of definitions so that courts can swiftly face this challenge, democracies will be defeated by Jihadism even in their most sacrosanct area: justice. The rule of law, a defining feature of democracy—and one that is so lacking in the radical Islamist and authoritarian states—will simply be unable to identify and prosecute the threat. In fact, defense lawyers, in order to win their cases, have gone to the extreme of arguing that Jihadism is not terrorism. Instead, what their new mission should be is to establish that their clients are not jihadists, not that Jihadism is fine. But while the West was struggling with its definitions, the battle of words was escalating further in the Arab world.

⊶⇒　⇐⊷

The third War of Ideas, triggered by the attacks of September 11, 2001, is about shaping the future perception of the parties to the War on Terror: democracies attempting to bring freedom and an alternative way of thinking to oppressed societies in the Greater Middle East and beyond versus jihadi forces and pressure groups trying to once again blur the democracies' vision of the conflict in order to keep the light of democracy from reaching Arab and Muslim societies.

CHAPTER ELEVEN

THE WAR ON LEARNING

IN WAR, IF YOU ARE ABLE TO DEFINE HOW YOUR ENEMY PERCEIVES you and acts toward you, you have virtually won. This is an important dimension of the War of Ideas. The jihadi world alliance is waging a two-front campaign: one objective is to control the Arab and Muslim world's perception of international affairs, particularly the War on Terror, while the other is to influence the Western public's view of events and realities in the Arab and Muslim world. This global strategy uses both madrassas in the East and colleges in the West. It also depends on the firepower of Arabic language media and friendly voices within the international press. For their part, the U.S.-led efforts to win the "war for the hearts and minds of Arabs and Muslims" are founded on the hope that civil societies will naturally evolve in line with the conceptions of social development shared by democracies. In fact, the War of Ideas is about the learning process, and more particularly, who controls it: whichever party can influence it can shift the tide of the current confrontation.

RESHAPING MINDS:
THE ARAB AND MUSLIM WORLD

"Al Harb ala ma yusamma bil Irhab": with this single slogan, which means literally "The war against what is called terrorism," Al Jazeera has influenced the Arab world and its diaspora to devastating effect, and much to the advantage of the jihadi bloc. No Western, American, or even Middle Eastern network has been able to counterbalance this Qatari-funded channel. Manned by skilled BBC-trained technicians and broadcasters, and guided intellectually and ideologically by Muslim Brotherhood cadres, Islamist TV was able single-handedly to turn the tide of the propaganda confrontation between

the U.S.-led campaign against terrorism and the militant regimes and organizations that oppose the West. Millions of viewers in the Arab world form their opinions based on the station's 24-hour programming, featuring political news reports "explaining" the world as it evolves by the hour, as well as heavy "indoctrination" shows. To millions of followers, there is no such thing as the War on Terrorism, because al Jazeera's political culture has transformed it into an "invention of America, Israel, and their agents."[1] The region is at the mercy of al Jazeera and its ideological bias; al Jazeera has won several rounds over the shy attempts by the United States to readjust the image.

The psychological or propaganda warfare delivered by al Jazeera is far superior to the programming of the former rigid state-run TV networks. Although the Qatari regime fully funds al Jazeera and endorses its messages (while hosting one of the largest U.S. military installations in the region), the channel is a power unto itself. Often, American foreign policy spokespersons have struggled to convey their messages to Arab audiences, only to have the Arabic-speaking commentators rip them apart. Years after 2001, after millions of minds had been influenced by al Jazeera, an Arab competition among al Arabiya, al Sharqiya, LBCI, al Mustaqbal, Abu Dhabi, and many other satellite networks emerged. In February 2004, the U.S.-funded al Hurra TV was established to compete with what many had dubbed "Jihad TV." It will be a while before balance is achieved between the two media lines in the region. Meanwhile, al Jazeera's Islamist audience is large and faithful. The prodemocracy public in the region is growing slowly, but none of the alternatives has gained the kind of power that al Jazeera wields over its own constituency.

The third War of Ideas, ignited by 9/11, hasn't altered the rapid growth of madrassas in the region, where future generations of jihadis are being molded. Despite the terror incidents inside Saudi Arabia and the clashes with al Qaeda, and even as the United States asked Riyadh to shut down its own madrassa and stop funding to these Qu'ranic schools around the region (and even within the United States), the Wahabi kingdom did not stop from spreading Wahabism. In reality, without reforms within the government and society, it is unlikely that the state or the emirs will suspend their funding to madrassas around the world, for the simple reason that the regime itself is Wahabi—even if the government wishes to adhere to international norms. The *rissala* (mission) of spreading the religion merges with the endorsement of the form of Islam the regime is based on; generations of young people are graduating from these Salafi-controlled ideological schools. The end result is that Wahabism produces the pupils, and al Jazeera and the Brotherhood harvest them. Immersed in the Wahabi indoctrination, youth also fall under the propaganda influence of Islamist media, such as websites and, at the top of the jihadi pyramid, al Jazeera itself. Already indoctrinated, graduates of the madrassas are further pounded by ideological slogans "explaining" the world—such as *al harbu ala Islam* (the War on Islam). Far from moderating, the most influential of the media available in the region is increasing its mobilization against the West.

Moderate media do exist, however, and have a role in balancing the radicals. Dailies such as *al Rai al Aam* in Jordan and *al Siyassa* in Kuwait, as well as others in Morocco, Egypt, and the Gulf, do criticize the radical trends. Even Saudi newspapers close to the government attempt to reduce the extremism of the ultra-Salafists. But these efforts are countered by the state-supported press in Iran, Syria, Sudan, Iraq (before 2003), and the Islamist media across the board. But with the fall of Saddam Hussein, Iraq has witnessed a media revolution, with the mushrooming of more than 120 newspapers and publications, and new TV and radio stations—most of which, interestingly, are antiterrorist. From Baghdad, one sees today a surge of alternative voices to Salafism and Khumeinism, even though the Khumeinists have managed to expand their media too. More centrist networks have also emerged in the region's Sunni milieu, such as the Gulf-based, Saudi-funded al Arabiya and the Lebanese al Mustaqbal TV. The once influential Lebanese Christian TV, LBC, remains docile toward the radicals because of the current geopolitics of Lebanon, where at opposite ends of the spectrum are, on the one hand, the very extreme and anti-Semitic al Manar TV of Hezbollah,[2] and on the other the most liberal website of the Arab world, the London-based elaph.com.

The Battles of Words

In the battle to gain control of the so-called Arab street, the jihadi media move from *Qadiya* to *Qadiya* (cause to cause). These "hot issues" feed the machine and usually begin their road on one of al Jazeera's shows or an Islamist website. From there they grow like a snowball, newscast after newscast, followed by press releases showered from the four corners of the globe. The message is stoked and reheated by on-air commentators and ideologues to such an extent that it would burn any moderate who tried to get close to it, let alone quell it. The jihadi *Qadiya* usually vanishes when a new *Qadiya* emerges. The chain of emotional volcanoes cooked up in the "jihadi kitchen" since 2001 looks more like a series of carefully staged psychological operations than the natural reactions people in the West imagined. The invention of each issue is remarkably clear and astoundingly controlled. Ironically, a documentary produced to criticize Western media for their performance during the War on Terror, *Control Room*, applies almost perfectly to the al Jazeera spin room and its stage managing of the propaganda war.

CRUSADING. One powerful example was the campaign to criticize President Bush's use of the term "crusade." He had said enthusiastically, after having declared the principles of the War on Terror and vowed to fight extremism and support moderates around the world, that this would be our "crusade." Instantly, al Jazeera and the Islamist coalition brewed up the *Qadiya*, accusing Bush of unleashing a Christian crusade against Islam. Evidently, there is an ocean of difference between the sociological use of the term "crusade" by Bush (or any other U.S. president or leader) and the deeply loaded meaning of *Hamla Salibiya* in Arabic, which is usually used to refer to the historic Crusades of the Middle Ages. The irony here is that while in the West, and particularly in Anglo-Saxon cultures, the term has evolved to express benign or more symbolic meanings, in Arabic, the term—if translated by Islamists with a jihadi "loading" and in a context of ideological mobilization—still means "holy war" as well. It would have been odd for a Western leader to declare a "real" crusade, almost 1,000 years after the last one ended, 400 years after the Enlightenment, and 200 years after the American and French secular revolutions. Furthermore, the off-the-cuff remark was made as Bush was rushing away from a press conference where he had outlined in detail what the War on Terrorism was and how it was in conformity with international law. But the "jihadi kitchen" disregarded the whole context (although it has enough scholars trained in the West) and went in for the kill.

Amazingly, intellectuals and scholars in North America and Europe, mostly apologists for Jihadism or highly partisan participants in domestic politics, would echo and amplify such messages, thereby aiding the other camp in its War of Ideas. Thus the al Jazeera *Qadiya* becomes a Western "political scandal," which academic and media elites seize upon and use at will in domestic partisan warfare. A whole literature has developed, for example, on the so-called American and European breach of what are deemed "Muslim sensitivities." As I will mention later, the Danish Cartoons, the Guantanamo Qu'ran issue, the French scarf affair, etc. will begin as incidents and end up as "manufactured" global crises. The War of Ideas launched by the jihadists has scored a second massive victory by forcing the mainstream establishment in the West to bow to these so-called "sensitivities," which do not actually arise from the Muslim masses but are manufactured by the jihadi propagandists. The proof is the fact that the Islamist militants and their Western apologists were never active on behalf of the sensitivities of Muslims in the Arab and Muslim world when they were under oppression by fascists and authoritarian forces. Where were the jihadi apologists, for example, when tens of thousands of Muslims in Algeria were savagely slaughtered by the Salafists during the 1990s and later? Where were they when genocide was perpetrated against the black Africans in Darfur? Or when thousands of Shiite and Kurdish Muslims were massacred by Saddam Hussein, not to mention when tens of thousands of other Muslims of all communities were persecuted or suppressed in Iran, Pakistan, and Lebanon? These examples show that the idea of "sensitivities" developed by apologists in the West is another form of psychological warfare against the democracies' sensitivities when it comes to their own citizens. But jihadists understand very well how democratic cultures work and how they protect their communities from physical and moral harm; hence they have inserted their ideology inside the West by camouflaging it as an issue of religious freedom and tolerance. Thus liberal democracies, themselves sensitive to the "sensitivities" of all communities, backed off from what could have been seen as moral aggression against Muslim communities. A weakness was exploited by the Islamists and their allies within the West, who gagged debate and granted exclusive rights to the jihadists to determine what is "sensitive" in Muslim culture.

The transformation of words into bullets has multiple dimensions. Historical memory can be played upon to incite emotional reactions. For example, Jews are as resentful of the Crusades as Muslims. Certain images and words evoke tragic episodes in Jewish-Christian history, particularly regarding the Jerusalem massacres and the Spanish Inquisition: many Jews died under religious persecution and under the banner of the cross. But modern Jewish communities that have lived in the West for centuries and been part of its evolving culture understand the contemporary and cultural use of the term "crusade." To American, European, and Australian Jews, for example, hearing non-Jewish leaders calling for a "crusade against drugs" isn't alarming. Christians in the Muslim world are sensitive to the word *kafir* because of its historic relation to centuries of oppression and persecution under the caliphates. Even today, as jihadists reuse the term in a real political sense, non-Muslim communities around the Arab and Muslim world—including Jews, Christians, Hindus, and Bahá'is—fear the return of sectarian massacres. But again, even Arab-speaking non-Muslims use terms such as *kufr* or even *jihad* sociologically, but stripped of their original theological sense. Hence the impact of words depends on their context and the ideological loading they are given.

After centuries of reform, reformation, and secularism, the use of the phrase "to crusade for" something in Western languages does not entail a revival of disturbing, intolerant ideologies of the distant past; a "crusade" against drugs, poverty, or injustice does not impinge on anyone's "sensitivities." But on the other hand, when Islamists today call for jihad, they are inciting theologically motivated war—especially when spokespersons of al Qaeda and other combat Salafists add that jihad is against "*kuffars*, Christians, and Jews." In this case, it is inescapably filled with historical meaning, even though most Muslim governments of the twenty-first century do not use the term anymore. But the jihadists, who see the world as it was in the Middle Ages, react to Western and international policies as if they were still an expression of the attitudes and conflicts of ancient times. One can detect the hypocrisy of the jihadist claim that the term "crusade" offends their sensibilities, when their use of "jihad" is explicitly a reactionary and totalitarian concept. The other major point one can see is that they play on Western guilt about errors of the past to muzzle criticism of their own agenda—jihad—which is openly a form of violent discrimination that the West has rejected.

SPREADING DEMOCRACY. Another highly publicized phrase in the war of words has been "spreading democracy in the Arab and Muslim world." Used often by U.S. leaders to explain the ultimate objective of the War on Terrorism, it was criticized by Islamists worldwide and their allies within the West, right- and left-wing alike. The jihadi campaign against the so-called "spread of democracy" builds on the argument that Arabs and Muslims reject the imposition of Western values and belief systems on other civilizations, and thus

U.S.- led international efforts to support democracies and organize elections are condemned as a form of neocolonialism. The critics went so far as to dismiss elections in Afghanistan and Iraq as masquerades, pitting themselves against the popular majorities of the new emerging democracies in the region. It may be correct that one cannot "spread" democracy from the outside, as one cannot force democracy on people who do not want it. The critics' caricature of this point is the image of soldiers forcing citizens with bayonets to go to the voting booths. But was that actually the case in the Middle East? Obviously not. First of all, the critics cannot claim that native Arab and Middle Eastern peoples are inherently opposed to democracy. This assertion is racist, as it implies that although other ethnic and linguistic groups can embrace democracy, Middle Easterners cannot. And in fact, the assertion that Arabs and Muslims will always reject democratization has been proven wrong on many occasions. When fascist and radical forces are kept at bay, as was the case in Afghanistan and Iraq, millions voted; and when repressive occupation was subjected to international pressure, millions took to the streets in Beirut. In Tehran, students are choosing to grasp at fragments of liberties on campuses or on the Internet at every occasion. Thus the U.S.-led call for the spread of democracy is not against the nature or will of the region's people, as is claimed by commentators on al Jazeera and prominent professors on Ivy League campuses.

A second astounding argument in this battle of words is the fact that jihadists and apologists often support the claims for democratization and liberalization in Arab and Muslim countries only if the claimants are Islamists and Pan-Arabists. For example, the critics often attack the Mubarak regime for obstructing the advance of the Muslim Brotherhood to power but reject similar demands by the Coptic Christian community and liberal Muslim Egyptians. The Copts, with a population of 14 million inside Egypt, are represented by 4 appointed legislators in a parliament of 400, yet the Islamists and their Western apologists do not criticize this underrepresentation. And when liberal writers in Egypt, such as human rights leader Saad Eddine Ibrahim and feminist activist Nawal El Saadawi, are persecuted by both the regime and Islamists, the so-called critics of "spreading democracy" remain silent. Democracy is acceptable to allow Islamists to gain power, but not when prodemocracy forces are struggling for pluralism. Hamas's victory in the Palestinian election in 2006 is a model for democracy, Islamist-style, but obviously the same does not go for the victory by millions of Iraqis

against Saddam Hussein and al Qaeda. These and other similar examples indicate that the critics of "spreading democracy" are mostly politically motivated, rather than showing real interest in furthering freedom for the masses
in the region. In American political thought, the Founding Fathers worried
about the "tyranny of the majority." The jihadist model seems to be to support democracy in places where they feel they can take a majority of seats
(like Hamas), so that they can then use this democratic "mandate" to tyran-
nize the rest of the population.

A third argument in this debate, and probably the most important, is the
will of the masses. For decades, the peoples of the region have been submitted to oppressive regimes and fascist ideologies. There has been almost no
space between authoritarianism and fundamentalism for civil societies. Unlike in Latin America or Eastern Europe, where societies had been exposed
to democratic culture for decades before losing it to either military or communist regimes, the Middle Eastern societies were ruled by empires and sultans before they were transformed into dictatorships and closed political
cultures. Ironically, and with the exception of Kemalist Turkey and Israel,
the few democratic practices and institutions allowed in Arab countries in
the mid-1920s were established by the European mandates: Egypt, Jordan,
Iraq, Syria, Lebanon, Morocco, Kuwait, and others. Within a few decades
after European withdrawal, most of the former mandates and colonies, although sovereign, reverted to authoritarian regimes in various forms, including some with genocidal practices, as in Iraq and Sudan. The regional
intelligentsia faced a fundamental crisis as regimes crushed the liberal element in the elite and the rest of the establishment turned to serve the interests of Baathism, Nasserism, Marxism-Leninism, or Islamism. By the end of
the Cold War, the liberal intellectuals in the Arab world and Iran were experiencing the apex of persecution. And after 9/11, when the West turned to
extend support to them, they weren't free to meet the offer halfway. The
"internal colonialism" in the region was and remains one of the most powerful tools of antidemocracy.

A fourth argument employed by the jihadists and Western apologists
is about the result of elections. They argue that the West encourages
democracy, but when Islamists win these elections, the U.S.-led coalition
criticizes the results, giving the examples of Muslim Brotherhood in
Egypt, the Hamas victory in Palestine, and Hezbollah's presence in the
Lebanese Parliament. Here again, the War of Ideas waged by the jihadists

selects what is needed for their slogans, as has been the practice of totalitarians for decades in the Soviet Bloc and Latin America. For example, the issue with the Muslim Brotherhood is not their wins in the legislative assembly—just the opposite. If Islamists would abandon Jihadism and opt for democratic political culture, the last obstruction to pluralism in the region would fall, opening its future to much better prospects. The issue with the *Ikhwan* (Brotherhood) is their antidemocracy and antipluralist agenda. Using the democratic system to disintegrate democracy is the problem. As was the case with the Front de Salut Islamique of Algeria in 1991, the issue wasn't their electoral victory, but their plan to dismantle the electoral process and replace it with a theological emirate. A parallel can be drawn with the National Socialists in Germany, who, after securing one electoral victory in the Bundestag, transformed the Weimar Republic into a genocidal Third Reich. The same was true of Mussolini's Fascists, who, from one victory in the Parliament, created a militia-controlled regime. The "democratic" installment of Nazis and Fascists in Europe, and the transformation of Germany and Italy into armed and expansionist regimes, led to the horrors of World War II. Islamist electoral victories, without reform in their ideological agendas, will ineluctably lead to the establishment of exclusionist Islamist states, unleashing jihadi war in the region. The electoral victory of Hamas in Palestine isn't the issue; its jihadi agenda is. The fact that Hezbollah obtained seats in the Lebanese Parliament isn't the concern, but rather its ideology and strategic support by Iran's oppressive regime.

Hence the real meaning of "spreading democracy" is not to send tanks to push voters to the ballot box, as the antidemocracy forces would have us believe; rather, it is the goal of offering assistance to oppressed civil societies for them to achieve democratization, human and civil rights, and freedoms. The international community can and should offer the necessary support for people to obtain freedoms, as was the case with Latin America, South Africa, and Eastern Europe. The Greater Middle East shouldn't be an exception, regardless of the claims made by ideologues in the Arab world and Iran and the apologist academics in the West. The people of the region have shown clearly what their aspirations really are, from Afghani women to Iraqi citizens to the youth of the Cedar Revolution in Beirut. The dozens of democracy websites and the hundreds of weblogs emerging from the borders of India to the Atlantic speak for themselves.

SHAPING THE MINDS OF THE WEST:
THE WAR ON LEARNING

The battle of words waged in the Arab Muslim world by the jihadists aims to maintain a state of enmity toward the *kuffar*, or infidels. In the West, the battle of ideas blurs the minds of the public so that it can't identify the threat and understand the agenda of the authoritarians, Islamists, and other antidemocracy ideologues. A 20-year observation of the Western "battlefield" shows two main trends: an effort to diminish the historical understanding of Jihadism and a campaign to deflect public attention from the modern threat of the jihadists. The ultimate goal is to paralyze the Western response to its enemies, particularly if that means reaching out to Muslim moderates and dissidents. By disrupting an alliance between democracies and democracy movements in the Greater Middle East, jihadi forces gain time to consolidate their power within the region and make inroads against the West. This explains why Arab and Muslim communities within the West are targeted and subjected to ideological penetration.

Since the 9/11 terrorist attacks, the assault against the Western mind has taken several shapes and forms. The "battles" have been raging in politics, education, media, arts, and other fields, but always between two main camps. Some have argued that the two camps are simply the left wing and the right wing, liberals and conservatives. The anti-Western political forces have attempted to blame the War on Terror on what they describe as "the Christian right wing and Zionists."[3] In fact, this charge not only is untrue, but also is a ruse to distance mainstream thinking from the global coalition against terrorism. The real fear in the ranks of the global jihadis and their allies in the West is that the public will distance itself itself from the formerly dominant elites, who are used to wielding influence over the masses' thinking. When terror attacks took place before 9/11 or wars erupted in the Middle East, the intelligentsia in general (with the oil-influenced academics at its center) had the upper hand in shaping the story. They used to explain that these things were happening because of the West, particularly America. But since 9/11, the U.S. public and those of other democracies have lost some of their blind trust in the intellectual elite. "They've alleged that jihad is a form of a spiritual yoga," keep repeating ordinary citizens in forums and chat rooms. "But the jihad that kills by the thousands, beheads civilians, and promotes world violence is not a spiritual yoga," they add. "Even if there could be such theoretical jihad, we don't see it, and certainly we don't see its promoters defeating the terrorists." The debate on jihadi terrorism is not merged anymore with the debate on social and economic questions. It has become glaringly evident over the years that the radical Islamists are far more antiliberal than any conservatives in any religion. The jihadists' first and most hated ideological enemies are feminists, Marxists, liberal thinkers, gays, socialists, and other parallel intellectual trends. Hence the Islamist tacticians in the West prefer to hide within the general progressive mainstream to obtain political cover, but this maneuver seems to no longer fool the masses, whose deep instincts seem to have become sharper.

The two camps in the battle for Western minds are the one that is opposing Jihadism and its derivatives and the one that is espousing its agenda. On the one side, a rising smaller intelligentsia that understands the threat is attempting to educate and mobilize both the public and governments. On the other side, the larger traditional intellectual elite is still in control of mainstream media and academia, mounting a rear-guard battle and clinging to its golden past. The newer, smaller group has its writers, analysts, and leaders, on the right and on the left; the older, pre-9/11 elite remains entrenched at the *New York Times, The Atlantic Monthly, Le Monde,* the *Guardian,* PBS, BBC, and TF1. The jihadists take advantage of this raging battle, using the precious time offered to accelerate their penetration of communities until it reaches urban guerrilla status in the future. The one overarching question is this: Is one of the two camps in the West aware of the penetration by the jihadists, which the jihadists themselves have enabled by preventing knowledge from flowing to the public? The answer is generally no. The War of Ideas within the West is fought mostly by proxies, who are unaware of their lack of knowledge. The large hub of intellectuals who serve as a shield to the jihadi machine are not necessarily part of it or acting in bad faith; rather, they are acting based on miseducation. Only the actual jihadists and their direct allies have a conscious strategy. Pro-Islamist lobby groups know the stakes involved in their action; some of their cadres have even been caught by the justice system for involvement in direct terrorist acts. This is unusual, but it has occurred.

The two main camps in this third and most powerful War of Ideas, which began in 2001, have been and still are vying for the collective conscience and awareness of the Western mind. One camp attempts desperately to delay the educational process, while the other tries fiercely to bring knowledge to the public.[4] The stakes are crucially high, as a fully informed and educated Western public would change the course of history by enabling the societies under the remaining authoritarian and jihadist regimes and organizations to rise and defeat the antidemocratic forces from the inside.

Academia's War of Ideas

In the West, the central battlefields over the perception of the world remain academic and educational. As detailed earlier, at least three generations of graduates of oil-funded programs have been launched into the national market, and thereby into the media, government, and arts. Even if new waves of petrodollars were stopped today, the funding over the last two decades has created a self-sustaining entity in Western, and particularly American, educational institutions. The penetration is too deep to be addressed in one generation. Three generations of scholars, researchers, and teachers have consolidated their positions, programs, and influence in about a thousand institutions. Even as the war with Jihadism is raging in the real world, and America is facing off with the most dangerous enemy infiltration it has ever known, the bulk of its students are being educated today by an elite that refuses to teach the real history and politics of the jihadists.[5] Post-9/11 politics and elections, regardless of the winners, will not affect this greater cultural crisis. Unless an intellectual revolution takes place and academic reform follows, it is unlikely that the United States will produce the talents needed for the current and future conflicts of ideas. Only a growing minority is competing with the traditional Middle East studies establishment, trying to shed light into the "black holes" in teaching and research programs. Eventually, administrative and parental leadership will push for such a reform, which is already happening in small part through the establishment of parallel departments not impacted by the Wahabists, such as security, counterterrorism, human rights, and new Middle East studies.[6] But the academic battlefield is still an open one, with no dramatic shift yet in view. This is the reality in the United States, Canada, Australia, and New Zealand, but it is much worse in European democracies. Academic institutions in Great Britain, France, Scandinavia, the Benelux, Spain, Germany, and Italy, to name the most important, are today what U.S. institutions could become in a few years: subjected to severe pressure by lobbies to corrupt Middle East studies, raising the profile of the jihadist agenda and its oil influence, suppressing struggling democratic movements in the Arab and Muslim world, and keeping the larger public uninformed.

The Battles in the Arts and Hollywood

Parallel to academia are the arts: literature, fine arts, television, and above all, cinema. In the Greater Middle East, the confrontation in the arts is raging and ever-expanding. The jihadists' agenda has a noticeable advantage: from al Jazeera to Hezbollah's al Manar, the Islamists have obtained the lead in the scope and content of their material. Their cultural machine influences tens of millions of adherents to their ideology, and without a counterbalance. Assuming that al Jazeera is financed by the Qatari regime and al Manar by Tehran's regime, other state-supported networks such as al Arabiya and Abu Dhabi, although more moderate, are also under pressure from the region's dominant ideologies. Of late, al Iraqiya in Baghdad, flanked by the U.S.-funded al Hurra, are struggling to claim some segments of the Arab audience, but it is an uphill battle. Jihadism and Pan-Arabism still dominate the arts and culture of the region, but not exclusively anymore. The democratic voice in the arts and culture is growing at a rapid pace. The cultural battle in the Arab and Muslim world, however, will depend largely on its parallel within the West. The trends developed across the oceans in Europe and particularly North America will either help or weaken the two competing currents in the Greater Middle East. For it is a world reality that whoever influences Hollywood can impact minds around the world. Hollywood is one of the most important players in the universal production of images and ideas.

Because American movies are watched from Seattle to Dacca, their message can make a huge difference psychologically on hundreds of millions of people. And Hollywood producers, writers, directors, and actors are, knowingly or not, shaping how we think about the future of the War on Terrorism. In this regard, American cinema (not to mention that of the Europeans) has been affected greatly by the academic and intellectual imbalance since the 1980s. Although Islamist lobbies have consistently accused Hollywood of distorting the image of Arabs, Muslims, and their causes, the reality is just the opposite.[7]

In fact, American visual art has engaged in cultural stereotyping since its inception but has rapidly evolved into integrationism. Indeed, the images of all nonwhite Anglo-Americans were painted ethnocentrically through the 1970s. It is not a secret that Native Americans, Hispanics, blacks, Eastern Europeans, Mediterraneans, Asians, Arabs, and others have all been portrayed in ways that reflected the ethnic relations and perceptions of American society at the time, and these were often negative. These portrayals were very visibly corrected with the evolution of America's race relations. Actually, Hollywood, one must admit, has been ahead of all other sectors in advocating integration and promotion of race relations. The anti-Semitic argument that the "Jewish element" inside Hollywood has been systematic in altering the image of Arabs and Muslims in movies can be proven wrong.[8] If anything, however, Hollywood, especially since the late 1980s, has clearly neglected the representation of the causes of minorities, women, youth, and liberals from the Arab world and Iran. Although many movies have covered the Arab-Israeli conflict, almost nowhere could one find prior to 9/11 movies about Sudan's genocide, slavery, and Darfur; the Kurds; Iranian dissidents; the Berbers' cultural oppression; Syrian occupation of Lebanon; Coptic religious persecution; and so on. In the 1980s, a couple of movies about the fate of women under Islamist regimes were made: *The Death of a Princess*, portraying female conditions in Saudi Arabia, and *Not without My Daughter*, describing foreign women's status in Iran. But as of the 1990s, the scissors of the Wahabi lobby cut off any other attempt, even at the height of the Taliban's oppression of women. Not to have one Hollywood movie tackling the genocide of women in Afghanistan would seem abnormal in view of the many other productions during that same decade on women's subjects related to other regions. Movies on the ethnic cleansing in Yugoslavia were produced in the 1990s, but not one story about the greater genocide against black Africans in Sudan. There were many stories on European dissidents against the Soviets, Latin American freedom fighters against military regimes, and the harassment of Muslims in the West (with the movie *The Siege*, 1998), but nothing on the many dissidents inside the Arab and Muslim world against Jihadism and authoritarian regimes. And regarding the road to 9/11, Hollywood in the 1990s released a number of terrorism-related movies, some hinting at jihadi terrorism, but only as a comedy plot line or unrelated to the real context, as in *True Lies* (1994).

When one looks into the reasons behind the blocking of Jihadism-related productions, one finds, perhaps not surprisingly, the influence of the Wahabi lobby and its various pressure groups. Thorough research would establish that the American cinema industry was besieged systematically so that it would not produce movies dealing with (at least) two subjects: human rights under oil-producing and authoritarian regimes, and Jihadism as an ideology and movement. The pressures applied were financial, exercised by multinational interests connected to the oil industry, and also ideological, by the Islamist lobbies within the United States, who equated any movie criticizing human rights under Islamist states in the region with an attack against the American Muslim community.[9] The Saudi pressure to prevent the movie *Death of a Princess* from being aired in the 1980s is one of many examples. Thus if a story related the saga of black Africans as slaves taken by the Islamist militia in Sudan, pro-jihadi groups in the United States would move to attack the company on the grounds of "insulting" an Islamist state, and therefore the feelings of the Muslim minority in America.[10] And with the very slight expertise Hollywood had on the issue, which only reflected the ignorance and systematic deprivation of information the whole country was experiencing, the coup would be successful—and in fact, it was successful throughout the 1990s and on until September 11, 2001. With hindsight, though, we might ask why not a single movie was made on the Taliban, Osama bin Laden, his fatwas, the first attacks against the Twin Towers in 1993, the attacks against the U.S. embassies in 1998, and so on. Nothing on the jihadi ideology paralleled the many productions on Communism, Yugoslav ethnic extremism, and the continuing Russian "threat," even years after the end of the Cold War.[11]

Since 9/11, one would have expected a revolution in Hollywood to address the revolutionary shift in national security and the War on Terror. Stunningly, it took this powerful industry half a decade before it produced *United 93* and finally *World Trade Center*. Instead of there being a rush to produce monumental movies with a Spielbergian scope on the tragedy of the century, Cold War–style thrillers continued to be made. Despite his infamous name and terrorist activities since at least 1996, Osama bin Laden wasn't featured in one single movie. That would be the equivalent of not one Hollywood movie being made on Adolph Hitler between 1941 and 1951. The problem for the industry is not bin Laden himself, as a personality, but how to present his ideology. Because a bin Laden movie would have to talk about jihad, and Jihadism and related subjects are taboo, the topic is simply too explosive for the lobbies. But a single movie involving a real depiction of the ideology would be the equivalent of years of teaching about the subject at college; it would inflict political damage on Wahabism, Salafism, and Khumeinism by exposing these ideologies for what they are to Americans, Westerners, and other audiences around the world. So powerful and universal is film as a medium that an accurate depiction of Jihadism on the big screen would trigger irreversible reactions worldwide. The situation might be compared to a dam ready to crack.

Additionally, there was not one movie about the liberation of millions of Afghanis, Iraqis, and Lebanese in the three years since the War on Terror began. And despite five years of women's liberation struggles in Kabul, not one good production with Afghan females as protagonists was produced. Even historical movies touching upon contemporary conflicts are being truncated, at the expense of accuracy so as not to offend lobbies. *The Kingdom of Heaven* is a challenging example. Cut from all historical context, detached from the real histories of the Christian Crusades and the Muslim jihads that lasted centuries, the producers reconstructed a slice of history based on today's lobbies' projected "sensibilities" instead of the realities of these times. Fearing a so-called "backlash" by Islamists, the Hollywood historians and academic advisors tailored the movie to be acceptable to the lobbies, even if it was insulting to history. For example, only the crusaders had bad guys; the Crusades were presented as the only wars of religion in that era; and last but not least, Saladin dismissed the defenders of Jerusalem, ordering them to depart to any Christian land—as if the Holy Land weren't itself partly Christian, or as if there weren't other Christian lands in the Middle East. This is not to defend the crusaders. An impartial reading of history would show that Crusades and jihads were of a single essence and reflected international relations as they were at that time. But when lobbies begin to impose political considerations on the description of events that took place centuries ago, the War of Ideas has truly become catastrophic in its distortion of the truth.

The American TV industry has gone through a similar crisis. In trying to produce television series to illustrate contemporary events, producers were also put under pressure by ideological lobbies. In the show *Over There*, which was supposed to describe the real situation of American troops on the ground and the various opinions of Iraqis, the series presented the U.S. personnel as primitive in their understanding of the war and the enemy, and Iraqis as deprived of all diversity. But more dramatic was the assault by the Wahabi lobby on the initially successful Kiefer Sutherland series, *24*. The 2005 season of the show, depicting al Qaeda's tactics, with no reference to religion or ethnic criticism, was so close to reality that it was gradually teaching viewers how to identify the organization. The Washington-based Islamist organization CAIR, which had built a powerful influence in the United States, mounted a campaign against the production company, forcing Sutherland to make statements about Islam (although the series wasn't about religion but terrorism). The following season of *24* switched the focus from jihadi terrorism to the Russian terror threat, shifting the attention of American viewers from post-9/11 realities to the pre-1990 Cold War, thus again keeping the truth from getting out to the public. This lobbying success on behalf of Western-based Wahabism can be termed a war "not to have any ideas" about the actual threat.

PREVENTING THE WEST
FROM UNDERSTANDING JIHAD

In the years that followed 9/11, two phenomena characterized the Western public's understanding of the terrorists' ideology. The first characteristic stemmed from the statements made by the jihadists themselves. More than ever, Islamist militants and jihadi cadres didn't waste any opportunity to declare, clarify, explain, and detail the meaning of their *aqida* (doctrine) and their intentions to apply Jihadism by all means possible. Unfortunately for them, though, those extremely violent means changed the international public opinion: the public now was convinced that there *was* an ideology of Jihadism, and that its adherents meant business worldwide. From Ayman al Zawahiri in Arabic to Azzam al Amriki in American English, via all of the videotapes made by "martyrs" in Britain, Iraq, and Afghanistan, the public obtained all the evidence necessary. Against all the faulty academic literature of the 1990s, the statements by the jihadists themselves were very convincing. The second phenomenon of help to the public was the surfacing of a new literature produced by alternative scholars, analysts, journalists, experts, and researchers who, from different backgrounds and countries, filled in some of the gaps in "jihadi studies." Producing books, articles, and blogs from Europe, India, the Middle East, and North America, a combination of Third World–born and Western-issued scholarship began to provide the "missing link" as to what Jihadism is all about. These factors came together to shift the debate from "Jihad is a spiritual yoga" to "Why didn't we know it was something else as well?" And this triggered in response one of the last attempts to prevent jihad from being understood.

In the 1990s, apologist literature attempted to convince readers and audiences in the West that jihad was "a spiritual experience only, and not a menace."[12] That explanation has now been shattered by bin Laden and Ahmedinijad. So in the post-9/11 age, a second strategy to delay public understanding of Jihadism and thereby gain time for its adherents to achieve their goals has evolved. It might be called the "good cop, bad cop" strategy. Over the past few years, a new story began to make inroads in Washington and the rest of the national defense apparatus. A group of academics and interest groups are circulating the idea that in reality, jihad can develop in two forms: good jihad and bad jihad.[13] The good holy war is when the right religious and political authorities declare it against the correct enemy and at the right time. The bad jihad, called also *Hiraba*, is the wrong war, declared by bad people against the wrong enemy, and without an appropriate authorization by the "real" Muslim leadership. According to this thesis, those Muslims who wage a *Hiraba*, a wrong war, are called *Mufsidoon*, from the Arabic word for "spoilers." The advocates of this ruse recommend that the United States and its allies stop calling the jihadists by that name and identifying the concept of Jihadism as the problem. In short, they argue that "jihad is good, but the *Mufsidoon*, the bad guys and the terrorists, spoiled the original legitimate sense."[14] When researched, it turns out that this theory was produced by clerics of the Wahabi regime in Saudi Arabia as a plan to prevent jihad and Jihadism from being depicted by the West and the international community as an illegal and therefore sanctioned activity. It was then forwarded to American- and Western-based interest groups to be spread within the United States, particularly within the defense and security apparatus. Such a deception further confuses U.S. national security perception of the enemy and plunges democracies back into the "black hole" of the 1990s. This last attempt to blur the vision of democracies can be exposed with knowledge of the jihadi terror strategies and tactics, one of which is known as *Taqiya*, the doctrine on deception and deflection.[15]

First, the argument of "good jihad" raises the question of how there can be a legitimate concept of religious war in the twenty-first century to start with. Jihad historically was as "good" as any other religious war over the last 2,000 years. If a "good jihad" is the one authorized by a caliph and directed under his auspices, then other world leaders also can wage a "good crusade" at will, as long as it is licensed by the proper authority. But in fact, all religious wars are proscribed by international law, period. Second, the authors of this lobbyist-concocted theory claim that a wrong jihad is called a *Hiraba*. But in Arab Muslim history, a *Hiraba* (unauthorized warring) was when a group of warriors launched itself against the enemy without orders from the real commander. Obviously, this implies that a "genuine" war against a real enemy does exist and that these hotheaded soldiers have simply acted without orders. Hence this cunning explanation puts "spin" on jihad but leaves the core idea of jihadism completely intact. The "spoilers" depart from the plan, attack prematurely, and cause damage to the caliphate's long-terms plans. These *Mufsidoon* "fail" their commanders by unleashing a war of their own, instead of waiting for orders. This scenario fits the relations of the global jihadists, who are the regimes and international groups slowly planning to gain power against the infidels and the "hotheaded" Osama bin Laden. Thus the promoters of this theory of *Hiraba* and *Mufsidoon* are representing the views of classical Wahabis and the Muslim Brotherhood in their criticism of the "great leap forward" made by bin Laden. But by convincing Westerners that al Qaeda and its allies are not the real jihadists, but some renegades, the advocates of this school would be causing the vision of Western defense to become blurred again so that more time could be gained by a larger, more powerful wave of Jihadism that is biding its time to strike when it chooses, under a coherent international leadership.

MUSLIM PERCEPTION OF JIHAD

One of the strangest, but not unexpected, battles of words and ideologies is over the claims made about the Muslim perception of jihad and Jihadism and their impact on public speech. I will analyze the various clashes on this level in the last chapter of this book, but it is appropriate here to introduce the essence of the ideological confrontation. In the three Wars of Ideas from 1945 to 2006, the heart of the Western engagement in the conflict was the understanding of two issues: what jihad was historically and what Jihadism is in modern times. These are two different but related phenomena. Jihad, like a number of other historical developments throughout the world, was a religiously based geopolitical and military campaign that affected large parts of the world for many centuries. It involved initial theological teachings and injunctions, followed by 14 centuries of interpretations by adherents, caliphs, sultans and their armies, courts, and thinkers. The historical reality of jihad is intertwined with the evolution of the Islamic state since the seventh century. It is emphatically *not* a modern, recent, and narrow creation by a small militant faction. It has to be seen in its historical context. But on the other hand, this giant doctrine, which motivated armies and feelings for centuries, also inspired contemporary movements that shaped their ideology based on their interpretation of the historical jihad. In other words, today's jihadists are an ideological movement with several organizations and regimes, who claim that they define the sole interpretation of what jihad was in history and that they are the ones to resume it and apply it in the present and future. It is equivalent to the possibility that some Christians today might claim that they were reviving the Crusades in the present. This would be only a "claim," of course, because the majority of Christians, either convinced believers or those with a sociological Christian bent, have gone beyond the Christianity of the times of the Crusades. Today's jihadists make the assertion that there is a direct, generic, and organic relation between the jihads that they and their ancestors have engaged in from the seventh century to the twenty-first. But historical jihad is one thing, and the jihad of today's Salafists and Khumeinists is something else.

As with all historical events, literary, analytical, and documentary efforts to interpret and represent past episodes frequently influence the psychology, imagination, and passions of modern-day humanity. Textbooks across the world detail battles, discoveries, and speeches that are the benchmarks of the formation of the national or civilizational identities of peoples. But even if the events in some nations' eyes are proud episodes, they are often considered disasters by other nations. The Native Americans obviously do not celebrate the Spanish conquests; the British Empire is a matter of pride to the English but not to the colonized peoples; and Napoleon's "liberations" are not fondly remembered by those who were conquered. And this is the perception of jihad among classroom pupils in the Arab and Muslim world: it is a matter of historical pride. For example, in the books from which I was tested for my history classes, a famous general of the Arab Muslim conquest, Khalid Ibn al Walid, is treated as a hero because he conquered Syria, Palestine, and Lebanon's shores. But to Aramaics, Syriacs, and Jews, he was a conqueror. He was what Cortés was to the Mexican Indians—an invader. In the same textbooks, Tariq bin Ziad, the general who led the Muslim armies into Spain, is presented as the hero of heroes; but in the eyes of the Iberians, he was a conqueror, and in the modern lexicon, he would be described as a colonial occupier. So historical perception is really in the eyes of the beholder. This is about Western guilt here. While the latter culture has largely demythologized its own conquerors and ideologies, once described as heroic—Napoleon, Gordon of Khartoum, "Manifest Destiny," etc.—it has accepted docilely ideas like the "spread of Islam," the benevolence of Arab occupation, etc. Westerners are schooled to repudiate the errors of the past in their own culture, but to overlook those of other cultures today. This is where the jihadi propaganda campaign deliberately harps on "Muslim resentment of the Crusades," in order to play upon this "guilt complex."

Historical jihad doesn't escape this harsh rule of history. Those who felt their ancestors' deeds were right—including military invasions and their violent consequences—see jihad as a good thing. And those who felt their ancestors were conquered and victimized see it as a disaster. This is the drama of the invading Arabs on the one hand and the conquered Persians, Assyro-Chaldeans, Arameans, Copts, Nubians, and Berbers on the other; of conquering Ottomans and conquered Armenians, Greeks, and Slavs. It should be noted that many of the conquered had been conquerors earlier, such as the Greeks, Persians, Assyrians, and Egyptians. World history is made up of such reversals. But the emotional perception of the past should stop at contemporary reality. Feelings and passions about the tragedies of the past cannot be erased and should not be forgotten, but they have to give way in the end to international law and doctrines of human rights. Many Christians today may believe that the Crusades were warranted at the time, but that cannot become a basis for military action under today's international consensus. The religious legitimacy of the Crusades or the Spanish *Conquista* no longer exists. Even the theological ground upon which many European Christians settled North America, although studied as a historical phenomenon, is irrelevant after the Constitution. And despite the fact that many Jews invoke religious Zionism as a basis for the re-creation of modern-day Israel, and that this is a deep conviction of many evangelical Christians, international law doesn't allow it as a component for the recognition of the state of Israel. In essence, twenty-first-century world society does not and cannot function as an extension of past centuries' theologies and philosophies. There is a full freedom of religion and thought for individuals and communities to believe in their faith's tenets regarding questions of land, nations, war, and peace. But these beliefs have standing under international law only insofar as they correspond to and fall within the world consensus on peace and coexistence. From this perspective, the question of contemporary Muslims and jihad cannot be an exception. Today's Muslim individuals and communities may have their feelings, passions, and readings of past historical jihads. Some may attach a religious value to them. But even if in the past jihad was a tool of the state and considered a legitimate form of warfare led by the caliphs (in the same way the Crusades and biblical wars were legitimate in the eyes of their peoples), under international law today there are no legitimate jihads. The theological authority of Charlemagne and Caliph Haroun al Rashid, and of Louis XIV and Suleiman the Magnificent may have been mainstream during their times, but not anymore. Hence neither French president Jacques Chirac nor Iranian president Ahmedinijad can invoke religion in his defense or when discussing international policies.

Thus the Muslims' relationship with this old and historical jihad is in the domain of past events and emotions; however, it can be reinterpreted to fit the form of modern society in such a way that it does not violate international law. Jihad as a personal "spiritual" dimension can exist, but only as different, separate, and distant from the historical jihad. The new proposition advanced by scholars in the West that a nonviolent, inner, and personal jihad is the "real one" can be tested only in the wake of a cultural, widely accepted principle that the historical, theologically endorsed jihad warfare is over, and not just suspended or hidden. Short of this fundamental reform in jihad perception, similar to the reputiation of the Crusades and biblical wars by Christians and Jews, any current political affiliation with the ancient jihad would be in contradiction with modern international law. Hence the argument that the Muslims have "sensitivities" regarding the issue of historical jihad, which therefore cannot be criticized or maligned, is at odds with the current structure of international relations and laws. As long as a world consensus exists on the nonreligious nature of international relations, the political and legal dimensions of the historical jihad cannot be played out in the international or public policy affairs of modern society. One cannot argue, for example, that jihad is the equivalent of self-defense in the modern international system. Self-defense doesn't relate to any theological concept. But if self-defense in Islamic religious law covers oral insults to Islamic values, then Muslim governments or a future caliph could declare wars of "self-defense" based on mere statements made by individuals and groups (thus, the Danish cartoons would have justified jihad against Denmark in the name of "self-defense"). Similarly, if to some Christian sects self-defense could be linked to an "end-time" theology, or if future religious groups thought self-defense could be a response to a divine order to reshape humanity by force, these interpretations could lead to a collapse of the planetary order. In sum, the basis of twenty-first-century peace is to abandon the racial, religious, and cultural legitimization of wars. International society, with its various nations and cultures, including the Muslim ones, has agreed on this since 1945, at least in principle.

MUSLIM "SENSITIVITIES" TO JIHAD

Many have advanced the idea of Muslim "sensitivities" to the concept of jihad to counter the democracies' opposition to Jihadism. One can respond to this idea on three levels. First, theologically, the Islamic faith has five pillars: witness, prayer, pilgrimage, fasting, and tithing. Jihad is only an unofficial pillar. Hence to start with, the concept is *not* among the five principal tenets that form the Muslim identity, but rather is recommended only in circumstances designated by rulers and scholars. It is therefore a matter of policy (though theology is in any event outside international law). On a second level of analysis, the democratic objection to Jihadism has to do with policy, and not with jihad as a pure idea. People can dream, believe, fantasize, imagine, and interpret historical and theological visions as they wish. But political and legal realities are something else. Religious Christians may imagine a crusade that would bring all humans under Christianity; biblically inclined Jews can dream of a divine intervention that would fulfill Hebrew prophecies; and fundamentalist Muslims can dream of Allah bringing the *deen* (religion) to cover the whole world. But in the real world of nations, civilizations, and modernity, the buck stops there: no wars in the name of theology. Democracy guarantees religious freedoms for all faiths, but democracies cannot recognize ideologies and movements that call for warfare based on theological grounds, meaning grounds beyond the scope of the people's will.[16] All "sensitivities" are accepted and recognized by democracies so long as they are not injunctions to violence, even if it is "religious" in origin. From this perspective, the principles of international law in general, and democratic societies in particular, can accommodate individuals and groups attached to values extracted from faith, but not those that would break the foundations of modern civil society and human rights.

The ongoing debate regarding Muslim "sensitivities" to jihad has an erroneous premise propagated by Western elites since the 1990s. They are

contending that Jihadism as an ideology and a movement is the representation of the historical jihad, and they even assert the divine right to apply it in
modern times. Muslims, including even mainstream conservatives, know that
historical jihad is a matter of past value, contemplation, and reinterpretation,
and not for direct implementation in twenty-first-century world affairs. It is
not an issue of whether it is authorized or not, licensed or not, legitimate or
not, because like crusades, such jihads violate international law. This is why
we can finally argue that Jihadism as a political philosophy and real militant
movement is in conflict with human rights and democracy. And this is why
criticizing Jihadism and banning it from international relations is not a criticism of Islam or an infringement on Muslim "sensitivities" or even religious
beliefs. Modern societies, including Muslim ones, cannot accept the jihadist
paradigm as it was launched by the Salafists in the 1920s and the Khumeinists
in the 1980s. To state otherwise would represent an attempt by the jihadists,
or radical Islamists, to shield a violent ideology under the guise of religious
freedom. The War of Ideas as it has developed since 2001 has witnessed
many desperate attempts to steer world opinion into misperceiving the nature of Jihadism as a legitimate religious duty of devoted Muslims. The reality is that the Muslims of modern times have severed their ties to the classical
jihad of the caliphate, just as Christians have severed their ties to the Crusades of the eleventh to thirteenth centuries. The jihadists are simply trying
to bring back the age of medieval empire. And the War of Ideas is about
learning this truth and turning the hearts and minds of people away from
jihad and back toward the international consensus on peaceful coexistence
and the observation of agreed norms of human rights.[17]

Some imams and Muslim liberal intellectuals have argued that nowadays
jihad can't emulate the old jihads. This "reinterpretation" could be a positive
step in the direction of removing violence from the concept. However, such a
redefinition can only be effective in the wake of a reform in Islam that
touches the theological level. For creating a "new" jihad, a form that would
be equivalent to some regimen of inner experience or meditation, needs a redefinition of the old as different. And that touches the core value of faith, a
matter that is possible to reexamine, as Christians, Jews, and many other religions have experienced. Outside the grand idea of reform, tactical slogans of
a "yoga-like" jihad would be merely a political ruse.

CHAPTER TWELVE

INFLAMING HEARTS AND FOOLING MINDS

AFTER SEPTEMBER 11, 2001, AND FIVE YEARS INTO THE CURRENT War of Ideas, a well-known phrase has constantly been employed: "the war to win the hearts and minds of Arabs, Middle Easterners, and Muslims." Often used by American leaders and politicians, this phrase makes it sound as if some forces have won over the thoughts and feelings of entire populations around the globe, as a result of which scores of militants emerged and joined the terror campaign against the United States, the West, and their friends and allies. The prescription is then to launch a counter informational, educational, and psychological campaign as a way to "win back" these hearts and minds. We have seen, since 2002, U.S. and other Western officials busily providing material aid to populations and sending envoys to meet leaders, intellectuals, and citizens in the Middle East. Government representatives and politicians have reached out to émigré communities in North America, Europe, and Australia to convince their citizens that the West is full of good intentions. But we have also seen Islamist leaders, media, spokespersons, and their allies in the West railing against these "simplistic, naïve, and arrogant" initiatives.[1] Indeed, the highest and most revealing segment of the War of Ideas has been the belief in the West that the issue is about public relations and image, while it is a firm conviction among the "makers of feelings" on the other side that their masses will respond solely to their emotional and cultural triggers, not to the "alien" messages of the Americans and Westerners. The question is, Who is winning this war in reality? To answer that question, one has to understand the evolution of the confrontation and examine underlying issues such as the following:

- Are the societies that resent the West conditioned to do so, or is it a freely developed attitude?

- Is the resentment deeply cultural, politically triggered by events, or is it constructed by an ideology that molds how people see the world?
- Are the ideological forces, namely the jihadists and other radicals, successful in building the enmity toward the West in an irreversible way? Are the masses trustful or fearful of these forces?
- Will civil society respond to the offered democracy and pluralism by rejecting or accepting liberation? Will Middle Eastern societies reject the liberation processes just because they are offered by the West, and the United States in particular?
- If civil societies in the East reject the Western "content" of democracy and human rights, do they naturally prefer the "content" of ideologies such as Jihadism and radicalism? Aren't there confrontations within the Arab and Muslim world as to the definition of these concepts and ideas?
- How does one explain the rising interest and participation in the Greater Middle East in democratic exercises, such as in Afghanistan, Iraq, Lebanon, and beyond? Were the millions of voters who hurried to participate in the elections and voted for majorities of nonterrorist candidates and parties mainly anti-American yet supporters of democracy? How can the one and a half million Lebanese demonstrators of the Cedar Revolution, who were supportive of democracy, human rights, and pluralism and valued U.S. and Western support for the evacuation of the Syrian army, be described in terms of the War of Ideas?
- How does one explain the electoral successes of the Muslim Brotherhood in Egypt's legislative elections and Hamas in Palestine?
- Which party in the War of Ideas is making progress within the other camp? Are the Islamists and their allies convincing more Americans, Westerners, Asians, Africans, and Latin Americans that jihad is a legitimate choice and Jihadism is a peaceful movement? Can oil influence turn the tide against Western-based efforts to spread conditions to enable freedom in the East? Or will American and other efforts break through the jihadi-authoritarian "shield" isolating the peoples of the region from international society? Are there today more activists for democracy and human rights and voting masses in the Middle East than before 2001?

Such questions go to the heart of the struggle between the two camps in the global War of Ideas. In chapter thirteen, I will review the developments and arguments of the antidemocratic offensive as of 2001, the multiple battlegrounds, the U.S.-led counteroffensive, and the rear-guard action of the jihadists up through 2006.

THE ANTI-AMERICAN OFFENSIVE

From the first few hours following the tragedy of 9/11, the anti-American conglomeration around the world—with the radical Islamists in the center, surrounded by a mix of authoritarian and neofascist currents—began to strike at the United States and try to scare other democracies from joining Washington's coalition. The jihadi architects launched a blitzkrieg of words and accusations against the victims of the attacks even as the smoke was still floating over lower Manhattan, the Potomac, and Pennsylvania. The psychological war led by the radicals aimed to preempt the U.S. response by stunning Americans and other Westerners with heavy accusations: "You are the criminals, not the jihadists; you are the terrorists, not al Qaeda," sang al Jazeera's Salafi commentators, along with Berkeley's radical militants. The offensive was fast and relentless: argument after argument, slogan after slogan, stereotype after stereotype hammered the slowly awakening citizenry. The purpose was to stifle the public's growing understanding by playing the guilt game. In college classrooms, radical professors slaughtered American and Western ethics, culture, and the West's very raison d'être, virtually shedding more psychological blood than the real blood shed by the 3,000 victims of 9/11. Think of the scholars who wished more 9/11s would occur and who equated the massacred population to agents of Zionism and imperialism.[2] I personally witnessed in classrooms and forums, on C-SPAN and NPR, more American self-immolation by academics and commentators than vituperation in the acerbic anti-American attacks by jihadi spokespersons on al-Jazeera and the Internet. A simple collection of the written and taped material from the fall of 2001 will show future historians that the jihadists' hope that the United States would crumble from the inside after the 9/11 strikes was not extremely unrealistic and might have occurred had the public been more deeply influenced by its elites. Hundreds of professors flooded the Internet and campuses with monodimensional criticism of America's essence, of its bias and "anti-Muslim" policies, which had "brought a legitimate retaliation against the country." These self-described "academic" evaluations of the root causes of the attacks not only attempted to crush the national resistance to terrorism, but also ignored the actual perpetrators and their aims, ideology, and strategies. In the thousands of statements, articles, papers, and interviews made by the bulk of the nation's elites, little was actually explained about the aggressor. Perhaps because the "aggressor" in the minds of the Wahabi-funded and influenced intellectual establishment was their own society. The same was true after the al Qaeda attacks in Madrid in 2004 and London in 2005. But in the United States, and in Great Britain to some extent, the public's survival instincts withstood the elites' message and affirmed the national consensus on a War on Terror.

The psychological war continued, however, with a second wave. Now the critics of the War on Terror, both before and after the beginning of the Iraq War, tried another guilt-inducing argument. An assortment of scholars and experts in Middle East affairs asserted that "the region is against America and the West; the whole region with no exception."[3] This second wave of criticism by jihadists and Western apologists aimed at stopping the upcoming counteroffensive against authoritarian forces. From their quarters in Iraq, Iran, Syria, and Sudan, and among the clerical circles of Arabia, the strategists of the ruling elites understood that something had changed deep within America. They saw that, in fact, their first line of defense within the United States itself had cracked. The sympathetic academics weren't able to erode the American will to resist from the inside; the facts of 9/11 were more powerful than arguments. Hence the second line of defense was to convince the American and Western public that any adventure in the region would be disastrous. Fearing for their power, the authoritarians and jihadists tried to persuade the public that any U.S. or Western intervention anywhere in the region against terrorism would end up creating a breach in the wall from which the peoples—hostages under these regimes—of the Middle East would be able to scream their pain to the international community. And if that happened, it would have a domino effect across the land. To avoid a "Normandy landing" in the region, and the turning of the tide toward democracy, the combined forces of Jihadism and authoritarianism struck preemptively, one blow after another.

THE "HATE AMERICA" MESSAGE

One of the most widespread arguments in the post-9/11 War of Ideas has been the relentlessly repeated claim that America is hated worldwide, increasingly since 9/11, and particularly since the Bush administration waged war "on Iraq." This plethora of ideas is assembled from various analyses and positions centered on one main thread: that the world was better off before the Bush administration originally declared its War on Terror and prosecuted it.

The contradictory reasons offered for the so-called "international hate of America" are revealing. For example, the critics of the United States (and also of its allies, such as the Aznar and Berlusconi governments before they were changed, the Blair government, and others around the world) pile up these reasons haphazardly: The foreign policy of the United States before 9/11 was responsible for the attack launched by al Qaeda. "Declaring" a War on Terror was wrong, as were calling regimes and organizations an "axis of evil"; committing the United States to the spread of democracy in foreign lands and alien cultures; sending forces to Iraq to remove Saddam Hussein; intervening in Darfur; criticizing the fascist movement within the Muslim world; and supporting Muslim moderates, liberals, and minorities. The irony of this aggregation of claims is the fact that the assertion that America is "hated" by Arabs, Middle Easterners, Muslims, and other nations is advanced by anti-Americans to start with. The overwhelming majority of writings, statements, and publications that coalesced against the U.S.-led efforts against Jihadism and authoritarianism in the Greater Middle East emanated from radical Islamists, supporters of Baathism, and left- and right-wing fascists and radicals around the world. This line of attack was seconded by domestic critics of the Bush, Blair, Aznar, and Berlusconi governments, particularly as the campaign against Saddam began. So from a political perspective, the "hatred of America" slogan has been reinforced opportunistically by opposition parties for simple competitive reasons rather than to present real strategic alternatives.

Indeed, if we analyze the ultimate goal of the critics of U.S. policy after 2001, we see one common denominator: removing the Bush administration and other governments involved in the War on Terror within the West and in India. But the critics never detailed an alternative agenda to the counterterrorist strategies initiated by the governments they opposed. Evidently, while domestic critics in the West want to grab constitutional powers, their "traveling companions" from the East, the jihadists and authoritarians, want to resume the terror against Western powers. It is not about Bush or Clinton in Washington, Blair and his successors in London, Aznar or Zapatero in Madrid, and Berlusconi or Prodi in Rome. It is about weakening the West's will for self-defense and its resolution to assist the democratic revolution in the Greater Middle East. Hence the claim that the world hates America is nothing but a retaliation against U.S. efforts (regardless of success or failure) to foster democracy in the region. The real answer to the argument that the world has been hating America since the Bush administration launched its War on Terror is very ironic: The forces of Jihadism and their allies in the

West began to hate America even more after the United States began confronting the jihadi and fascist regimes and organizations in the Arab World and the Greater Middle East. It is, in fact, that simple. The supposedly newfound hatred is not a reversal of mass love for America, as the critics claim. It is an organized, massive response by the antidemocratic forces in the region, including the Taliban, Saddam Hussein, Iran's mullahs, and the Assad regime in Syria, as well as their political allies within the West itself, against the change of course by Washington and other capitals. It is not surprising that the United States was hated by Salafi Islamists after the downfall of the Taliban, despised by Baathists after Saddam's removal, or vilified after the issuing of UN Security Council Resolution 1559 and the pulling out of Syrian occupation forces from Lebanon. To understand why the jihadi regime of Khartoum joined the fray of anti-American hatred, one has simply to look at the U.S.-led UN initiative to support the oppressed black Africans of Southern Sudan and Darfur. It is not so difficult to see that Hezbollah is frustrated with Washington because the latter stood by the Cedar Revolution of Lebanon in its quest to disarm the Khumeinist militia, or to understand that the Ahmedinijad regime is vociferously against the United States because of UN efforts to stop the Iranian nuclear threat. It is obvious that the Muslim Brotherhoods, al Jazeera, and the madrassas around the region are frustrated by the calls to democratize and free women in the Muslim world. Even Turkey's "soft Islamist" government voiced criticism of Washington, not because of the Iraq invasion, but because of the determination of American leadership to enable Iraqis to choose their government through pluralism and the recognition of minorities.

Thus the so-called hatred of America—or, as they paint it, of this specific administration—is, in fact, a manufactured political and ideological mobilization against the agenda that the Bush-Blair alliance has pushed in response to rising fascism in the region. Such an agenda would be opposed by the Islamists and authoritarians after Blair and Bush are gone—and for years to come, regardless of who is pushing for it, liberals or conservatives, left- or right-wing governments. As I wrote in several articles in 2002 and 2003, peoples in the region, or more precisely, certain segments of societies, were "conditioned to hate" whomever the regime bosses, the militant cadres, and al Jazeera's ideologues targeted for hating.

Ironically, the critics who charge that the War on Terror triggered hatred of the West and the United States were actually calling for stopping any intervention in support of the underdogs in the region. Therefore, following their line of thinking to its logical conclusion, to avoid being hated, Washington and its allies should have followed another agenda that did not involve prodemocracy intervention. Here are a few possible alternatives:

- Not removing the Taliban in Kabul. This would have led to tens of thousands more women becoming victims and an increase of jihadi influence among Pakistan's fundamentalists.
- Not removing Saddam Hussein (in any shape or form). This would have left the Shiia and Kurds to be further persecuted and let Iraq's Baathists redevelop unconventional weapons.
- Not asking Syria to leave Lebanon. This would have left its civil society under the oppression of the Baathist intelligence services and Hezbollah's weapons.
- Not intervening to assist the Africans in Darfur. This would have abandoned them to ethnic cleansing and genocide, which is still occurring.
- Not promoting democracy and human rights in the region. This would have meant ignoring abuse, oppression, and persecutions.

So had America not pursued its War on Terror and War of Ideas after 2001, perhaps the hatred of the United States would not have increased! Certainly, it would not have been manufactured on a mass scale, because the jihadists and fascistic regimes and organizations would have been busy with their internal victims or preparing for future enterprises. It is easy to understand that the jihadi-crafted hatred was systematically disseminated in the region and worldwide, for the very clear reason that a status quo had been disrupted by Uncle Sam. And in order to stop America and its allies from turning the tables on regional totalitarianism, the combined resources of jihadists and authoritarians were put into the mother of all propaganda wars. The "hatred manufacturing" can be controlled, cultivated, and unleashed when needed. Indeed, during the 1990s, the hatred of the West and America was on a back burner, cooking slowly in the minds of the adherents for future jihads. It was instilled gradually through the educational systems and via the media outlets, until the war broke out. From that moment on, the pace was accelerated by the "jihadi kitchen." As the United States moved its forces into the region, as elections were organized in Afghanistan and Iraq, and as demonstrations filled the streets of Beirut, the "hate America" message was served up in the region and inside the West. This War of Ideas initially may not have been understood by the public because of the mass deception campaign, but it will be in the days to come.[4]

CREATION OF TERRORISTS WORLDWIDE

Another repeated attack against the U.S.-led War on Terror has been the charge that military action has created more terrorists than there were before. Multiple reports from academic institutions and government agencies have concluded that the Iraq War has increased, rather than lessened, the number of jihadists. A 30-page National Intelligence Estimate (NIE) completed in April 2006 stated that the U.S. invasion of Iraq "has become the primary recruitment vehicle for violent Islamic extremists, motivating a new generation of potential terrorists around the world whose numbers are increasing faster than the United States and its allies are eliminating the threat."[5] But the analysts' use of particular words has created confusion.[6] For example, the report stated that the number of potential terrorists is "increasing faster" than the elimination of "the threat." But the analysis didn't say how the threat could be eliminated. By killing terrorists? Reducing their recruitment or suppressing the recruiting ideology? Apparently, the critics of the war reduced the progress of the war to a quantitative measurement: if there were 30,000 armed jihadists in 2006 versus 10,000 in 2001, for example, that would be an indication that the war is being lost. But a quantitative measurement alone won't provide a thorough assessment. In comparison, Hitler had less advanced equipment deployed in 1940 than in 1944; would that mean that after Normandy and Stalingrad, he was winning the war? An analysis of a war is not limited to the numerical count of the enemy's troops at a particular time, but includes many other factors. The following also need to be taken into consideration in determining who is winning the war:

- Do al Qaeda and the jihadists still have a historic and strategic advantage to undertake a massive surprise attack against the West?
- Although many jihadists have been traveling to join the "holy war" against U.S. and coalition forces in Iraq, did they defeat the antijihadi forces in their own countries of origin? (In fact, terrorists who leave Algeria or Chechnya to fight in the Sunni Triangle of Iraq have reduced terror resources on these other battlefields.)
- Are more Salafists joining the jihad? Surely they will go wherever the "battlefields" are; this is part of their essential character. Unless

all combat Salafists and Khumeinists are contained worldwide by all counterterrorism powers combined, one rationally has to expect that as soon as a prodemocracy or antiterrorist move is made against them at any spot on the planet, the jihadists will come from all points to combat that initiative.[7] The fact that jihadists have rushed to counterattack the United States in Iraq or elsewhere is not a measure of success or failure; jihadists moving to reinforce antidemocratic power in Iraq is (or should have been) one of the expected results of the engagement.[8]

- Although more Islamist recruits are joining the fighting jihadists, are more antijihadist resources being mustered as well? Against each terrorist joining the fray, one must count the policeman, soldier, democratic demonstrator, and voter arising on the other side of the equation. It is only when the final showdown between the two sides occurs (that is when enough Iraqi troops are sufficiently trained to stand up to the jihadists and a democratic political culture is deeply rooted) that a rational analysis can be given.

From these and many other arguments, we ought to realize that the War of Ideas waged by the jihadists and those who share their views is not always on solid ground. Rather, most of their arguments are aimed at a quick gain in the propaganda battle to score psychological or political points. In addition, many of the analyses of the state of the war are based on a Western model of interpretation, such as sheer numbers of casualties, or on a collection of media reports, especially fragments from TV and radio reportage. Many among the sincere but failed attempts to criticize the war coherently are to be blamed on the initial misunderstanding of the politics and ideologies of the Greater Middle East. For if military, security, and strategic analysts in the West are not taught that behind local conflicts in Iraq, Afghanistan, Sudan, and other areas there are transnational ideologies and movements fighting a global war against the West and democracies, then the "big picture" will be missing; and if the local analysis lacks a full geopolitical framework, those analysts, political scientists, and government planners won't see, for example, that "foreign" jihadists are going to meet U.S. and allied forces anywhere on the planet, regardless of the "political validity" of the intervention, and they won't be able to recognize the actual turning point of any of the battlefields—nor, more importantly, will they see this global conflict's shifting trends.

JIHADISTS' ALLIANCE
WITH THE ANTIWAR MOVEMENT

Oddest of all is the open alliance between the jihadists and the so-called "antiwar movement" in the West. The original source was the growth of the Islamist–left-wing collaboration in the 1990s. Even though the Wahabis fiercely fought the Soviet Communists in Afghanistan, the Muslim Brotherhood and the Marxists have been at each other's throats for decades, the Salafists butchered left-wing intellectuals in Algeria and assassinated progressive bureaucrats in central Asia after the Soviet collapse, the Taliban killed socialists and shut down arts institutions, and last but not least, the Khumeinist regime in Iran decimated more than 50,000 members of the Tudeh Communist Party in the 1980s, the left-wing collaboration continues. Despite the Islamist–left-wing mutual bloodshed across the Mediterranean and throughout the Middle East, an unnatural alliance was established by the two groups of elites even while the blood was being shed in the 1990s. Setting ideologies and history aside, the Islamist tacticians and left-wing pragmatists gradually converged on a two-lane path against liberal democracies and the specter of a free market and pluralist Middle East. The jihadi concern with Western involvement in the region is logical: free societies in the Arab and Muslim world, joined finally to the international community, would shatter Islamic fundamentalism's control of the regions' political cultures. To have Arab and Iranian youths, in addition to minorities, hooking up directly with the peaceful and prosperous societies of the West would leave the Islamists without a base to recruit from. The jihadists' violent opposition to democratization is not surprising—but unexpectedly, a cohort of left-wing groups, including Marxists, Trotskyists, Maoists, Anarchists, and Neo-Leninists, have espoused the jihadists' "causes": globalization is mixed up with caliphate, class struggle with Wahabism, proletariat with infidels, and North Korea with Palestine.

One of the strangest phenomena of pragmatic "realism" took place between two antipodes, the post-Soviet international Marxist left and the international jihadists. The rise of dissidence in the region and the aligning of the international post-Soviet neo-left with oppressive regimes is evidence of the neo-left's fascistic leanings. While still bleeding each other in reality and in the indoctrination rooms, the Reds (neo-left) and the Dark Greens (Islamists)[9] have conducted a joint offensive against both democracy-pushing

America and the democracy-craving Middle East. This rapprochement between the two ideological opposites against their "common enemy"—liberal democracy—produced another even stranger alliance between the jihadists and the antiwar movement. Highly ironically, Jihadism is joined with the antiwar movement even while promoting "holy war," which is the essence of their *rissala* (mission). The ideology of the Salafists and Khumeinists is to prepare for, mobilize for, incite, and engage in a constant war of jihad against the infidels, who are supposed to be all those who aren't Islamists, as well as moderate Muslims. Theoretically, the jihadi connection to the antiwar concept is impossible. But in the realm of reality, it did occur, mainly because of the mutating "pragmatism" of both antidemocratic movements. The radical Islamists, as I argued in *Future Jihad*, have undergone a strategic mutation that has allowed them to coalesce tactically with ideological foes, among them Baathists, Neo-Marxists, and anarchists. The last group, under an international neo-left umbrella in the West, created the antiwar movement, which is reminiscent of the old Cold War Communist-controlled "peace movement." What is revealing is the fact that the Islamists found it easier to insert themselves as partners in an antiwar movement than a peace movement. Effectively, in the jihadi *aqida* (doctrine), seeking permanent peace with others is a nonissue, given that jihad is constant, regardless of its form. Jihadism cannot accommodate a peace movement in principle; however, a jurisprudence based on *al Haja* (necessity) would allow the jihadists to accept an interim cessation of war and work in more sophisticated ways to stop wars that they cannot win. Thus it is in the interest of the radical Islamists to stop a war that can't be won by them, at least until the balance of power is restored and a winnable war becomes possible again. In the case of the War on Terror, the "political Islamists" joined the "no-war" crowd in order to stop the military efforts by the United States and its allies against the terrorist forces of the jihadists. Hence Islamist militants marched in the demonstrations against the wars in Afghanistan and Iraq as a way to give respite to the Taliban and al Qaeda: as I wrote in an op-ed in 2003, "against the war, yes, but against all wars, not just the ones waged by the Jihadists."[10] Indeed, the antiwar movement exposed its broken rationale when it marched against some wars but not against all wars. It demonstrated against the military efforts to overthrow the Taliban and Saddam but ignored the wars waged by the Sudanese regime against the African peoples in the south and Darfur; it marched against the Israeli occupation of the West Bank, but ignored the Syrian occupation of Lebanon.

Worse in the eyes of millions of Middle Easterners were the highly publicized "red buses" filled with antiwar militants who headed to Iraq to "support" dictator Saddam Hussein. They traveled from London, Berlin, and Rome through Eastern Europe without a word in remembrance of its struggle against the Soviet occupation and crossed Syria without comforting the thousands of political prisoners tortured and assassinated by the Baathist regime. And for an apex of irony, the buses rolled through sinister Halabja, a Kurdish town gassed by Saddam in 1988, and past the Shiites' mass graves, stopping only to "shield" Saddam's castles, built from oil revenues that rented the buses and lodged their occupants in fancy hotels. This antiwar movement was convenient for the jihadists, as it was a form of war against the rise of democracies in the region. For the movement, mostly bourgeois in nature, never showed up in Darfur, among Berbers in Algeria or Lebanese under Syrian occupation, or to shield women executed under the Taliban. Hence it wasn't surprising for viewers around the world to see the Islamist militants in Europe taking to the streets alongside the "bourgeois Neo-Marxists" to protest the governments that supported the War on Terror. In Europe, the most revealing action of the Islamist militants was when—in the same year as the red buses—they marched in support of the French government against U.S. intervention in Iraq, and then burned shops and cars in 200 French cities and towns during a "French intifada." The jihadi manipulation of the bourgeois–Neo-Marxist "struggle" has played a central role in the so-called "mass demonstrations" in the West since 2002—the demonstrations themselves an important component of the War of Ideas against democracy. On campuses, both in North America and Western Europe, the jihadi-antiwar axis has planted deep roots, and thanks to the skills of university-based anarchist groups, the jihadists have found a cover they can hide under, instead of simply becoming members of the typical Muslim Student Unions. But this "marriage of convenience" with the extreme left has not deterred jihadists from conducting another, simultaneous, wedding with the extreme right.

JIHADISTS' ALLIANCE WITH NEO-NAZIS

Much of the literature disseminated by radical Islamists on the Internet and in the Arab world is produced by extreme right-wing ideologues in the West. Even though in cahoots with the extreme left, jihadi tacticians have embraced the Neo-Nazis in at least two areas. One is the Neo-Nazi anti-Semitic literature, massively copied in Arabic, such as the infamous *Protocol of the Elders of Zion*. The racial attacks against Jews initiated and promoted by the Third Reich constitute a large portion of the arguments used by jihadist propagandists to engender deep enmity toward Jews among Arabs and Muslims. Often seen on Salafist and pro-Khumeinist websites, but also heard in the statements of al Jazeera guests and commentators, the anti-Jewish material shows its obvious Nazi origin, in that the "cases" cited are about Jewish conspiracies against white Europeans. The Hezbollah-controlled al Manar TV went so far in its anti-Jewish productions and shows that even European countries (usually slow to censor) put a ban on al Manar broadcasts.[11] But from the Nazi inspiration, the rhetoric has mutated into a constant accusation against "Jewish lobbies," who, according to the jihadists and other authoritarians, "have taken control of the minds and decision-making process of America and other governments." Islamist propaganda often spreads the views of Western academics and intellectuals who push "Jewish conspiracy" as an explanation for U.S. and Western policies.[12]

But beyond the "Jewish" element of the jihadi alliance with the extreme right lies another important component of the War of Ideas: the drive toward American isolationism. The logic of this objective is clear. First, the United States has had a history of isolationism in the past, particularly in the early twentieth century. Second, the Neo-Nazi groups in the United States have continually argued for a U.S. withdrawal from the United Nations and other international organizations, a pullback of U.S. forces to the American mainland, and U.S. noninterference in overseas affairs. Although this is an ideological position taken mostly by white supremacists (but also elements from the conservative-isolationist wing), this trend falls in perfectly with what the international jihadists dream of: having American power restrained, restricted to the domestic sphere, and generally weakened. The immediate effect in the Greater Middle East would be for jihadi and authoritarian forces to crush civil societies and democracy movements, allowing the Islamists to emerge as the only alternative to the authoritarians. To engineer this appealing possibility requires allies within the United States—allies who, for their own reasons, want to roll back American influence and overseas presence. The overlap between the Neo-Nazis in the United States and the jihadists is even greater than that between Islamists and the extreme left. Many times on al Jazeera, the prominent leading cleric, Sheikh Yussef al Qardawi, has declared that "the best thing America should do, is to remove its forces and presence from around the world and keep itself inside its borders."[13]

BATTLES OF RHETORIC

Another line of attack by the jihadi propaganda machine has been developed on linguistic and cultural grounds. An extension of the 1990s guilt build-up by most of the intellectual establishment in the West, the new tactic has been to depict the United States and the West as a constant producer of aggression with a "grand design" of hurting Islam. The jihadists' tactic is to shield them- selves behind religion, just as the National Socialists hid behind the cloak of German identity and protecting German populations. The rhetoric forged during the second War of Ideas in the 1990s is a lexicon staple of al Jazeera and Islamist websites, as well as in the West, where critics of the War on Ter- ror have repeated jihadi-coached claims about Muslim anger against the West. The list is very long but consistent; here are a few examples:

- *Al harb ala ma yusamma biul irhab:* "the war on what is called terrorism." Al Jazeera, the promoter of this line, has never recognized that the war against al Qaeda, the Taliban, or other combat jihadists is a war against "terrorism." Even when translating speeches by international officials, the Qatari-funded station does not interpret "War on Terror" verba- tim, but always uses the phrase "war on what it is called terrorism." This phrase alone has been repeated tens of thousands of times over the years, in a way that has left audiences not believing that terrorists actually are just that. Obviously, such a psychological inculcation of the masses facilitates the absorption of other ideological content.
- *Al harb ala al Islam:* "the War on Islam." This second powerful phrase has been as widely disseminated as the previous one and has left an even greater impact on viewers, listeners, and readers. For it interprets any and all actions and sayings by the West and democracies as an ac- tual war against the Muslim religion and Islamic identity. Any political attitude not accepted by the Islamist agenda ends up automatically under the rubric of the "War on Islam" list, with predictable conse- quences, including retaliations and retributions, ranging from intimi- dation and threat all the way to physical harm.
- *Al harb ala Iraq:* "the War on Iraq." In American, Western, and inter- national rhetoric, the war waged by the coalition, regardless of its just- ness and timing, is described accurately as a war "in" Iraq, against Saddam Hussein or the terrorists and insurgents. But al Jazeera and

the international jihadi network present it as a war against the "whole of Iraq." And despite the three massive elections and the open relationship between the elected Iraqi government and the United States and its allies, the conflict is portrayed as an American-Jewish war "on all Iraqis," aiming at their destruction. The same rhetorical ploy is used in the case of Afghanistan, where the war supposedly was not waged to remove the Taliban government, which gave aid to al Qaeda, but against Afghanistan and its people.

- *Qasf li:* "bombardment of a whole country." From Afghanistan to Iraq and Pakistan, all NATO, Western, and UN military operations against terrorists have been explained to the public as a "shelling of the whole country." Take this one linguistic example from a U.S. missile strike launched from Afghanistan against a supposed hideout of al Qaeda's number two, Ayman Zawahiri, inside Pakistan's territories: al Jazeera and others quickly put out the slogan *qasf Bakistaan,* "the shelling of Pakistan." A few hours later, as I was participating in a panel on al Jazeera, I asked the former director of Pakistan's intelligence service, who was also on the panel and was a critic of the attack, if this was a shelling of all of Pakistan. "Was it even a bombardment of the whole village?" I questioned. The panelist, a professional military man, said no. So I then asked whether it was not, in fact, a "strike against Zawahiri inside Pakistan." Obviously my words didn't change the editorial line.

THE BATTLE OF "AFFAIRS"

The battle of words and definitions, as we have seen, is an essential component of the War of Ideas. It has practical effects in such high-profile crises as the prisoner treatment and the alleged desecration of the Qu'ran at the U.S. detention center at Guantanamo and the Iraq Abu Ghraib prison scandal, as well as in homeland security affairs.

Guantanamo

The first of these "affairs" raised by the jihadi movement worldwide, its allies, and genuinely concerned human rights circles was the treatment of detainees in Guantanamo, Cuba. The anti-American groups, including Islamists, Baathists, and authoritarians, in addition to the critics of the War on Terror, claimed there was systematic abuse of human rights. The jihadists went as far as to accuse the United States of opening detention centers specifically for Muslims. So what is the reality of Guantanamo? Captured on battlefields in Afghanistan or arrested in other places, alleged terrorists were brought by U.S. authorities to a detention center at the U.S. military base in Cuba. The affair had multiple dimensions, not all related to the War of Ideas, but the first question was how to classify the armed jihadists arrested on the battlefield, even though they may not have been on the front lines. During all wars, including World War II, the Korean War, the Vietnam War, the Gulf Wars, and the Arab-Israeli wars, military personnel arrested physically far from the battle lines were naturally considered "prisoners of war" by all parties. In the laws that regulate conflicts, the legal determination of "combatants" is exclusive to those in the trenches or shooting. A German tank and its crew captured 100 miles from the front line was an enemy tank still, and its crew members were treated as enemy combatants under the Geneva Conventions. The Taliban, with al Qaeda under its wing, was an organized army serving a regime in control of a country, even though de facto and not necessarily recognized by the United Nations. In international law, the Taliban was a caretaker of the country until a legitimate government replaced it. Thus when the United States and its coalition, with support from the United Nations, invaded Afghanistan and removed the Taliban, the Taliban forces and their al Qaeda auxiliaries (international volunteers serving in Afghanistan) were supposed to be considered as "enemy fighters." The prisoners were to be classed as "enemy combatants" under international law and tradition. Hence these prisoners were supposed to be detained by coalition forces until the conflict was resolved and an agreement was reached between the United States and the new government in Kabul.

But among the captured elements were al Qaeda individuals (and also Taliban and other jihadists) who were involved in war crimes. These persons would have qualified as being enemy combatants who had committed either war crimes or crimes against humanity. These cases would be put under U.S. (or coalition) custody until a trial could be organized. Evidently, the two types of prisoners—regular enemy combatants and persons accused of war crimes—are supposed to fall under the custody of the invading force and allies until a series of decisions is made by Washington and another series of agreements is concluded with the Afghan-elected government and the appropriate international organization.

But because of the War of Ideas waged on behalf of the jihadists and their allies, the normal processing of the Guantanamo detainees was obstructed and slowed. For to process prisoners of war, the custodian government (the United States) needs a domestic legal framework as well as an international legal one. If these detainees are considered as combatants in a war, they cannot be processed via the normal judicial structure reserved for nationals, residents, and visitors, as well as international criminals who must be brought to justice. But these weren't categories under the War on Terror against al Qaeda and the Taliban—the U.S. Congress has not declared war on the jihadi "enemy" (it may still be a valid case for discussion in 2007). This might solve the issue. But here again there is inside opposition to a declaration of war against the world jihadist movement, mounted by their U.S.-based sympathizers. So, in the logic of the critics, the government can neither consider the terrorists as enemy combatants nor declare war against their movement. Only one alternative remains, and this meets the interest of the jihadists: to process the captured terrorists in American courts, which is against the nature of war. This would be the equivalent of having sent German and Japanese troops to regular criminal courts. Worse, however, the accused jihadists would be represented by defense lawyers who (along with their hired experts), instead of proving that their "clients" aren't terrorists or have no link to al Qaeda and Jihadism, would spend public dollars to prove that Jihadism is not a terror ideology. Thus if the persons on trial were found far from, or even near, the combat areas but not in actual combat, they would simply be treated as individuals who happened to have weapons and be Salafists, whom the Wahabi-funded "scholars" would argue were just practicing their freedom of thought. They would become the equivalent of Nazi soldiers or officers who happened to be apprehended with weapons just outside a French village but could be prosecuted only for illegal possession of firearms.

The "Wahabi lobby" in America and the West opposes a declaration of war against Jihadism, or even considering the ideology as an equivalent to Fascism or Nazism. Their offensive has been successful so far in preventing America and other democracies from declaring war on Jihadism and obstructing the allies from considering the (alleged) terrorists as enemy combatants, thus attempting to force the authorities, through the debate, to process the detainees in U.S. and other courts as criminals. Were that done, and if the individuals concerned were found not guilty of bearing arms and shooting, their cases would be dismissed. But democracies should process detainees based on the War on Terror and the Geneva Conventions, regardless of whether al Qaeda and the Taliban recognize international law and the United Nations. The detainees should be considered as "enemy combatants" until the war is over; it is up to Congress to decide when the war is over, which means that U.S. legislators will have to discuss and legislate in that direction and deal with the definition of "Jihadism." These are unavoidable matters if democracies are to roll back terrorism. Enemy combatants should not be tried, but war criminals and perpetrators of crimes against humanity should. Special tribunals must be established for such cases, rather than trying them in the regular criminal courts. Finally, the U.S. government should ask the United Nations and the international community to declare war on jihadi terrorism and establish the appropriate courts. If the international institutions aren't ready, then democracies can handle the legal dimension of the War on Terror. But to do so, the publics in these democracies should be informed, educated, and equipped to face the War of Ideas waged against them.

Abu Ghraib

The second public-relations clash between the United States and the jihadists has been over the series of incidents that took place in the Iraqi prison of Abu Ghraib and its reporting worldwide. In a state of war or outside it, occupation forces have the responsibility of ethical conduct regarding prisoners of war. In Iraq, U.S. and allied forces have followed the Geneva Conventions and other ethics codes of the armed forces. But in 2004, in the Abu Ghraib prison, a number of American servicemen and women exhibited unethical behavior toward Iraqi detainees. The pictures from Abu Ghraib were on every TV screen and in every newspaper around the world, muddying the image of U.S. forces and offending many Iraqis and Arabs as well. A loud debate took place in Washington for months, ending in blaming the responsible authorities and sending U.S. personnel to courts and to prison. That is how democracies with systems of ethics act, and that is what many Arab commentators concluded: "What dictatorship in our past and in our present would severely punish its soldiers and officers for badly treating political prisoners, or any prisoner?" lamented writers in the daily *as siyasa*, on elaph.com, and elsewhere in the media. In our oppressed countries, stated liberal intellectuals, the average mistreatment is torture, and we don't get pictures out of our prison; besides, even if we do, it is not the guilty soldiers who go to jail, but the ones who sneaked the photos.

But though it impressed many liberals and moderates in the Middle East that the United States investigated and prosecuted the offenders, the Abu Ghraib episode also gave the jihadists and their authoritarian allies a chance to inflame U.S. domestic politics. From al Jazeera and other podiums, the Salafists, Khumeinists, and Baathists accused America of "insulting the Muslims on purpose." The commentators attempted to inflame sentiments by insisting there was an American intention to "assassinate the dignity of Arabs and Muslims." The war of propaganda is relentless. But former victims of Saddam and other similarly oppressive regimes were in disbelief in the face of the al Jazeera campaign. Callers to its live programs shouted, "Where have you been when our sons and daughters were tortured daily in the same Abu Ghraib prison under Saddam?" Indeed, the same building was the host of horrific tortures under the previous regime, but was never the subject of inquiries by the media, including al Jazeera. The callers and blog writers continued, "What about the greater torture houses in Syria, Libya, Sudan, and Iran?"[14] The Abu Ghraib scandal left a significant trail behind: It showed Iraqis and Arabs how future governments should punish the perpetrators of torture—another reason why the authoritarians had second thoughts about the rush to tarnish America's image because of the behavior of a few of its soldiers. For Abu Ghraib taught Iraqis and Arabs how to reform the region's jails and revolt against the oppressive systems that manage them.

The Qu'ran Desecration Affair

A third "crisis" in the war of propaganda was the alleged desecration of a copy of the Qu'ran in Guantanamo. Unconfirmed reports, published by *Newsweek* magazine, alleged that a member of the U.S. military flushed a copy of the Qu'ran down the toilet.[15] By ethical standards, such an insult to beliefs is forbidden, especially if it contributes to psychologically harming the detainee. U.S. authorities quickly investigated and reported on the matter. But critics of the War on Terror insisted on turning it into a cheesy, tabloid-style affair by publishing and broadcasting the story of the incident. When the jihadists got hold of the incident, they inflamed the TV and radio audiences of the Arab and Muslim world with conspiracy theories that the "crusaders" were on a campaign to offend the Prophet and their religion.[16] Violent incidents took place in central Asia, leaving some people dead and others injured. In the end, the initial report that started the whole affair appeared to have been false, and the matter was closed.[17] But as liberal Muslim commentators noted, "The radicals are concerned about one unconfirmed report about a copy of the holy book, while thousands of Qu'rans have been destroyed and desecrated in Pakistan, Iraq, and Darfur, with entire mosques burned to the ground."[18]

Homeland Security Affairs

The jihadi propaganda machine has also tried to make an issue of the pressures that Muslim-Americans (and their counterparts in Canada, Europe, and Australia) have supposedly been put under because of the War on Terror and its attendant measures. Although pressures do indeed exist as far as the discomfort of the public is concerned—and that includes all of its subgroups—the propaganda machine has transformed this into a "singling out of Muslims" within the West. With each effort made by authorities to confront terrorism, the other side has raised an objection to any measure targeting Jihadism. The repetitive campaigns organized by Islamist lobbies show a trend: overall, they represent an effort to slow the national and international mobilization against terrorism. One single issue, the "eavesdropping affair," illustrates the general trend. Critics of the U.S. administration say the executive branch cannot eavesdrop on U.S. citizens' phone conversations without a special court's permission. The government responded that it has war powers, bringing back the debate to square one: is America at war legally or not? But beyond the legal debate, the radical Islamists propagated the issue as a full-fledged collapse of democracy in America, seconded by their extreme-left and far-right allies within the country. In fact the matter has exploded because of two reasons: One is the conflict arising between the war powers the U.S. executive is claiming in fighting al Qaeda and its critics' claims that a state of war hasn't been declared and thus the War on Terror has to be prosecuted strictly under present legislation. Two is the fact that not all judges and other civil servants have a clear understanding of Jihadism, and thus don't grasp the need to respond quickly in terrorism cases. But while the debate is ongoing in the United States, a number of European countries have begun to address both issues: In England, special legislations allow a wider, but specific power to the executive branch during the War on Terror. Another example, in France and Spain, is the formation of counter terrorism judges, who can ensure the proper judicial process and are trained to understand the jihadi threat.[19]

WAR ON THE GREATER MIDDLE EASTERN "DEMOCRACIES"

Since the idea of taking the War on Terror from the Atlantic theater (the U.S. mainland and Europe) to the east and south of the Mediterranean found popular support in the West, the terrorist axis has responded strategically at every turn. From Afghanistan to Iraq, Lebanon to Sudan, the American-supported push for freedom has been confronted by the authoritarians and radicals as a "new imperialist" enterprise. From al Jazeera to Western campuses, the spin put on the War on Terror has been that it constitutes attacks against the "democratic Greater Middle East."

By the winter of 2002, jihadists and authoritarian regimes in the region were projecting an American "move" eastward. Islamists and Baathists alike prepared for the upcoming offensive by mounting preemptive campaigns. An Arab summit in Beirut during the spring of 2002 rushed through a reconciliation between the Assad and Saddam regimes and a solidarity move with the Sudanese regime, all in preparation for meeting the heat coming from across the Atlantic. It was amazing for observers like me, who shift analysis from one cultural zone to the other, to watch the debates taking place on opposite sides of the planet. In the Arab and Muslim world, although bin Laden wasn't especially loved by the ruling elites, the general feeling was that the West, and especially America, had been struck hard by the "follies of Osama." The dominant establishment, particularly in Tehran, Baghdad, Damascus, Khartoum, and to a certain extent Tripoli, knew instinctively that it was soon going to be on the receiving end of something to come. The sight of the Taliban regime being taken out deeply intimidated these other regimes. Even though licensed by the United Nations, it was still technically a regime change—the unspoken threat to all dictatorships' survival. Radical organizations such as Hamas, Islamic Jihad, and Hezbollah, having witnessed the purging of al Qaeda from Kabul, also got nervous. On their part, the mullahs of Tehran looked strategically at U.S. forces deploying to their east, removing the Taliban, and opening the path for a potential democracy in central Asia. The "hyenas" of the east, the jihadists, were already preparing for preemptive wars, while the donkeys and elephants in Washington were drowning in the politics of quicksand. The jihadi wars that followed the invasion of Iraq in 2003 had already been prepared for in January 2002; supporters of al Qaeda in Waziristan, of Hamas in Gaza, of Hezbollah in southern Lebanon, of the Janjaweed in Darfur, and of Salafists from Somalia to Bali and from Madrid to London, were sharpening their teeth. They were ahead of the most daring strategists in Washington at the time, and what they were watching for was the landing zone of U.S. intervention. Inside the United States, the debate was about the idea of initiating a regime change in the Middle East. In the region, the debate was about where the move would come, and how. On al Jazeera, the forums swung from one prediction to another: would it be Iran, Iraq, Syria, Sudan, or Lebanon? In D.C., the discussion was still about "Why do they hate us?"

THE WAR "ON" IRAQ

As soon as the Bush administration started to build the case against Iraq at the end of 2002, the region's "authoritarian shield" began thickening. Intense diplomatic activity was initiated by Arab League diplomats in an attempt to gain time and propose solutions. As a general pattern, most Arab leaders dislike each other, but the bloodiest regimes practice among themselves a sort of a "brotherly solidarity." In secret encounters, dictators acknowledge to each other, "If it happens to me, it would happen to you." Hafez Assad hated Saddam Hussein, but Bashar Assad was concerned that the fall of the Baathists in Baghdad would lead to the fall of their sister party in Damascus. Iran's Khamenei was horrified by the idea that political change would be rolling ahead on his two borders. The Islamists were on the fence; on the one hand, they disliked Saddam, but on the other hand, they resented another Karzai-like situation being created in Iraq. Hence al Qaeda prepared itself for all probabilities. This whole political mobilization translated into al Jazeera's editorial line *al Harbu ala Iraq*, "the War on Iraq." Before, during, and after the invasion, the War of Ideas dictated a full-fledged campaign to disqualify, delegitimize, and demonize the whole U.S.-led campaign. Instead of being seen as the liberation of a people oppressed by a dictator, the intervention was reframed as an "imperialist, infidel, crusader war against the Muslims, which has ultimately failed."[20]

Regardless of the decision to select Saddam as a target, invade Iraq, and execute a regime change from the outside—matters that are still under debate in the United States and worldwide—the ideological war peaked with the conflict in Iraq. The U.S. agenda started as a campaign to remove weapons of mass destruction (WMDs), disrupt a purported link between Saddam and al Qaeda, and help the Iraqi people liberate themselves. At the time, I hoped the agenda would be flipped upside down. In front of 550 students in Florida, I argued that Washington should have followed another route: first, liberate the Iraqi people; second, intercept the jihadists; and third, preempt the rearming of Saddam with WMDs. I wasn't wrong, for already in the region, the foes of the United States were preparing to fight on the third issue, "people's liberation," while leaving the first two to be ripped apart by the domestic partisan debate in Washington. In fact, the Baathists and Islamists feared that if one Arab people was freed, others might follow. That was what the regimes and terrorist organizations were fighting about, not Saddam or his vanished WMDs. The United States and the West were busy wrestling over the ethics of the war, while the forces of Jihadism were busy unleashing a regional and international campaign to cripple a future Iraqi democracy—two worlds with concerns light years away from each other. The rest of the events since 2003 only demonstrate the evolution of the two sides. The Islamists, Salafists, and Khumeinists have been fighting the political process in Iraq or trying to dominate it. Their common goal is to obstruct the rise of a pluralist democracy that could link up with the world's other democracies. In the United States and Europe, the issues in the debate were always narrower: the calculation of casualties (not why and against whom soldiers were dying) and the time schedules. The bigger picture seemed always to be lost.

THE CEDAR REVOLUTION

The fall of Saddam opened the closed space in the region to other claims. One of them was by Lebanese civil society, which had suffered Syrian occupation for 30 years. Emboldened by the public discourse on "spreading democracy," Lebanese-Americans first, then the diaspora as a whole, pressured both the United States and France to present the matter before the United Nations Security Council. The action by the Lebanese themselves encouraged the two democracies to pass UN Security Council Resolution 1559, asking Syria to withdraw and Hezbollah to disarm, an act previously thought out of the question. I had the privilege to be a part of some of the work leading to that resolution. The interaction between democracies at work from Washington and Paris to Beirut—even under occupation—was a new experiment in the War of Ideas. On the other side, the Syrian-Iranian axis lacked arguments. Two great powers, with the support of Lebanon's civil society, were putting their influence behind a second underdog country in the region (after Iraq). Losing its temper, Damascus responded à la Saddam—with assassinations. In February 2005, Sunni former prime minister Rafiq Hariri was killed by the Syrians. But in March, the Lebanese masses broke the chain of fear and, despite the Baathist army, put one and a half million people on the streets of Beirut. This was known as the Cedar Revolution.

Beirut will become a crucial arena for the War of Ideas. With many universities, TV and radio stations, art institutions, banks, and intellectual forums, as well as being a multiethnic and multireligious society, Lebanon is poised to fan the highest flames of democracy in the region. Because of their past democratic experience, and the suppression to which they were subjected for decades, the Lebanese—at least a majority of them—will be to the region what Poland was to Eastern Europe: a beacon of early freedom. But because of this privileged situation, the country has already been under a counterattack by the Iranian-Syrian axis through Hezbollah. The Cedar Revolution has been under attack through assassination since 2005: legislators, journalists, and activists have been killed. During the summer of 2006, Hezbollah attempted to turn the country back from a renewed democracy movement into a battleground in an Iranian-Syrian war with Israel, mounted on Lebanon's territory. But despite the attempts by the jihadists and Baathists to turn back the clock at the end of that year and in the beginning of 2007, the breach of freedom is too wide to close. Like Afghanistan and Iraq, Lebanon is fighting its own War of Ideas and may in the near future lead that movement in the entire region—even if the West remains uncertain of the region's natural inclination.

THE GENOCIDE IN DARFUR

For decades, the Islamist regime of Khartoum pushed the agenda of Jihadism, engaging in ethnic cleansing in the south and racial discrimination to the west. Amidst a heavy Western silence—mostly ensured through oil contracts on both sides of the Atlantic—the black Africans of Sudan were, even more than South Africa's native people, the most brutalized on the continent. But when 9/11 occurred, Sudan's regime felt the shock. Starting in the mid-1990s, an antislavery movement in support of the black people of Sudan arose in the United States, propagating waves in the United Kingdom: Charles Jacobs, Keith Roderick, and Samuel Cotton, with whom I worked during these years, charged Jihadism with genocide in Sudan, first in the south, and then in Darfur, the black Muslim western province of the country. By 2000, the U.S. Congress, thanks to bipartisan efforts, had legislated on this tragedy, calling for sanctions. But when bin Laden, who had assisted Sudan's Hassan Turabi in the early stages of the genocide, perpetrated an American genocide in Manhattan, the United States finally put Darfur on the radar of the United Nations. Sudan's Islamist regime felt the wrath of international public opinion coming its way. The Bashir regime, to gain additional time, accepted concessions with Southern Sudan (a Christian majority province) to avert a UN-assisted revolution in the Muslim province of Darfur. Islamists are more sensitive not to lose influence among other Muslims than among *kuffar.* Despite the support by authoritarians and Islamists in the region, and the diplomatic backing by the Arab League in general, the Khartoum regime was losing the battle of ideas on the international stage. For after it had silenced the African south for so long, the world would not easily be convinced that the regime that authorized taking slaves by the hundreds of thousands was a legitimate Third World partner.

Sub-Saharan Africa then shifted away from Sudan's Islamists: Kenya, Eritrea, Zaire, post-Amin Uganda, and other states formed a southern belt to stop the Turabi jihad from thrusting into the heart of the African continent. But the most recent successes in public policy against the terror-supporting regime in Khartoum were also due to a marriage between the American campaign to "spread democracy" on the one hand and the will of this African people to join in on the other. As is the case in Afghanistan, Iraq, and Lebanon, Sudan's Darfur region and southern provinces haven't yet obtained full freedoms, and the antidemocratic forces still have the upper hand; however, it has joined the combat between Jihadism and democracy—and on one of Africa's most inhumane battlefronts.

WAR ON IDEAS: JIHAD PLAYS ETHICS

In the clash between democracy and Jihadism, there are two classic and opposed movements: jihadi efforts to penetrate the West and the spread of democracy in the Muslim world. But the international war room of the jihadists—mostly articulated by the highly skilled Muslim Brotherhood, Wahabi financial powers, and al Jazeera's vast influence—has created a third battlefield: international ethics. Playing on the colonial guilt complex of Western democracies, the Islamists and their allies have been pounding the

European and North American elites for decades to repent for the sins committed by their ancestors. Surely, no one from the West is retaliating against
historic jihad (in the form of a crusade) or resurrecting colonialism. Because,
in all simplicity, the Western public has not conceived of the notion of equiva-
lence between Jihadism and Western imperialism. Hence, as of the 1990s, an
intellectual movement instigated in Europe by Wahabi influence pressured
the West to apologize for the Crusades. Delegations of scholars and journalists began visiting the Middle East asking for forgiveness. This jihadi-insti-
gated move, which attracted Western apologists, would have been a success
story had it been in the framework of historic atonement for past histories—
all histories, including Western and Islamic. Apologizing for events perpetrated by ancestors centuries ago is by itself a very precarious and delicate
process, as all races and nations (or the overwhelming majority of them) have
at some point massacred, oppressed, or violated the rights of other populations—from the empire of the Incas to that of the Mongols. The Europeans
colonized Muslim nations in the modern era; before that, the Ottomans conquered and occupied half of Christian Europe; earlier still, the crusaders subjugated the mostly Muslim eastern shores of the Mediterranean; and centuries
before, Arab Muslim dynasties had conquered the Middle East, North Africa,
Spain, Persia, and beyond. Just imagine how many nations ought to apologize
to how many others, over how many layers of occupation.

But that wasn't what the jihadist radical clerics wanted to achieve. Behind
the veil of demanding a unilateral apology, and borrowing the model from
the politics of anti-Semitism in Europe and racism in the United States, the
imams of Salafism and Khumeinism thought that they could use this ethic of
atonement to weaken the resolve of Western democracies in spreading
human rights and pluralism across the Mediterranean. Indeed, the smart
strategy was to pressure intellectuals to perform a pilgrimage to the areas
where their ancestors had sinned, so that they could thereby become a privileged "caste" in the West. Cultivating the Western apology to the Eastern
dominant elites would enable the latter to continue to oppress their own societies without external intervention—intervention itself being a mode of oppression and colonialism in the first place. For as the guilt culture grew in
Europe and North America, all attempts by mainstream Western elites to demand respect for human rights in the Arab world were met by this answer:
"How dare you to ask us to comply—you, the masters of colonial times. You
should rather apologize for your ancestors." And by obstructing Western sol-

idarity with civil societies in the East, the authoritarian elites of the Arab and Muslim world would be able to thrive for decades more.

But after 9/11 and the Iraq invasion, the guilt equation is not as ironclad as before. The publics in Western democracies are becoming more inquisitive and asking more frequent questions. "What happened before the Crusades?" ask students nowadays. Recently, a prominent European leader, former prime minister of Spain José María Aznar, responded to the challenge by replying to the radical Islamists who are criticizing the *Reconquista*'s records against Arab settlers of Andalusia: "And who would apologize for the conquest of Spain?" This statement, although it ignited several attacks on al Jazeera, nevertheless marked a change in the discourse on both sides of the divide. Ironically to Westerners, al Qaeda and its cohorts use the term *Salibi* ("crusaders") to describe their enemies, showing the fruits of decades-long warfare by their intellectuals.

The complex cultural and propaganda battle exploded after 9/11, and ethic and religious clashes have been rapidly seized upon by the jihadists and used against democracies. In 2003, a crisis erupted over the banning of the Muslim scarf (chador) in French schools; the famous *Hijab affaire* signified the beginning of cultural clashes in France, soon to spread across Europe. France opposed the Iraq invasion, and yet during the fall of 2005, thousands of Arab Muslim youths, incited by radical clerics, set fire to thousands of cars in dozens of cities across the country, drawing new geopolitical battle lines inside the largest nuclear power of Europe. The French *intifada* (urban uprising) interpreted as socioeconomic, was in fact a test of French tolerance of future jihadi uprisings. In September 2005, a Danish daily published cartoons of Prophet Mohammed, which were deemed offensive by mainstream Muslim standards. But what followed the normal political protests was a rapidly spiraling wave of violence in Europe and the Middle East. Here again, the "jihadi kitchen" backed by al Jazeera tried to set the tone internationally as a way to shape the issue for jihadi benefit. While the cartoons could be seen as obnoxious to many Muslims, the real battle wasn't about the drawings; it was about the capacity of an international jihadi command to set the rules of engagement in the War of Ideas. The Muslim Brotherhood used the "cartoon offensive" to preempt future Western intervention to assist Muslim liberals engaged in criticism of religion and clerical power.

The cartoon crisis was followed by another international incident involving an Afghan citizen who converted from Islam to Christianity and was sentenced to death by a Taliban-influenced tribunal in Kabul. The plan behind the sentencing was to use religion to push the envelope even further in international relations and strain the mission of multinational forces in Afghanistan. And to top off the series of incidents, Pope Benedict II delivered a lecture in Germany about theology during the summer of 2006 that touched a sensitive Muslim nerve about the Prophet.

Once more, the subject of discord can be dealt with intellectually in academic forums, but the mass protests and violent expressions incited by the radical clerics and some regimes fuel the war of anger among civilizations—an objective perfectly suited to the jihadists. In the months and years to follow, the radical Islamists will attempt to trigger more "ethical crises" as an advanced line of defense internationally to deter the questioning, reasoning, and ultimately reform that might take place in their midst. The real objectives are to prevent the West from intervening in the Muslim world's internal tensions—even verbally—and to prevent a connection from being made between those in the West with newly opened eyes and those in the East with awakening and liberated minds.

The final question in the War of Ideas is the following: What is the force that works to blind the West and democracies, denying them understanding of the freedom-crisis in the East? If jihadists are the foes of democracies, who then, is aiding them inside the West? In fact, the most dramatic consequence of the jihadist penetration of Western political, academic, and informational spheres over the past two decades has been the development and spread of what I coin *Jihadophilia*. This new concept in terrorism studies, and more particularly in Jihadism studies, defines those forces, groups, and individuals who are not essentially believers in the ideologies or the ultimate theological goals of Salafism or Khumeinism per se, but support their strategic objectives and legitimize their methods by covering up for them. In short, the *Jihadophiles*, or the backers and sympathizers of Jihadism, support efforts to weaken and defeat Jihadism's enemies, mostly democracies.[21] The mostly Western Jihadophiles trivialize the threat of Jihadism, minimize its importance, and simultaneously assert that jihadists in their essence are in fact a legitimate "resistance" caused by Western and other foreign policies, not an ideological movement aiming at world domination. Therefore the crux of the War of Ideas boils down to a match within the West between the expanding influence of Jihadophiles and the capacity of the intellectual resistance to Jihadism to win the minds of the public. This will be the Bastogne of the War of Ideas.

CHAPTER THIRTEEN

WAR ON THE MESSENGERS

TO READERS AND FUTURE RESEARCHERS IN THE FIELD, PERHAPS THE messengers are less important than the message. The catastrophic dimensions of the clash of ideas worldwide, especially after 9/11, have overshadowed the little histories of those authors, researchers, scholars, and journalists who have been attempting to enlighten readers, listeners, and viewers about the simple fact that the War of Ideas was in existence long before the War on Terror and about what it would take to address the ideological conflict in order to end the violence and its future spread. The messengers in the War of Ideas are not the ideologues per se, but the people who have observed the rise and expansion of the jihadi movement and witnessed its impact in the Arab and Muslim world; intellectuals who have analyzed the state of political culture in the East and compared it with the collective understanding of it in the West. The messengers are those, born and educated in the Greater Middle East or the West, who have come to the conclusion that a massive misunderstanding has existed for at least the last half century between two kinds of global societies: those that have progressed into democracies and those that have been denied that progress.

Even during the Cold War, while most scholarship and research in the West concentrated on the Soviet threat, a number of writers and essayists out of the Middle East were dedicated to warning the Free World of the rise of the modern jihadi menace. These messengers, whether Muslims, Christians, or Jews, were at first mostly from the region and had seen the War of Ideas up close during its earliest stages. Among them, from those I have known personally, were Muslim Mustafa Jeha, who wrote *Mihnatu al Aql fil Islaam (On the crisis of mind in Islam)*; Jewish writer Bat Ye'or, who penned *The Dhimmi*; and Christian Fuad Afram al Bustany, the erudite author of several volumes. There are many others around the region I could also name. These early commentators on the first War of Ideas have attempted to raise consciousness among the region's elites and masses as to the seriousness of the war on learning and the spread of the madrassas' jihadi culture. Little of their work appeared in the West until 1990.

In 1979, while still living on the Mediterranean's east coast, I added my first book, *al Taadudiya (Pluralism)*, to the contemporary intellectual efforts of the messengers. In the years following its publication, I experienced (as any intellectual dissident has) the heat of the dominant paradigm: Islamist, Baathist, left-wing, and right-wing authoritarians alike resented the new conclusions, which at the time didn't do more than state historical facts. But the revealing of these facts, concerning the jihad-related conquests of the seventh century through modern times, had the dominant elite concerned about their impact on the native populations of the Middle East. In the rebuttals, no contrasting facts were introduced. No historian, for example, was able to deny the happening of the battle of Yarmuk in 636 AD/CE,[1] and no political scientist was able to perform a different reading of Sayyid Qutb's modern writing, as long as both of us read Arabic and understood it equally.[2]

But, speaking of Arabic, most of my original writings didn't make it to American universities or into Western academic journals before the 1990s. Even the works of a giant in the field, the erudite al Bustany, were never allowed by the Wahabi lobby to make it to the researchers in America and Europe. Bat Ye'or's publications of the mid-1980s on the conditions of non-Muslims in the Muslim world did slowly make their way into Western libraries, but under a barrage of fire by the Wahabi lobbies and their academic friends. Many Muslim critics of Jihadism, who went further than analysis and engaged in advocacy for reform, met a tragic end. Mustafa Jeha, for example, who published volumes and articles on intellectual terrorism in the 1970s and 1980s, was assassinated. As a Muslim liberal, his fate was a prelude to that of many other dissident intellectuals and academics who paid with their lives for their daring publishing enterprises in Algeria, Lebanon, Egypt, Turkey, Bangladesh, and other countries. Others were forced to emigrate into exile. But in general terms, what held back the acceptance of the knowledge shared by these pre-1990 messengers was the Western inability to see the global threat emerging. This blindness had two causes: the priority of the Cold War and the effects of the 1973 oil crisis. With the spread of Wahabi, Khumeinest, and apologist influence, the voices of dissident researchers were drowned out by white noise.

THE 1990S

During the 1990s, wider scholarly dissent opposed the Wahabi-influenced academic order in North America and Europe. Out of the old continent, more writers, including Swiss-based Bat Ye'or, French historian Paul Fregosi, and emigré Indian Muslim author Ibn Warraq, produced a wave of books and monographs exposing the party line in Islamic history. Across the Atlantic, two high-profile scholars fired the first salvo into the thick wall of academic jihadi denial. The first, Professor Samuel Huntington of Harvard, shook off the thinking of the elite with his 1993 *Foreign Affairs* article on the "Clash of Civilizations," followed in 1996 by his book of the same name. An ocean of critics emerging from all quarters of the social sciences, as well as journalists and activists, blasted this leading Western scholar in international relations for his assertion that "some force was provoking a clash of religious civilizations."[3] Huntington's critics may have neglected to read the declarations of the Khartoum Jihadi Conference,[4] but they couldn't have missed the first attack against the Twin Towers, both in 1993. During this same decade, the elite of Middle East and literary studies, impacted by Jihadophilia, led by professors John Esposito and Edward Said, repeatedly attacked another American icon of Near East history, Professor Bernard Lewis. Born in London before he emigrated to the United States in his adulthood, Lewis wrote extensively on the region's history and Islam, never accommodating his views to the post-1973 oil influence. Also in the 1990s, more messengers rose to the occasion in America. I will only name a few, but the work of many others is accessible in libraries and archives. Scholar Daniel Pipes, head of the Middle East Forum, and Professor Martin Kramer were among the first academics to expose the bias in U.S.-based Middle East studies. Courageous journalists such as Steve Emerson, freeing themselves from the Jihadophile diktat, investigated the depth of jihadi-terrorist penetration in America. Human rights activists such as Charles Jacobs, Keith Roderick, and African American Samuel Cotton, despite the general silence of the human rights community, raised the issues of Sudan, Mauritania, and minority persecution in the whole region. Occasionally even mainstream journalists spoke out, such as Abe Rosenthal of the *New York Times*, who wrote against radical Islamist oppression in the Middle East, and Robert Kaplan, who in the *Atlantic Monthly* exposed the "Arabist" influence at the U.S. State Department.

In the decade preceding 9/11, the second War of Ideas was fought fiercely by a very few in the West and scattered pro-democracy Middle East underdogs, many seeking asylum and exile. During the 1990s, most of the few and the brave who dared oppose the Wahabi lobby were verbally harshly attacked. All of the above-mentioned intellectuals were harassed by Islamist watchdogs: for example, Huntington and Lewis were verbally denounced by Wahabi-funded academics, and Pipes and Emerson by Islamist lobbies. But more dangerously in the years before 9/11, a witch hunt systematically targeted the ethnic dissidents. Middle Eastern activists, Muslim and Christian alike, were the subject of militant and vicious media attacks. The talons of Jihadism dug deeply into the social structure of the intellectual and political establishment. Sudanese, Copt, Assyrian, Lebanese, Kurds, Shiite, and moderate Sunni community workers were submitted to various jihadi pressures. Jobs were cut, grants were canceled, professional sanctions were applied, and in some cases direct threats were made. Before their 2001 strike on the Twin Towers in New York, jihadists spent a whole decade attempting to silence the voices of the witnesses of their past activities in the Middle East and the experts who uncovered their ideology in the West. These messengers were the real heroes of the second War of Ideas.

SINCE 9/11

In the United States and the rest of the West, an uphill intellectual battle has been fought fiercely by a few messengers against an army of academics, scholars, and former government analysts who oppose the War on Terror and defend regimes and radical movements. But in this battle of ideas, which has been totally unbalanced in terms of numbers, a quantitative change has been noticed over the past five years. Slowly the intellectual ground has been shifting. The public, disregarding the old paradigm of apologists, has shifted to new media or new voices in the old media. The message has finally been breaking through the Wahabi–oil money wall. The new American classroom has had enough of the apologist teachers, but unfortunately the obstacle remains in place. In the educational system, the elite co-opts the elite, and the Jihadophile academic lobby continues to hire more of the same. But today's intuitive youth want to get the facts, and instead of going into the field of Middle East studies, more and more students are shifting toward security and counterterrorism studies, new areas in which the elites are less entrenched. In a nutshell, academia will have to accommodate seekers for real answers about the War on Terror.

Around the nation, and progressively in Europe and beyond, new think tanks have been arising to meet the challenge, some on terrorism studies and others on democracy advocacy. In Washington, older institutions have been promoting new programs to educate the government and the public, and new ones such as the Foundation for the Defense of Democracies (FDD), led by Cliff May, have signaled the emergence of a new generation of multitasked NGOs, whose goal is to catch up with more than a decade of research and close the educational gap. The field of counterterrorism has seen a new class of projects, such as the Investigative Project of veteran Steve Emerson, the counterterrorism blog of Andrew Cochran, and the faculty's Summer Workshop on Teaching about Terrorism (SWOT). These are only a few examples from a growing force in the War on Terror in the United States. Similar alternative analysis entities are developing around the world, from Toronto, Brussels, London, Paris, Istanbul, and Baghdad to Singapore and Sydney. In addition to the think tanks, a myriad of Internet-based news services have also emerged in the West and in the Arab world. Cyberspace has become the widest battlefield of all, with hundreds of sites expressing the views of all the contending streams in the third War of Ideas. In addition to the Western critics of the War on Terror, mostly entrenched on campus-based home pages, the Salafists, and to some extent the Khumeinists, have carved out their own web space to launch their indoctrination blitz.

But the most interesting phenomenon has been the explosion of a weblogging culture by a growing opposition to the traditionalist oil apologists. The "bloggers," from New York to Beirut and Warsaw to Baghdad, are overwhelming the jihadists online, suggesting a future turning of the tide in the War of Ideas. For while Iranian president Ahmedinijad blasted the U.S.-led democracy efforts at the United Nations in Manhattan, Iranian bloggers out of Tehran were chanting a popular slogan about the days to come: "No, No to the Taliban, from Kabul to Tehran."[5]

DESPERATE JIHAD AGAINST THE MESSENGERS

With the intellectual revolution brewing in America and many democracies around the world, the old axis of jihadists, authoritarians, and their Western advocates has turned to desperate attacks against the men and women of the new dissident school. In newspapers and weeklies, on TV and radio shows, and widely on the Internet, extreme-left and ultraright cadres and academics from the 1970s, along with Islamists, radical scholars, and media activists, have concentrated their fire on the front-line messengers to discredit them and distance them from the public—but to no avail. The Wahabi lobby, in conjunction with the Neo-Marxist network and their political allies within democracies, unleashed a systematic campaign against both the messengers and the message. To each trial involving alleged jihadi terrorists, the Wahabi lobby has been sending lawyers and their own countermessenger "experts." In many courtrooms, as in the Virginia cases in 2006,[6] the jihadi lobbies have attempted to discredit the new experts on Jihadism, such as Evan Kohlmann and others.[7]

Interestingly, some of the jihadis verbally attacking the messengers in the U.S also happened to be involved in terrorism activities. As I noted in *Future Jihad*, Ismael Royer, who is now serving a sentence for participating in the Virginia jihad "Paintball" network, was the lead pen in bashing many experts and think tanks between 1998 and 2003. A number of jihadi preachers, activists, spokespersons, and members of alleged human rights groups on both sides of the Atlantic were found to be linked to or guilty of terror-related actions. This is indicative of the fine line that exists between ideological activism and literal violence. The assassination of filmmaker Theo Van Gogh in Holland was a chilling example of how incitement to ideological hate can lead to physical violence.

In the United States and the West in general, jihadophiles' attacks against intellectuals often include vilification of scholars and experts who expose Jihadism or reveal oppression under Islamist or authoritarian regimes in the region. Commentators on Middle Eastern affairs such as MESA President Professor Juan Cole have accused others of playing "sinister roles" and called for Inquisition-like "investigation" of colleagues who teach and testify on Jihadism. Some instructors, displaying an even more radical stance, have demonized counter-terrorism scholars. For example, Berkeley's As'ad Abikhalil (who has admitted meeting with Hezbollah terror group leader Hassan Nasrallah) accused U.S. experts of endorsing or being morally or politically linked to overseas massacres. The campaign against experts testifying on Jihadism in U.S. and Western courts began in the 1990s and has continued, undaunted by 9/11 and the War on Terror. An *Atlantic Monthly* article of

September 2006 by Amy Waldman, for example, vilifies those experts who expose Salafi Jihadism and praises the ones who claim Salafism is a spiritual experience.

The list of attacks on writers who attempt to educate the public about Jihadism is endless, and will be as long as the War of Ideas goes on. The point is not that this or that person attacked me or another scholar; it is that even though well-meaning and open-minded Americans take academic freedom and impartiality so much for granted that they may find it hard to believe that Wahabi oil money has influenced the jihadi-friendly "party line" put out by the Middle East studies establishment over the last 30 years—it's true, and the above are just some of the examples. Even more worrisome is the overlap between the campaign by the Wahabi lobbies in America and the West and the verbal attacks by the new experts on Jihadism and al Qaeda. In one of his most important al Jazeera video addresses, al Qaeda spokesperson for America Adam Gadahn, a.k.a. Azzam al Amriki, named a number of pioneering messengers in the United States, including Pipes, Emerson, and author Robert Spencer. Very interestingly, he praised British politician George Galloway and journalists Seymour Hirsh and Robert Fisk for being supportive of his jihad.[8] The apparent lesson here is that the terror jihadists and the apologists in the West are indeed in one trench.

The jihadist ideologues and strategists are not as isolated as one would think. In their global war to reach their goals, they display a remarkable ability to reach out to the other opponents of democracies and use their energies fully. The jihadi "politicians" have excelled in conducting a war of ideas with the resources of their enemies, against the best of their adversaries, striking at the most efficient of their foes in the midst of the latter's own societies.

CONCLUSION

LET'S LOOK AT THE BIG PICTURE OF THIS WAR OF IDEAS, ASK THE remaining major questions, and look to the future. My primary goal is to show how best to understand it, prepare for it, or even deal with it as it comes. In these last analyses, I am offering a global look at the connections between the two campaigns, the consequences of this ideological war and its prolongation, the real choices available to democracies and to Muslim societies, and what is being done as of 2007, along with a short set of prescriptive guidelines. I'll highlight the central message of this book and the central challenge of this war.

THE EAST AND WEST ARE INTERCONNECTED

The West and all other democracies worldwide, including India, Russia, and those in Latin America, have the most important role to play in ending the War on Terror by winning the War of Ideas. The United States, in the center of the Free World, has an even more crucial mission to fulfill. Because of its resources, its power, its ideals, and the generosity of its people, America finds itself leading campaigns around the globe to assist societies in peril that are facing off against terror organizations and regimes. But the U.S.-led campaign needs to be backed by a determined, unified, and convinced public. This is where the rise of consciousness would turn the tide of the ideological conflict. If Americans are enabled to understand the realities of the menace, they will in turn enable their government to act credibly, strategically, and with a consensus behind it. Democracies must educate their own publics on the history, evolution, and future development of Jihadism and its allies. Without full public awareness, the West will waiver through a long and costly war. And, once ready to engage in a rational program of international resistance to terrorism, the West's most important task will be to extend vibrant, long-term, and comprehensive help to the peoples of the Greater

Middle East seeking freedom and peace. A major conclusion of my research over the past quarter of a century, before the Cold War and after, before 9/11 and since, is that the conflict is global and interactive in nature. Maybe some world leaders have stated this equation in their own words since the War on Terror started in 2001, but in the years before, many of my research colleagues and I hopelessly warned that in this conflict there are no limits or safe places. Either the peoples of the region will be liberated or the terrorists will wreck world peace and stability for generations. The latter is not really a choice, of course; a focused and enlightened West must move the international community to reach out to the oppressed masses of the Arab and Muslim world and empower their free-minded, emerging forces. It is only then that Jihadism as an ideology will be confronted in its own habitat and rolled back in favor of reform.

But the East also has a neglected duty toward the West. Civil societies in the Greater Middle East have to produce and encourage the rise of a younger, newer, and determined elite, ready to engage in the War of Ideas through reform, socialization, and political change. The democracy movements in Iraq, Syria, Iran, Lebanon, Egypt, and the rest of the Arab and Middle Eastern region should meet existing democracies halfway. The popular uprisings in Lebanon, Iraq, and Afghanistan should encourage similar democratic uprisings in the region and embolden youth, women, and minorities to reach out to the international community. In addition, the democrat, liberal, reformist, and humanist elements in the Muslim world, particularly in the Greater Middle East, must make their views known to the Western public so that it can support them. For example, the peoples of Iraq and Afghanistan must address the American and international public directly on the importance of political change in these countries to counter the arguments of those lobbies who claim that democracy, as a Western "interest," is being forced upon Muslim nations. The historical opportunity has opened in the early twenty-first century for liberation to spread in this long-oppressed region. The opportunity has to be seized fast so that peace can still be tasted by this generation and lived fully by the next.

CONSEQUENCES OF THIS WAR OF IDEAS

If the War of Ideas drags on, and the efforts for increasing awareness in the West and democratization in the East stall, fail, or are reversed, two major consequences are to be expected. First, the War on Terror will be extended into the next generation, and potentially the following one as well. Our grandchildren will still be dying on battlefields around the world and in our cities and towns. This projection is not a fruit of imagination but a rational calculation. Indeed, if the public within democracies is not enabled to understand and sustain the campaign, its support for liberating the East will collapse. And if that happens, then the Greater Middle East will fall back into an extreme and lethal radicalization. And as a boomerang effect, Western societies will see their security shattered. The cycle will continue in spirals as the West responds with more and more devastating force. In very sober words, if democracies don't win and democracy doesn't spread, the War on Terror will last for generations.

Second, if the conflict of ideas and ideologies continues for some time, the impact of improved technology and science will be catastrophic.[1] On the security level, the longer these wars last, the higher the probability that the terrorists will use advanced technologies. Science in principle doesn't go backward, and the lethalness of its military dimension increases. Time is not a positive factor in the War on Terror, and therefore the shorter the War of Ideas, the better for a bleeding humanity. On the development level, this war (like all wars) consumes energies, resources, lives, and talents and slows down discoveries in the fields of health and exploration, and advances in the quality of life. Sadly, the holy war waged by the Salafists and Khumeinists is an obstruction to the development of science and improvement of the human condition. Had al Qaeda, Saddam, the Taliban, and the radical mullah regime of Iran not existed since the 1990s, the end of the Cold War would have spared the world another decade and a half of warfare and military spending. The estimated $600 billion spent by all players in wars provoked by the jihadists and Baathists since 1990 could have been used to solve a number of medical problems challenging humanity and to hasten the conquest of space. Instead, kids today from Pakistan to New York City are taught to become suicide bombers for Allah.

WESTERN CHOICES

The practical question in 2007 is this: What are the choices available to the West as the War of Ideas unfolds—for policymakers, the media, strategic planners, individuals, and communities? The worst choice, an unacceptable option, is to dodge the debate, flee the intellectual confrontation, and play the ostrich, putting our heads in the sand and convincing ourselves that the problem doesn't exist—and indeed, as has been shown, the Wahabi lobbies are only too ready to support the "choice" of believing that jihad as a violent, totalitarian ideology is not a reality.[2] The West already has liberties, tolerance, and pluralism. Its elite should not defect and abandon the inquiry process. It would be disastrous to western societies if their scientists were finding more and more answers to scientific problems while their politicians and academics were backing off, just because of lobbying pressures applied by their foes. In fact, since 9/11, many Western political and academic establishments have generally caved in to the jihadi intellectual offensive. With the exception of some leaders, the mainstream elite in America and the bulk of European politicians, instead of denouncing antidemocratic Jihadism as an ideology and a movement, have looked the other way. Missing the entire equation, and falling into the trap of jihadi lobbies, badly advised European commissioners have been setting the clock back and exposing their populations to further confusion, and hence to future breaches in their national security. At the European Commission in 2006, a special committee was tasked to create a "Lexicon" for bureaucrats, politicians, and legislators on how to use terms related to Islam as a religion. In fact, the special committee as of the end of 2006 was advising commissioners not to use the terms "jihad," "Jihadism," and "Islamism" in European speeches, but instead to employ phrases such as "terrorists who are using a religion for their activities." Naturally, after investigation, it was revealed that among the members of the advisory board were notable apologists for Wahabism and even jihadi scholars, such as Dr. Tariq Ramadan.[3]

In the United States, a similar campaign was unleashed against President Bush and congressional leaders from both parties when they began to use terms such as "Islamo-fascism" in their speeches.[4] These "offensives" are triggered as rear-guard actions to prevent the use of terms that might awaken the public to the reality of the War of Ideas.[5] Obviously, the users of the terms—politicians or commentators—aren't the ultimate experts in the field, since most scholars shied away from the issue decades ago.[6]

Nevertheless, political jihadis' battles to slow down the awareness process in the West can only prolong the War of Ideas; ultimately, the bottom-up "discovery" of the terrorists' ideology will happen irreversibly, if only because the jihadists themselves are constantly reminding the world of their goals. From this perspective, the West should hasten its own self-education about the matter, through the media, debates, and the like, for at least two reasons: to identify the jihadists and their strategies, and to further distinguish the Muslim community's majority of law-abiding citizens and peace-loving members from extremists, radicals, and terrorists. The West's responsibility to speed up the process of national and international education is crucial in this regard.[7]

MUSLIM CHOICES

In the Muslim world and within its diasporas, what is needed is for more democratic and reformist currents to rise up and express themselves on the essence of the issue and for less formal interviews with clerics and officials who always deny the link between terrorism and religion. Muslims should not be put on the defensive about their faith. The questions about the theological interpretation of the *wajib al jihad* (the duty of jihad) should be separated from the actual jihadist movements that are using religion in their ideology. It is up to Muslims, not non-Muslims, to reject the jihadist interpretation of "jihad" in modern times. These debates and similar ones can be rekindled, much like the debates that took place centuries ago in other religions, which then led to reforms. And even if the West and the international community help in the process of opening space for freedoms, the responsibility is on Muslim intellectuals, scholars, and commentators to initiate and widen the debate within their own cultural and political space. The reality is that the debate already exists but is extremely limited, in view of the state of liberties within the Muslim world. While the Islamist-jihadists have been enjoying an open field to advance their agenda and interpretations, the antiji-hadists, or humanists, have been suppressed.

In the West, the debate within Muslim communities is also developing, but with a strong advantage to the jihadists so far. Aided by the apologists and lobbies, the jihadists have placed themselves in the driver's seat of the Muslim communities. They, not the moderates, represent the communities, speak on their behalf, set their agendas, and define the public discourse. For example, the influence of the Islamists in the West and in the United States enables them to penetrate the prison system and oversee Muslim religious teaching and counseling. Practically, this allows them to facilitate the recruitment to Jihadism among a critical, vulnerable population.[8] Nonjihadi Muslims in Europe, North America, and Australia are misrepresented or unheard from on the most important issues, although Muslims who identify with moderate views are numerically a majority, albeit a silent one. Hence, to use an American expression, nonjihadi Muslims should benefit from the equivalent of "affirmative action." They should be empowered, granted public space, and when needed, funded with public spending. Ideally, nonjihadi Western-based Muslims should become the leading reformist force in the Muslim world, as they are able to understand both cultures and at the same time have chosen democracy and pluralism.

WESTERN AND AMERICAN MEASURES

The present (mostly American) measures to contain Jihadism include the so-called campaign to "win the hearts and minds" of Arabs and Muslims around the world. Polls conducted on behalf of U.S. and Western institutions[9] regularly show, depending on how the questions are framed, that America and its allies have bad images in Muslim countries. Even intelligence estimates, five years after 9/11, still link the rise of Jihadism to poverty and global attitudes instead of seeing it as a result of mass mobilization by jihadist ideologues and movements. The measures taken by the European and Canadian governments in the War of Ideas up to now have been completely reliant on their mostly Islamist advisers, with few exceptions. In the United States, at least since 2002, measures have been mostly defensive and based on a series of highly funded public-relations campaigns to "win" those hearts and minds. The bureaucracy in charge of the measures focuses mainly on attempts to better explain the positive intentions of the U.S. government toward the Muslim world. But the jihadists are mobilizing radicalized Muslims not on the grounds of America's image, but to follow "the injunction of Allah," and hence no PR campaign can defeat them unless it defeats the premises of the jihadi ideology. At the higher levels of the state in the United States, United Kingdom, Australia, Germany, and somewhat in France, the rhetoric is attempting to single out the ideas and ideology of the terrorist enemy, but not always with the requisite precision and adequate information. Presidents and prime ministers are executive leaders, not experts. If they are not backed by lower-level expertise and systematic educational campaigns, their work will be gone with the wind. It is curious, for example, that although U.S. presidents and legislators from both parties have made excellent speeches on the subject, the tax-funded PBS and NPR, and the cable public service C-SPAN, have not followed their lead, but on the contrary criticized the speeches. For the Arab-speaking world, the U.S. Congress has funded a broadcast system to send a message of democratization, human rights, and counterterrorism via the Virginia-based al Hurra TV and Radio Sawa. These outlets, although professional media that are increasingly viewed and listened to in the region, still need to reach the level of al Jazeera's incitement—but for democracy and against the jihadists' ideology.

It is also very important for the United States and the rest of the West to support dissidents and democracy groups. Again, as with the PR campaigns, though national leaders have been advancing powerful arguments and making significant pledges of support to dissidents and to human rights and democracy groups, the rank and file in the War of Ideas still trail behind the leadership vanguard and aren't meeting public expectations. Billions of dollars have been spent on the military and security fight against terrorism since 2001, but very little has been granted to real, effective, and committed currents of democracy in the region or in exile. And, just as important as spending money on such groups is recognizing the dissidents as leading and respected forces in their societies. But up until now, in both Europe and North America, it is the radicals and jihadi sympathizers, not the moderates, who have been received by governments as "partners" in the dialogue. Stunningly, and at various levels of bureaucracy, it is mostly the apologists and radicals, not the democracy advocates and nonjihadists, who end up being recognized as experts, translators, analysts, and leaders.

Last but not least, in the general War of Ideas, it is in United Nations' discussion and dialogue that the future of democracies and Jihadism can be measured. Although the United Nations originally sought to promote democracy and freedoms, as set forth in its charter in 1945 and the Universal Declaration of Human Rights in 1948, its political culture has shifted so that it now supports authoritarian regimes and legitimizes totalitarian ideologies, including Jihadism. Unfortunately, when historians unearth the UN records of voting and interventions for the last few decades, they will see that it was mostly oil-driven agendas that sent the UN peacekeepers, the Blue Helmets, into particular areas and not others, and obstructed them from saving populations endangered by terrorism. In this clash of ideas, the United Nations has to reposition itself as a defender of freedoms and not the status quo. And it has to recognize that freedom's most lethal enemies today are terrorism and totalitarianism.

POLICY RECOMMENDATIONS

To end this book, I leave the reader with the following strategic recommendations, which I suggest be made to NGOs, governments, and international organizations as a way to rebalance the debate about terrorism and democracy and open alternatives in the War of Ideas.

- Open the debate about Jihadism, and vote for laws that would ban ideologies that discriminate within societies, divide humanity into enemy zones and peace zones, and legitimize violence outside international law. The U.S. Congress, European Parliament, United Nations, and legislative branches of all democracies around the globe, including those in the Muslim world, must do so.
- Open national and international debates and forums (including legislators and intellectuals) to identify, clarify, and specify the terrorist roots of the Salafist and Khumeinist jihadi doctrines.
- Support free-minded democratic movements, groups, leaders, and intellectuals in their resistance to the surge of fascist, radical, and terrorist ideologies.
- Within the United States and other democracies and among partners in the War on Terrorism worldwide—including those in the Muslim world—reform the educational system to advance public awareness and counter the radicalization of certain societal segments.
- Use public media for education and information. Reserve appropriate space for educators who can provide material and research on terrorism and Jihadism, and for dissident voices from the Muslim world and the Greater Middle East who can testify to the persecution, oppression, and radicalization taking place at the hands of the jihadists, as well as to the necessity of enabling civil societies to acquire democratic institutions, rights, and processes.
- Welcome and embrace all Muslim reformers who seek freedom, democracy, and pluralism, and distinguish them from the Islamists and jihadists who oppose all of these.
- Expose the jihadi network and lobbies and explain their strategies to the public.

NOTES

INTRODUCTION

1. Walid Phares, Lecture, Florida Atlantic University, Lifelong Learning Society, "The Politics of Civilizations," November, 1998.
2. French celebre expression used to describe those fundamentalists "crazy about Allah."
3. See for example Faisal Devji, *Landscapes of the Jihad: Militancy, Morality, Modernity* (Ithaca, NY: Cornell University Press, 2005).
4. Neil Gregor, ed., "The Psychology of Nazism," in *Nazism*, Oxford Readers Series (New York, NY: Oxford University Press, 2000), p. 42.

CHAPTER 1

1. See Walid Phares, *Future Jihad: Terrorist Strategies against the West* (New York: Palgrave Macmillan, 2006), chapter 1.
2. Samuel Huntington, "The Clash of Civilizations?" *Foreign Affairs* (Fall 1993).
3. See Richard E. Rubenstein and Jarl Crocker, "Challenging Huntington," *Foreign Policy*, No. 96 (Autumn 1994), pp. 113–128.
4. Francis Fukuyama, *The End of History and the Last Man* (New York: Free Press, 1992).
5. Samuel Huntington, *The Clash of Civilizations: The Remaking of World Order* (New York: Simon and Schuster, 1996).
6. See criticism of Huntington in Albert L. Weeks, "Do Civilizations Hold?" *Foreign Affairs*, September/October 1993; Fouad Ajami, "The Summoning;" *Foreign Affairs*, September/October 1993; Kishore Mahbubani, "The Dangers of Decadence: What the Rest Can Teach the West," *Foreign Affairs*, September/October 1993; Edward Said, "The Clash of Ignorance," *The Nation*, October 4, 2001. See also response from Huntington, "If Not Civilizations, What? Samuel Huntington Responds to His Critics," *Foreign Affairs*, November/December 1993.
7. See Karl Marx and Frederick Engels, *The Communist Manifesto* (Pamphlet), 150th Anniversary Edition (n.p.: Charles H. Kerr Publishers, 1998).
8. See Dennis Sherman, *Western Civilizations: Renaissance to the Present*, 4th ed. (New York: McGraw-Hill, 2003).
9. See Lee Harris, *Civilization and Its Enemies: The Next Stage of History* (New York: Free Press, 2004).
10. Walid Phares, *al Taadudiya fi al Aalam* (Pluralism in the world) (Mount Jordan, Lebanon: Kasleek University Press, 1979).
11. See Bernard Lewis, *The Crisis of Islam: Holy War and Unholy Terror* (New York: Random House, 2004).
12. See Jeanne Morefield, *Covenants without Swords: Idealist Liberalism and the Spirit of Empire* (Princeton, NJ: Princeton University Press, 2004).
13. See Sir William Muir, *The Caliphate*, new ed. (New Delhi, India: Cosmo Publications, 2005).
14. See Allister Heath, "The Jihadists Are Coming," *Business Journal*, August 6, 2006.
15. See Lorenzo Vidino, "Democracy in the Muslim World," *Boston Globe*, September 24, 2006.
16. In *al Sharia wal hayat*, al Jazeera TV, October 24, 2003.
17. See John B. Dunlop, *Russia Confronts Chechnya: Roots of a Separatist Conflict* (Cambridge: Cambridge University Press, 1998).

CHAPTER 2

1. Paul Berman, *Terror and Liberalism* (New York: W. W. Norton, 2004).

2. Jamie Glazov, "Round Table: Is Democracy in the Middle East Possible?" frontpagemag.com, September 26, 2006. See also Natan Sharansky with Ron Dremer, *The Case for Democracy: The Power of Freedom to Overcome Tyranny and Terror* (Cambridge, MA: Public Affairs, 2004).

3. Mordechai Nisan, *Minorities in the Middle East: A History of Struggle and Self Determination* (New York: McFarland, 1992), conclusion.

4. From various editorials in the London-based weekly *al Quds al Arabi*, Syria's daily *Teshreen*, and al Jazeera's panels on Arab nationalism.

5. See Paul M. Johnson, *Modern Times: The World from the Twenties to the Nineties* (New York: Harper Perennial, 2001).

6. See Michel Aflaq, *al Baath* (Beirut: Dar al arabi, 1957); also Omayma Abdel-Latif, "Is Baathism Dead? " *al Ahram*, April 28, 2004; also Lee Smith, "It's an Arab Nationalist Thing: Osama's Islamism and Saddam's Baathism Are More Alike than You Think," *Slate*, October 22, 2004.

7. Walid Phares, "The Jihadists," in *Future Jihad: Terrorist Strategies against the West* (New York: Palgrave Macmillan, 2006).

8. In Niall Christie, "A Translation of Extracts from the *Kitab al-Jihad* of 'Ali ibn Tahir Al-Sulami (d. 1106)." The Arabic text, with a French translation, may be found in Emmanuel Sivan, "Un traité Damasquin du début du XIIᵉ siècle," *Journal Asiatique* 254 (1966): 206–222: "Abu Hamid Muhammad al-Ghazali said: 'Whenever a year passed without an expedition every Muslim (who was) free, responsible and capable of taking part in an expedition went out on one, seeking by it to exalt the word of God (who is praised), to demonstrate his religion, to suppress by it his enemies the polytheists, to achieve the reward which God (who is praised) and His Prophet promised him from (fighting) the jihad in His cause, and to gain their (the enemies') wealth, women and lands, until there were, of those who came to face them (the enemy), enough to fight them in it (the expedition). That is to say that the jihad, however, is an obligation of sufficiency."

9. See definitions in Andrew Bostom, *The Legacy of Jihad: Islamic Holy War and the Fate of Non-Muslims* (Amherst, NY: Prometheus Books, 2005); also Thomas F. Michel, ed., *A Muslim Theologian's Response to Christianity: Ibn Taymiyya's Al-Jawab Al-Sahih* (Delmer, NY: Caravan Publishers, 1985). Also Ibn Taymiya, *Public Duties in Islam: The Institution of the Hisba*, trans. Muhtar Holland (n.p.: Kazi Publications, 1982).

10. See Bostom, *The Legacy of Jihad.*

11. This interpretation was advanced by the Wahabis inspired by Muhammad abdel Wahab and the Muslim Brotherhood, founded by Hassan al Banna. Shaykh M. Kabbani, *Salafi Movement Unveiled* (n.p.: Kazi Publications, 1997).

12. Walid Phares, "Jihadism as an Ideology," lecture at Harvard Law School, February 2002; also interview with author Fuad Afram Bustani, Beirut, March 1983. Also see Quintan Wiktorowicz and Grover Gardner, *The Name of the Enemy: Jihadi Salafis*, Pocket University audio CD, July 2004. See also *Salafi Tapes: Authentic Salafism* at www.salafitapes.com; *Salafi Islam* at www.globalsecurity.org/military/intro/islam-salafi.htm; *Salaf* at www.salaf.dk/; also Salafi Publications at www.spubs.com/sps/sp.cfm.

13. The dogma of the "Mandate of the Wise" is at the foundation of Shiite politics. It claims that the Muslim state will be ruled by the Wisest until the return of the missing Imam. See Shaul Bakhash, *The Reign of the Ayatollahs: Iran and the Islamic Revolution* (New York: Basic Books, 1984); and Homa Omid, *Islam and the Post-Revolutionary State in Iran* (New York: St. Martin's Press, 1994).

14. See Said Saffari, "The Legitimation of the Clergy's Right to Rule in the Iranian Constitution of 1979," *British Journal of Middle Eastern Studies*, No. 1 (1993): 64–67; and Nikkie R. Keddie, Introduction, in *The Iranian Revolution and the Islamic Republic*, ed. Nikkie R. Keddie and Eric Hoogland (Syracuse, NY: Syracuse University Press, 1986).

15. James Turner Johnson, *The Holy War Idea in Western and Islamic Traditions* (University Park, PA: Pennsylvania State University Press, 1997); also see Gilles Kepel, *Jihad: The Trail of Political Islam*, trans. Anthony F. Roberts (Cambridge, MA: Belknap Press, 2002).

CHAPTER 3

1. From Osama bin Laden speech, al Jazeera, October 20, 2001.

2. From several speeches by bin Laden and his supporters on al Jazeera and *al ansar*'s Web site, 2001 to 2005.

3. From *al ansar*'s Web site, September 2, 2006.

4. See Quintan Wiktorowicz, *Global Jihad: Understanding September 11* (Winchester, VA: Sound Room Publishers, 2003). Also Walid Phares lecture, "Jihadism," at George Washington University, October 12, 2005.

5. Al Azhar is the Islamic religious university in Cairo, considered the most influential theological center in the Muslim world. The sheikh of al Azhar is the top Muslim Sunni cleric.

6. Speeches by Osama bin Laden and Ayman al Zawahiri between 2001 and 2006, the last of which by Zawahiri was a video aired by *al Sahhab* on September 29, 2006. See also Walid Phares, "Prime Minister of Jihad Zawahiri," *The Counter Terrorism Blog*, September 30, 2006.

7. Zawahiri video messages in September 2006, from al Jazeera, dailies, and other media.

8. From *ansar al sunna wal hadith* chat room, January 17, 2006.

9. From *al-Khilafa* chat room on www.Paltalk.com, March 12, 2006.

10. From several statements by Sheikh Yussuf al Qardawi on *al Sharia wal hayat* on al Jazeera, 2003 to 2005; from *al ansar*'s chat rooms and speeches by al Qaeda's leaders, 2004 to 2006.

CHAPTER 4

1. On this subject see Paul Fregosi, *Jihad in the West: Muslim Conquests from the 7th to the 21st Centuries* (Amherst, NY: Prometheus Books, 1998).

2. Osama bin Laden, videotape, on al Jazeera TV on December 26, 2001, and in the *Washington Post*, December 27, 2001.

3. From *ahl al sunna* web cast on www.Paltalk.com, September 15, 2003.

4. See Samuel Huntington, *The Clash of Civilizations: The Remaking of World Order* (New York: Simon and Schuster, 1996), conclusion.

5. Walid Phares, *al Taaddudiya fi al Aalam* (Mount Jordan, Lebanon: Kasleek University Press, 1979).

6. On al Jazeera's *al Sharia wal Hayat* weekly program, 2002 to 2006.

7. From al Jazeera's program "al Sharia wal hayat," several times in 2004–2005.

8. From Osama bin Laden and Ayman Zawahiri's video and audio speeches on *al Jazeera* and *as Sahab* (al Qaeda's official production outlet online), 2002 to 2006. See also "Hindu, Enemy of Islam," Dhimmi Watch.com (media group that monitors the persecution of non-Muslims by jihadists), from *Outlook India*, October 2, 2006; also Serge Trifkovic, "Islam's Other Victims: India," frontpagemag.com, November 18, 2002.

9. See Ali Abunimah, "Electronic Intifada," August 22, 2001, at http://electronicintifada.net/features/articles/20010822kpfk.html; also on *ansar al sunnah* chat room, www.PalTalk.com, June 20, 2006.

10. In "Bayan li Hezb al Tahrir an Lubnan" (press release from Hizbu Tahrir on Lebanon), *Sawt al Mashreq* (weekly), December 1982.

CHAPTER 5

1. See Ibn Taymiah's *fatwa*s in Ahmad A. M. Qasim and Muhammad A. A. Qasim, comps., *Majmu' Fatawat Shaykh al-Islam Ibn Taymiyah*, vol. 9 (Riyadh: Matba'at al-Hukumah, 1996).

2. From *ahlul sunna* web chat room, August 2005; also several statements on al Jazeera, especially on "al Sharia wal hayat," Fall 2004.

3. From discussion with Sheikh Yussuf al Qarqawi, "al Sharia wal hayat," al Jazeera, Fall 2004; also on *al khilafa* chat room, www.Paltalk.com, June 2004.

4. Ibid.

5. See Abu al-A'la al-Mawdudi, Hasan al-Banna, and Sayyid Qutb, *Al-Jihad fil-Islam* (Beirut: Dar al-Fikr and al-Ittihad al-Islami al-'Alami, 1969).

6. Qardawi, "al Sharia wal hayat." See also Bernard Lewis, *The Political Language of Islam* (Chicago: University of Chicago Press, 1988), p. 72.

7. In *al salaf al salih* discussion chat room on www.Paltalk.com, May 15, 2006. The Salafi Group for Call and Combat Site Institute, February 23, 2005. Also Associated Press, "*Algérie: Le Groupe salafiste pour la prédication et le combat (GSPC) rejette l'amnistie du gouvernement*," October 2, 2005; Jean Chichizola, "Al-Qaida trouve un soutien en Algérie," *Le Figaro*, September 14, 2006.

8. "Profile: Somalia's Islamic Courts," *BBC World News*, June 6, 2006; also Christina Nwazota, "Islamist Control of Mogadisshu Raises Concerns of Extremist Future," on PBS's *Newshour*.

9. From a discussion in the chat room *ahl al sunna wal jihad*, self-declared discussion forum on www.Paltalk.com "to express al Qaeda's views," May 1, 2005. For comments on partial elections held in Saudi Arabia: Associated Press, "Islamists Dominate Saudi Arabia Elections," April 24, 2005. The discussion was between those who defended the Saudi decision to allow elections and those pro al Qaeda who rejected it. Also a press release by the al Qaeda in Iraq Jihad Committee: "elections are only deceptive," January 31, 2005, from *Global Terror Alert*; Also PBS, discussion of Zarqawi and Iraqi elections: "Democracy Is Evil, Don't Vote."

10. "Prince Alwaleed Bin Talal Donates $20 Million to Support the Harvard University Islamic Studies Program," *Harvard Gazette*, December 12, 2005; also Suzanne Gershowitz, "The Prince's Money: It's Probably One of the Last Things Harvard and Georgetown Needed," *National Review*, December 20, 2005.

11. See Freedom House Annual Report on Religious Freedom, 2002 to 2005.

12. Shukri al Qawatli, director of the Sharia Council, Beirut, in *as Safir*, August 1975; *American Journal of Islamic Social Sciences*, No. 3 (Summer 2002). *As Safir*, August 1975.

13. Pastor Mehdi Dibaj had converted from Islam to Christianity 45 years ago. On December 21, 1993, he was sentenced to death on charges of apostasy. Released on appeal, his body was found on July 5, 1994. Pastor Haik Mehr, superintendent of the Church of the Assemblies of God, who had campaigned against Dibaj's death sentence, was found dead on January 20, 1994. On July 2, 1994, the body of the Pastor Tatavous Michaelian, chairman of the Council of Protestant Ministers in Iran, was found with several gun shots to the head. Cited by Iranian Christian International; Christian Solidarity International (news agencies).

14. Paul Fregosi, *Jihad in the West: Muslim Conquests from the 7th to the 21st Centuries* (New York: Prometheus Books, 1998).

15. Antoine Najem, *Lan Naish Dhumiyeen* (We won't live as dhimmis), al Kasleek, 1980. Bat Ye'or, *The Dhimmi: Jews and Christians under Islam* (Rutherford, NJ: Fairleigh Dickinson University Press, 1984); Fuad Bustany, interview in *Mashrek International Weekly*, May 1985; Sami Fares, editorial, *Sawt al Mashreq*, March 1982. See also Rod Dreher, "Damned If You Do: Historians Dare to Criticize Islamic *dhimmitude* at Georgetown and Pay a Price," *National Review*, October 29, 2002. The article described verbal attacks on author Bat Yeor during a lecture at Georgetown University for addressing the persecution of non-Muslims under the caliphate.

CHAPTER 6

1. From discussion in *al ansar*'s www.Paltalk.com chat room, September 30, 2004.

2. Often repeated by Sheikh Ysuf al Qardawi in "al Sharia wal Hayat" (Sharia and life) on al Jazeera TV, 2003 to 2004.

3. In hearings before the U.S. Senate on August 9, 2004, Senators Charles Schumer and Susan Collins said that the Saudi government has continued to violate the right to freedom of thought, conscience, religion, or belief.

4. See report on the life and assassination of Lounes Matoub in *Al-Ahram Weekly*, July 2–8, 1998. The GIA has claimed responsibility for the death of Berber singer Lounes Matoub. "It is common knowledge that the slain Lounes Matoub was among the most stubborn enemies of religion and the Mujahideen (holy warriors)," their statement read. (Agencies).

5. *The Guardian*, August 2, 2004.

6. See testimony, Professor Walid Phares, before the U.S. Senate Committee on Foreign Relations, Near East and South Asia Subcommittee on religious persecution in the Middle East," Washington DC, April 29, 1997.

7. From author interviews with: Dr. Shawki Karas, president of the American Coptic Association, New York, 1995; Louis Shenouda, founder of the Coptic Middle East Committee, Beirut, 1984; Ghassan Yunan, Shuraya Assyrian organization, Germany, 1999; Professor Joseph Saouk, Uppsala University, 2005; Dr. Dominic Mohammed on Sudan's history, Florida International University, 1994; Professor Frank Salameh on the Maronites, Boston College, 2006. On Muslim military conquests, see Hugh Kennedy, *The Armies of the Caliphs: Military and Society in the Early Islamic State* (New York: Routledge, 2001); George F. Nafziger and Mark W. Walton, *Islam at War: A History* (New York: Praeger, 2003); Paul Fregosi, *Jihad in the*

West: Muslim Conquests from the 7th to the 21st Centuries (New York: Prometheus Books, 1998), p. 8. Cursing one's religion is very extreme in the Arab world. Many expressions about "your" (*deen*) religion exist.

CHAPTER 7

1. Erich Fromm, *Love, Sexuality, and Matriarchy: About Gender*, ed. Rainer Funk (n.p.: Fromm International Publishing Corporation, 1999).
2. Malcolm McKesson, *Matriarchy: Freedom in Bondage* (New York: Heck Editions, 1996).
3. See Geraldine Brooks, *Nine Parts of Desire: The Hidden World of Islamic Women* (New York: Knopf Publishing Group, 1996).
4. Amina Wadud, *Inside the Gender Jihad: Women's Reform in Islam* (Oxford: Oneworld Publications, 2006).
5. These statements are often made by female and male activists from the Salafi and Khoneinist currents. Also by Sheikh Yusuf al Qardawi on al Jazeera's *al Sharia wal hayat* from 2002 to 2004. On this position see in general Leila Ahmed, *Women and Gender in Islam: Historical Roots of a Modern Debate* (New Haven, CT: Yale University Press, 1992); also Jan Goodwin, *Price of Honor: Muslim Women Lift the Veil of Silence on the Islamic World* (New York: Penguin Group USA, 2002).
6. See Khalida Messaoudi, *Unbowed: An Algerian Woman Confronts Islamic Fundamentalism*, trans. Anne C. Vila (University Park, PA: University of Pennsylvania Press, 1998). In an article titled "GIA Leader's Death Not the End of Algeria's Troubles," *Daily Star*, Februrary 14, 2002, Atmane Tazaghart wrote in that the Salafi commander Antar Zouabri "permitted the rape of 'infidel' women and girls as 'spoils of war.' Women were kidnapped and taken to remote mountain strongholds, where they were treated as slaves, raped by Zouabri's followers, and forced to cook and clean for them."
7. Rosemarie Skaine, *The Women of Afghanistan under the Taliban* (Jefferson, NC: McFarland & Company, 2002).
8. See Phyllis Chesler, *The Death of Feminism: What's Next in the Struggle for Women's Freedom* (New York: Palgrave Macmillan, 2005).
9. According to the Conference of the Coalition for the Defense of Human Rights in 1999, these statements were made by pro-Taliban students and supporters on many campuses, including Harvard, UCLA, Georgetown, and as witnessed by the author on his campus at Florida Atlantic University in 1999. On this debate see Cinnamon Stillwell; "Duke Feminist Gives Thumbs Up to Taliban," frontpagemag.com, September 27, 2004.
10. See Alyssa A. Lappen, "For a Feminist Foreign Policy," frontpagemag.com, November 22, 2005.
11. Osama bin Laden, interview on al Jazeera, October 2001.
12. The "Revolutionary Guards," the regime's ideological militia.

CHAPTER 8

1. From *"istiqra' sirat al Jeehad"* (rereading the march of Jihad), a series of online lectures in *al ansar*'s www.Paltalk.com chat room, June 2005.
2. On the subject, see Charles Allen, *Terrorists: The Wahhabi Cult and the Hidden Roots of Modern Jihad* (New York: Da Capo Press, 2006). Also see Stepehen Schwartz, *The Two Faces of Islam: The House of Sa'Ud from Tradition to Terror* (New York: Doubleday, 2002).
3. They used the term *jihad* to refer to the Great History of the Arabs, without overstressing the theological component. The various caliphates were described as "Arab" achievements, the Islamic conquest was seen as "Arab" conquests, and so on. See "Al ARabi wal Urubi" (The Arab and the Arabist) in Walid Phares, *Hewar Dimucrati* (Democratic dialogue) (Beirut: al Tajamoh, 1981).
4. Michel Aflaq, *al Baath* (The Baath) (Damascus, 1957).
5. Since 1954 Egypt under Nasser allied itself with the Soviet Union. In 1977 President Sadat signed the Camp David Agreement with Israel and the United States and became an American ally.
6. Interestingly, the progressive Arab regimes, although not religious officially, used a sociologically religious terminology, the "old jihad," or "historical jihad," to refer to past glories.

7. See the analysis on the subject in Walid Phares, *Khalfiyat al Thawra al Khomeiniya al Islamiya al Iraniya* (The background of the Khomeinist Islamic revolution of Iran) (Beirut: Dar al mashreq, 1987).

8. The Takfiris are the most radical among Islamists who use the doctrine of Takfir, that is, to accuse someone of being a Kafir, and hence submit that person to punishment. See "Definition of Takfir," in *Perspectives on World History and Current Events* (www.pwhce.org/). Also see Trevor Stanley, *The Quest for Caliphate: Islamist Innovation from Qutb to al-Qaeda* (Melbourne, AU: La Trobe University, 2003).

9. See Andrew G. Bostom, *The Legacy of Jihad: Islamic Holy War and the Fate of Non-Muslims* (Amherst, NY: Prometheus Books, 2005). Also Walid Phares, "Spain's 9/11," frontpagemag. com, March 14, 2004.

10. See Martin Kramer, *Ivory Towers on Sand: The Failure of Middle Eastern Studies in America* (Washington, DC: Washington Institute for Near East Policy. 2002). Also see Lee Kaplan, "The Saudi Fifth Column on Our Nation's Campuses," frontpagemag.com, April 5, 2004.

11. See Rachel Ehrenfeld, "Jihad on the American Mind," frontpagemag.com, March 11, 2005.

12. Charles Allen, *God's Terrorists: The Wahhabi Cult and the Hidden Roots of Modern Jihad* (New York: Da Capo Press, 2006).

13. Zbigniew Brzezinski, National Security Adviser to President Carter at the time, disclosed this aim of U.S. funding for the Mujahedeen, and that it commenced before the Soviet invasion. Interview in *Le Nouvel Observateur*, January 15–21, 1998. See also Zbigniew K. Brzezinski, *Grand Chessboard: American Primacy and Its Geostrategic Imperatives* (New York: Basic Books, 1998). In October 2001, CNN aired a documentary showing Brzezinski addressing a crowd of Mujahidins in the late 1980s calling on them to "fight a Jihad for religion."

14. Edward Said, *Orientalism* (New York: Knopf, 1979).

CHAPTER 9

1. By "liberal patriotism," we mean western democracies that did not suppress citizens' freedoms because of patriotic ideas.

2. Most intelligence analysis accused Hezbollah and Iran of the attack. See Louis Freeh (former FBI director), "Khobar Towers: The Clinton Administration Left Many Stones Unturned," *Wall Street Journal*, June 25, 2006.

3. See "Backgrounder," Council on Foreign Relations, September 17, 2006: "The 1992 bombing of the Israeli Embassy (killing twenty-nine) and the 1994 bombing of a Jewish community center (killing ninety-five)."

4. On these issues see Steven Stalinsky, "Mixed Signals: Iraq Turns Off al Jazeera," *National Review*, August 11, 2004.

5. See Stephen F. Hayes, "Al Jazeera: 'Fair,' 'Balanced,' and Bought," *Weekly Standard*, May 28, 2004; also Ian Richardson, "The Roots of Al-Jazeera's Journalism Are Firmly in the BBC World Service," *Press Gazette* (London), April 11, 2003.

6. See Dr. Khaled Shawkat, "al Jazeera, Controlled by Muslim Brotherhood," Elaph.com, July 29, 2006.

7. See Hugh Miles, *al Jazeera: How Arab TV Challenged the World* (London: Abacus, An imprint of Time Warner Book Group UK, 2005), p. 28. Many critics of al Jazeera point at Sheikh Yussuf al Qarqawi as the mentor of the Jihadi ideology. See Ian Richardson, "The Failed Dream that Led to al Jazeera," *Press Gazette* (London), April 2003.

8. On the U.S. foreign policy pre-9/11, see Robert Kaplan, *Arabists: The Romance of an American Elite* (New York: Free Press, reprint, 1995). Also a theme recurring on various al Jazeera TV shows, chiefly *al ittijah al Muakess* (Opposite directions).

9. See, for example, Jonathan Dowd-Gailey, "Islamism Campus Club: The Muslim Students' Association," *Middle East Quarterly* (Spring 2004); also Cinnamon Stillwell, "Duke Feminist Gives Thumbs Up to Taliban," frontpagemag.com, September 27, 2004; Jim Kouri, "Yale University: Taliban Yes; US Military No," *American Chronicle*, March 3, 2006.

10. Criticism often leveled by Arab reformers against the regimes, particularly on dissident web sites and publications such as Elaph.com, al Naqid, al Nahar Daily, and democracy chat rooms on paltalk.com.

11. Often cited by al Jazeera commentators.
12. See the archives of the American Anti-Slavery Group (Boston), various documents.
13. See Minoo Southgate, "Slavery Ignored—Black Slavery in Sudan and Mauritania," *National Review*, October 23, 1995; also Kim Brockway, "Using Smooth Stones, 'Warrior-Philosopher' Fights African Slavery," *Columbia University Record*. September 25, 1998; also "The Slavery Issue: A Crisis in Black Leadership," *City Sun* (New York weekly), April 5, 1995.
14. See panel on Islamists in Algeria, Middle East Studies Association Twenty-fifth Annual Meeting, November 23–26, 1991, Washington, D.C.
15. See pro-Sudan Alex De Waal, "Self Serving, Sensationalist or Lazy Journalism? Panorama of Darfur," ESPAC (European Sudanese Public Affairs Council), December 23, 2004.
16. Walid Phares, "Al-Taqiyya: The Muslim Method of Conquest," paper presented at the Freeman Center of Strategic Studies, December 1997; "The Taqiya," Ismaeli.net, 2006; also Syed Saeed Akhtar Rizvi, *al Taqiya* (Dar es Salaam: Bilal Muslim Mission of Tanzania, 1992).
17. See the article "There are a billion plus Muslims in the Arab world, 90 percent of whom support Hamas," www.jihadwatch.org (Feb. 26, 2005), criticizing Bernard Haykel's article "Defense in Terror Trial Paints a Rosier Picture of 'Jihad,'" in the *New York Times*.
18. Examples of the positive treatment of "Jihadism" in academia can be found in Benjamin Barber, *Jihad vs. McWorld* (Toronto: Ballantine Books, 1996); Muqtedar M. Khan, *Beyond Jihad And Crusade: A New Framework for U.S. Policy in the Islamic World* (Washington, DC: Brookings Institution Press, 2006); Rudolph Peters, *Jihad in Classical and Modern Islam: A Reader* (Princeton Series on the Middle East) (Princeton, NJ: Markus Wiener Publisher, 1996).
19. See John Esposito, *The Islamic Threat: Myth or Reality?* 3rd ed. (New York: Oxford University Press, 1999).
20. See Martin Kramer, *Arab Awakening and Islamic Revival: The Politics of Ideas in the Middle East* (New Brunswick, NJ: Transaction Publishers, 1996), p. 297; also "Ballots and Bullets: Islamists and the Relentless Drive for Power," *Harvard International Review* (Spring 1997):16–19, 61–62.
21. See Matthew Yglesias, "Kabul on the Charles: The Harvard Initiative for Peace and Justice Will Achieve Neither," *Harvard Independent*, September 27, 2001.

CHAPTER 10

1. Lorenzo Vidino, "The Muslim Brotherhood's Conquest of Europe," *Middle East Quarterly* (Winter 2005).
2. These statements were made by a number of activists and commentators on al Jazeera between the fall of 2001 and the summer of 2004, mainly on the show *al ittijah al muakes* (Opposite directions).
3. Ibid.
4. Jalil Rawshandil, *Jihad and International Security* (New York: Palgrave Macmillan, 2006).
5. Emerging Web sites, such as www.elaph.com, or think tanks, such as al Naqid, testify to this dissident new trend. I have often argued with Islamist and Arabist classical intellectuals on al Hurra and al Jazeera TV networks, including on al Hurra's "Eye on Democracy" on July 20, 2006.
6. The author reviewed court cases in Canada and the United States as an expert. Also March 1999 interview with Charbel Barakat from the Canadian Lebanese Human Rights Federation on "cases against political asylum seekers from southern Lebanon"; September 1998 interview with Charles Jacobs, chairman of the American Anti-Slavery Group, Boston, on cases from Sudan; and September 1998 and June 2000 interviews with Keith Roderick on cases from Egypt, Indonesia, and Iran.
7. Walid Phares, Testimony to the Subcommittee on Terrorism, Committee of International Relations, on "Islamist Threat, Five Years after 9/11," September 7, 2006.
8. See Timothy R. Furnish, *Holiest Wars: Islamic Mahdis, Their Jihads, and Osama Bin Laden* (Westport, CT: Praeger Publishers, 2005).
9. See Muqtedar M. Khan, *Beyond Jihad and Crusade: A New Framework for U.S. Policy in the Islamic World* (Washington, DC: Brookings Institution Press, 2006); also Daniel Pipes, "Jihad: How Academics Have Camouflaged Its Real Meaning," History News Networks, December 2, 2002.

10. For an example on the "reading" of the War on Terror, see Katrina vanden Heuvel, "It Is Not a 'War' on Terror," *The Nation*, September 8, 2006.

11. For example, see the highly publicized statements by Columbia University assistant anthropology professor Nicholas De Genova. Rejecting the war as a War on Terror, he said at an antiwar teach-in Wednesday night that he would like to see "a million more Mogadishus." "Professor Calls for 'Million More Mogadishus,'" CNN, March 29, 2003.

12. See, for example, George Soros, *The Age of Fallibility: Consequences of the War on Terror* (New York: Public Affairs, 2006).

13. Paul Marshall, "Four Million: The Number to Keep in Mind This November," *National Review*, August 27, 2004.

CHAPTER 11

1. These accusations were constantly aired in numerous shows, such as *al ittijah al muakiss* (Opposite directions), *ma wara" al khabar* (Behind the news), and *al sharia wal hayat* (Sharia and life), from 2004 to 2006.

2. See Avi Jorisch, *Beacon of Hatred: Inside Hizbollah's al Manar TV* (Washington, DC: Washington Institute for Near East Policy, 2004).

3. See As'ad AbuKhalil, *Bin Laden, Islam and America's New "War on Terrorism"* (New York: Seven Stories Press, 2002).

4. On minimizing the deep ideological meaning of Jihadism, see, for example, Fawaz A. Gerges, *The Far Enemy: Why Jihad Went Global* (New York: Cambridge University Press, 2005).

5. The academic literature that minimizes the Jihadi threat is still dominant and spreading in the West in general and the United States in particular. Examples are Noah Feldman, *After Jihad: America and the Struggle for Islamic Democracy* (New York: Farrar, Straus and Giroux, 2004); David Cook, *Understanding Jihad* (Berkeley: University of California Press, 2005); Michael Bonner, *Jihad in Islamic History: Doctrines & Practice* (Princeton, NJ: Princeton University Press, 2006); and Judith Wren, *Crusades and Jihads: Killing Infidels* (Frederick, MD: PublishAmerica, 2005).

6. See Harvey Mansfield, "At Universities, Little Learned from 9/11," *Boston Globe*, September 13, 2006.

7. Paul Bond, "Fox vs. CAIR," frontpagemag.com, September 23, 2002.

8. See Akbar S. Ahmed, "Hello, Hollywood: Your Images Affect Muslims Everywhere," *New Perspectives Quarterly* 19, No. 2 (Spring 2002): 73–75; also see Daniel Mandel, "Why Hollywood Is Not the Villain," *The Age*, May 15, 2004.

9. A number of documentaries in the 1990s were rejected by producers in Hollywood and other studios around the nation on the basis that they raised issues that would be criticized by the Islamist lobbies in the United States. From October 2000 interview with Keith Roderick, secretary general of the Coalition for the Defense of Human Rights in the Muslim World.

10. October 2000 interview with Dr. Charles Jacobs, founder of the American Anti-Slavery Group, Boston.

11. "Anonymous," in "Osama's Hollywood," frontpagemag.com, December 22, 2005, wrote: "*Syriana* [the film] is the Jihadist's version of recent Middle East history. Without the slightest equivocation or apology, it states the moral justification of the Islamists' war on America and the West." See also Jacob Laksin, "Hezbollah's Hollywood Hero," frontpagemag.com, July 6, 2004; Jason Apuzzo, "Hollywood's New War Effort: Terrorism Chic," TownHall.com, August 12, 2005; Debbie Schlussel, "Terrorism, Hollywood-style," WorldNetDaily.com, December 11, 2001.

12. See John Esposito, *The Islamic Reality: Myth or Reality?* 3rd ed. (New York: Oxford University Press, 1999).

13. The practice of not using the terms "Jihad" and "Jihadism" was lately defended by two academics at the National Defense University (May 23, 2006), who based their arguments on a study published by a Washington lobbyist, Jim Guirard, in the *American Muslim* in August 2003, "Hiraba versus Jihad." On June 22, 2006, Jim Garamone, writing for the American Forces Press Service, published the study of Douglas Streusand and Harry Tunnell under the title "Loosely Interpreted Arabic Terms Can Promote Enemy Ideology." Streusand told CNN that "jihad is a term of great and positive import in Islam. It is commonly defined as striving or struggle, and can mean an internal or external struggle for faith." See Henry Schuster, "Words

in War," CNN, October 19, 2006. The article was posted under the title "Cultural Ignorance Leads to Misuse of Islamic Terms" by the U.S.-based Islamist organization CAIR, quoting the American Forces Press Service on June 29, 2006. Since then the "concept" of deflecting away from the study of Jihadism has penetrated large segments of the defense newsletters and is omnipresent in academia.

14. See James Fallows, "Declaring Victory," *Atlantic Monthly* (September 2006).

15. According to the *Encyclopaedia Britannica*, *Taqiya:* "spelled *Taqiyah*, Arabic *Taqiyah* ("self-pro-tection"), in Islam, [is] the practice of concealing one's belief and forgoing ordinary religious duties when under threat of death or injury to oneself or one's fellow Muslims. The Qur'an al-lows Muslims to profess friendship with the unbelievers (3:28) and even outwardly to deny their faith (16:106), if doing so would save them from imminent danger," on the condition that their hearts remain attached to faith. Also see Larry Stirling, "On 'Taqiya' and 'Fatwas,'" *San Diego Source*, September 25, 2006; also Walid Phares, "*al-Taqiya:* The Muslim Method of Con-quest," Freeman Center for Strategic Studies, December 1997.

16. Germany is a democracy, but national socialism as a Nazi ideology, as well as any use of its symbols (above all the swastika), is illegal there. The same is true in Italy of fascism.

17. Nihad Awad, executive director of CAIR, believes "Bush should not even mention Islam when referring to the would-be terrorists." But radical Islam critic Daniel Pipes said, "For the presi-dent to articulate who the enemy is so clearly and unambiguously is a huge step forward. . . . You cannot diagnose and treat a disease without first identifying and naming it. So, a strategist cannot defeat an enemy without first identifying it and naming it." Alison Espach, "Muslim Group Upset by Bush's Use of 'Islamic Fascists,'" CNSNews.com, August 11, 2006.

CHAPTER 12

1. From a debate on *al ansar* web talk on the "American War of Ideas," September 2005. Also de-scribed as "naive, provincial, and evangelical" by American journalists in David E. Kaplan, "Of Jihad Networks and the War of Ideas" in *US News & World Report*, June 22, 2006.

2. "Colorado University Professor Compares 9/11 Victims to Nazis," TheDenverChannel.com, January 28, 2005.

3. See Youssef M. Ibrahim, "Arab Winds Blowing against America," *USA Today*, November 9, 2004; also Patrick Seale, "The Rebellion against American Policy," Middle-EastOnline.com, September 10, 2006.

4. Robert Satloff, *The Battle of Ideas in the War on Terror: Essays on U.S. Public Diplomacy in the Middle East* (Washington, DC: Washington Institute for Near East Policy, 2004).

5. See, e.g., Karen De Young, "Spy Agencies Say Iraq War Hurting U.S. Terror Fight," *Washing-ton Post*, September 24, 2006.

6. See Mark Mazzetti, "Spy Agencies Say Iraq War Worsens Terrorism Threat," *New York Times*, September 24, 2006.

7. See Craig Whitlock, "Al Qaeda finds New Partner: Salafist Group Finds Limited Success in Native Algeria," *Washington Post*, October 5, 2006.

8. See Walid Phares, "The Continued Misunderstanding of the Salafi Jihad Threat," *World De-fense Review*, October 9, 2006.

9. In this description, dark green is the color of the Islamists, not the environmentalist "Greens" in the West.

10. Walid Phares, "End All Wars," www.walidphares.com, October 23, 2003.

11. "France Pulls Plug on Arab network," BBC TV, December 14, 2004; also Sebastian Usher, "French Seek Anti-Semitic TV Ban," *BBC World*, December 2, 2004.

12. See John Mearsheimer and Stephen Walt, "The Israel Lobby," *London Review of Books*, March 23, 2006.

13. This is a literal translation from Arabic; the sense in English may be altered. The citation was said often during the show *al sharia wal hayat* (Sharia and life).

14. Often cited on Arab liberal Web site Elaph.com and on many Middle Eastern blogs.

15. *Newsweek* reporters Michael Isikoff and John Barry published "Gitmo: SouthCom Show-down," May 9, 2005, an article accusing the United States of flushing the Koran in one of the Guantanamo detention center's toilets.

16. See the original *Newsweek* article.
17. Howard Kurtz, "Newsweek Retracts Guantanamo Story: Item on Koran Sparked Deadly Protests," *Washington Post*, May 17, 2005.
18. Radio Mashreq, May 25, 2005.
19. From a briefing by the author, Walid Phares, to the Justice Subcommittee at the U.S. House of Representatives, May 24, 2006.
20. As defined on al Jazeera TV, al Manar TV, *al Quds al Arabi* weekly, *al Ahad* weekly, and on Salafist Web sites.
21. As I argued in my initial introduction of the concept (see "Jihadophilia," www.walidphares.com; also in *World Defense Review*, January 2007), Jihadophilia started slowly in the early twentieth century with an exaggerated colonialist romance. British voyagers and regimes in Muslim lands unearthed the history of the Jihad as a means to pit Arabs against Ottomans. Initially a mere diplomatic maneuver, the praise of the idea was borrowed by western (Anglo-American) lobbyists and academics in the late 1970s during the Cold War to trigger similar sentiments among Muslims against communism But this primitive Jihadophilia got reversed by the Wahabis in the 1980s and later the Khumeinists in the 1990s. Oil funds and influence began spreading Jihadophilia on multiple levels on both sides of the Atlantic, deepening its roots and widening its scope. The modern Jihadophiles became political agents for the contemporary ideological movement identifying itself as Jihadism.

CHAPTER 13

1. In this battle, the Arab Muslim armies led by Khalid Ibn el Walid defeated the Byzantine army on August 5, 636, and invaded Syria, Iraq, and the rest of the Middle East, establishing the High Caliphate. This battle is considered as the turning point for the Arab conquest of the region by the native populations. See *The Origins of the Islamic State, being a translation from the Arabic of the* Kitab Futuh al-Buldha *of Ahmad ibn-Jabir al-Baladhuri*, trans. P. K. Hitti and F. C. Murgotten, Studies in History, Economics and Public Law 68 (New York: Columbia University Press,1916 and 1924), vol. 1, pp. 207–211.
2. Sayyid Qutb, *Milestones* (n.p.: Kazi Publications, 1993).
3. See "Responses to Huntington" in *Foreign Affairs*, 1993 and 1994.
4. Releases about this conference were published in the Arab press during December 1993. See for example, *al Hayat, al Safir*, and *al Nahar.*
5. Popular Iranian slogan chanted during the 2002 student uprisings. See Michael A. Ledeen, "Fish Are Better than Women," *National Review Online*, January 8, 2003.
6. "Virginia Jihad Investigations Have Led to 10 Convictions," NBC, September 16, 2005.
7. Matthew Barakat, "Judge to Allow Terrorism Expert to Testify," Associated Press, March 18, 2005.
8. *As Sahhab's* al Qaeda Web site, August 31, 2006. Also Walid Phares, "The Longer Reading of the al Qaeda Tape," Counter Terrorism Blog, September 6, 2006.

CONCLUSION

1. See Gary R. Bunt, *Islam in the Digital Age (Critical Studies on Islam Series): E-Jihad, Online Fatwas and Cyber Islamic Environments* (Sterling, VA: Pluto Press, 2003); also David D. Newton, *Jihad: The Second Wave* (Lincoln, NE: iUniverse, Inc., 2006).
2. On the western effort to end the War on Terror, see George Soros, *The Age of Fallibility: Consequences of the War on Terror* (New York: Public Affairs 2006).
3. See Patrick Poole, "Britain's Tariq TV," frontpagemag.com, May 25, 2006.
4. See Katha Pollitt, "The Trouble with Bush's 'Islamofascism,'" *The Nation*, August 26, 2006.
5. See, for example, Lisa Miller and Matthew Philips, "Caliwho?" *Newsweek*, October 13, 2006.
6. Walid Phares, "The Caliphstrophic Debate," Counter Terrorism Blog, November 1, 2006.
7. See Will Marshall, Kevin Croke, and Randolph Court, eds., *A Progressive Strategy to Defeat Jihadism and Defend Liberty* (Lanham, MD: Rowman & Littlefield,2006).
8. "Out of the Shadows: Getting Ahead of Prisoners' Radicalization," Special report by the George Washington University Homeland Security Policy Institute, 2006.
9. Such as by the Pew Research Center.

INDEX